# Naked Emperors
*Essays of a Taboo-Stalker*

# GARRETT HARDIN

# Naked Emperors
## *Essays of a Taboo-Stalker*

*William Kaufmann, Inc.*   *95 First Street*   *Los Altos, CA 94022*

**Library of Congress Cataloging in Publication Data**

Hardin, Garrett James, 1915–
  Naked emperors.

  Bibliography: p.
  Includes index.
  1. Human ecology—Addresses, essays, lectures.
  2. Human evolution—Addresses, essays, lectures.
  3. United States—Emigration and immigration—
  Addresses, essays, lectures. 4. Language and
  languages—Addresses, essays, lectures. I. Title.
  GF49.H37     304.2     82-7209
  ISBN 0-86576-033-0     AACR2
  ISBN 0-86576-032-2 (pbk.)

10   9   8   7   6   5   4   3   2   1

# CONTENTS

LANGUAGE, THE SUBTLE ENEMY

# 1

## *What Heretics Are For*

"Myths," said Salustios, are "the things that never happened but always are." Though distinguishable from myths, the best of the fairy tales share this paradoxical relation to reality. A truth we are reluctant to acknowledge can be insinuated into the mind by the account of an event that never happened. Hans Christian Anderson's *The Emperor's New Clothes* tells just such a story. His emperor is a fiction, unnamed and unplaced in time ("many years ago"), but he is also all of us at all times—and no fiction.

The swindlers who fleeced the Emperor first caught him in a neat logical trap. The exorbitantly priced and nonexistent clothes they tailored had the wonderful quality, they said, of being invisible to anyone who was "hopelessly stupid or unfit for his office." Given the Emperor's acceptance of this criterion of reality, his loyal subjects were psychologically bound to see the invisible. Behold, then, the noble Emperor, naked as a jaybird, marching in parade to the enthusiastic plaudits of the throng! The denouement comes when an innocent child protests: "But the Emperor is naked!"

This scene, first projected on the mind's eye of a delighted, giggling child, is periodically recalled by the realities of the external world. Every generation brings new swindlers (many of them, curiously, self-deceived) and more new clothes for credulous emperors. At any point in time a sizable wardrobe of such clothes is being paraded in the marketplace of ideas. There are far too few children, too few iconoclasts (to use another image), to keep up with the busy loom of the weavers of invisible cloth.

The story of *The Emperor's New Clothes* no doubt strikes completely socialized, other-directed adults as preposterous, but reality outrages myth. In Anderson's story the child's outcry leads to a rapid erosion of faith among the spectators: truth strips the Emperor naked. Unhappily, in real life, majority opinion frequently overwhelms perception.

Some experiments carried out by the social psychologist Solomon Asch are most enlightening. Asch asked a small group of college men to identify the longest of several lines drawn on paper. Unbeknownst to one of them, all the others had been instructed to agree on a preposterously wrong answer. Choices were announced in open meeting. As the responses forced the "odd man out" to become aware of his position, he not infrequently gave way to the majority and expressed his agreement with them. It does not take an Inquisition to make heresy painful. ("Heresy" comes from a Greek word meaning "to choose for oneself.") Out of 123 men subjected to this ordeal, 37 percent conformed. (Is it significant that this is about the same percentage as that of "placebo reactors," people whose pain is reduced by the administration of a placebo, a medication known to have no beneficial effect?)

Asch's experiments might tempt a cynic to rewrite the Anderson story to make the little child yield to adult opinion. We would not accept such a rewriting, of course, because the cynical version would deprive us of hope. The progress of science—indeed of all positive knowledge—depends on the courage of Thoreau's "majority of one" in the face of nearly unanimous error. Yet there are many naked emperors parading the streets of learning, and we need a few people who have the Anderson child's confidence in their own senses and judgment. Statistically speaking, the populace may well be right more often than wrong—but sometimes the Emperor is indeed naked.

What follows is one heretic's attempt to point out some of the naked emperors of our time. Heresy is no guarantee of truth; but let us not forget (as T. H. Huxley said) that every new truth begins as heresy.

# IMMIGRATION

# 2

# Immigration—America's Peculiar Population Problem

In 1974 the journal *BioScience* published my essay "Living on a Lifeboat" almost simultaneously with the publication of a simpler version, "Lifeboat Ethics," in *Psychology Today*. From the theory of the commons I derived two practical conclusions: (1) the global distribution of food in accordance with need, so long as population is uncontrolled, will ultimately produce universal hunger; and (2) uncontrolled immigration, without population control, will also result in globalizing and universalizing need and misery. These publications evoked over two hundred letters, some agreeing with me, others not. Remarkably, all the comments referred to my first conclusion only, to the condemnation of world food banks. No correspondent said a word about immigration. Evidently, as of 1974, this issue was beyond the pale of discussion. I was the little child who had been so insensitive to social values as to call attention to the Emperor's nakedness.

Slowly, in subsequent years, the crowd started murmuring that perhaps we did need to reexamine our views on immigration. The topic graduated from taboo to controversy. The problems are immensely complicated and will take a long time to untangle. General principles, qualitative in their wording, must be measured against quantities, rates, limits, and ultimate consequences. We are now in a position to begin the analysis.

"We are a nation of immigrants," said President Kennedy, and from this purely factual statement—which, be it noted, applies to every nation in the world—some people derive the conclusion that America must forever admit new waves of immigrants without limit. The conclusion is gratuitous, not logical. We need not linger over logic. What is most needed is an examination of the consequences of the various policies we might pursue: consequences for ourselves, consequences for our children and grandchildren.

We need some numbers. In the beginning of the 1970s the *net* immigration into the United States—in-migration minus out-migration— was about 400,000 per year. By the end of the decade it was close to a million per year. This was legal immigration only.

What about illegal immigration? By its nature and extent, illegal immigration is hard to estimate. In 1979 the Immigration and Naturalization Service (INS) apprehended slightly more than a million people trying to enter illegally. The significance of this figure is not obvious. On the one hand, it tends to overestimate the extent of illegal immigration because the same person caught four times is counted as four apprehensions. On the other hand, many illegal immigrants are not apprehended at all. How many? Some INS spokesmen think that for every person apprehended four get through without being caught. If this estimate, which can hardly be checked, seems too high to you then consider this significant fact: the number of INS personnel patrolling the two thousand mile Mexico-U.S. border is less than the number of policemen assigned to Capitol Hill in Washington, D.C.

For scale, let us compare immigration to "natural increase," which is defined as births minus deaths. In 1980 the natural increase of the United States was 1.6 million. On even the most conservative assumptions it seems unlikely that the number added to our population by immigration was less than this figure. This means that we have now reached the condition in which more than half of our yearly increase of about three million people is contributed by immigration. Most of the immigrant-increase is of young adults looking for jobs in a country that already has 6 to 8 million unemployed. It is not too much to say that for the United States, with the low fertility of its resident citizens, the population problem has now become an immigration problem.

Migration occurs for understandable reasons. Given an acceptable minimum degree of comfort few people choose to leave their native land and move to another, particularly one where a different language is spoken. But economic necessity can overcome this reluctance. Many impoverished Latin Americans enter through the portals of Puerto Rico and the Virgin Islands; immigrants from China and Taiwan come in illegally from Canada into the Pacific Northwest; but by far the largest group of illegals is that entering from Mexico.

The economic motivation of the Mexicans is easily understood. The Coordinator General of Mexico's National Population Council has given the 1976 rate of natural increase as 3.8 percent per year—an absolute increase of 2.3 million people. This was 100 percent more *in absolute numbers* than the natural increase in the United States for the same year (though the U.S. population was 3.6 times larger). The unemployment rate in Mexico is estimated to be between 20 and 40 percent (as compared with 8 percent in the United States) and the differential in pay on the two sides of the U.S.-Mexico border, for the same kind of work, is 10 to 1. Farther south of the border Mexicans earn still less. Why Mexicans emigrate is no mystery.

How do Americans view the influx? They are ambivalent. The existence of limits on the statute books argues that we want to restrict immigration, but the multitude of the illegal entries suggests that we don't. How can the contradiction be reconciled? Only by noting that the word "we" does not always stand for the same group. Who is the *we* who would like to restrict immigration? And who is the *we* who encourages it? If you don't know who the players are in this drama you can't understand the play.

The most effective players are easy to identify: they are the business managers who believe their economic survival depends on low-paid labor. In the cities this means owners of hotels, restaurants, and laundries. In the country it means farmers, particularly those who grow vegetables and fruits that must be picked by hand. The political power of these commercial enterprisers is significantly augmented by that of thousands of householders whose lives are made pleasanter by low-paid domestic help. In San Antonio, a housewife can get a maid for four dollars a day thus freeing herself to earn four dollars an hour in work outside the home. In Washington, D.C., a scandalous legion of Americans employed by the legal government enjoy the low-cost services of illegal domestics.

There are those who say that the legal quota of immigrants per year is too low, maintaining that a higher limit would meet the economic "need" better. This proposal misses an important point: illegality is part of the "need." Many employers say that our minimum wage is too high. Illegals are often employed to do the dirty work of industry at subminimum wages. The fortunate (and unfortunate) people who take such jobs know that if they inform on their employers they will be turned over to immigration authorities and deported. That is why illegality is an essential part of the "need" for immigrant labor.

At the level of public policy, illegality can never be defended. Tolerated illegality breeds disrespect for the law. This point is not mentioned by the kindhearted people who would like to ignore the immigration problem. Simple compassion might lead one to say that we ought to open wide the doors and let in all who want to come. In fact, no responsible statesman urges this policy. Those who call themselves compassionate generally content themselves with wrapping the policy issue in a blanket of silence.

An even larger issue is missing in the thinking of "compassionate" people: the threat of the tragedy of the commons. Since 1833, when the English economist William Forster Lloyd first pointed out the logical consequences of uncontrolled access to common property, it has been clear that *shortages cannot be solved by sharing*. Given uncontrolled population growth, wealth cannot be shared. Were we to dismantle all barriers to migration, the gains one nation might make by adopting a zero population growth policy would be totally absorbed by in-migration from neighboring nations not committed to population control. Mexico (the most immediate population threat to the United States) merely stands as an example of all nations that depend on the safety valve of emigration to relieve overpopulation. The United States is an illustrative instance of all prosperous countries that have a low rate of population growth. The logic and the conclusions of the argument are general, not particular.

In a world of limits prosperity can be maintained only if population is contained. This means that a nation that hopes to remain prosperous must insist that its resources are not to be regarded as a commons to be dipped into by the world's poor. Exporting resources without recompense is one way of creating a commons. Importing poor people is another. Both lead to disaster for the rich, uncompensated for by any enduring gain to the poor. Poverty is the consequence of an unfavorable population-to-resources ratio. Technology makes some expansion of the resources component possible—a consideration Malthus missed—but the exponential growth of population can still overwhelm the resource base (which was Malthus' essential point). If we want to help the poor of the world to become self-reliant and reasonably prosperous we must persuade them to bring their population into balance with the resources of their own territory. Dismantling national barriers to create free commons is suicidal. Whether the barriers are liquidated by legal or illegal means is a secondary matter.

What are we to do to keep immigration from creating a ruinous commons? The difficulties can be treated under three aspects: technological, political, and educational. Let us take up the easiest first.

Entry through seaports is easy enough to control. If we are not doing this sufficiently well now, we can do better. Entry by land is a more difficult matter. Our border with Canada is over 3,000 miles long; with Mexico, over 2,000 miles. At the moment—this conceivably could change in the future—the southern border is far more important; so let us look only toward Mexico. Can we prevent illegal immigration across a 2,000 mile line?

There are a number of possibilities. First, we might build a wall, literally. Unfortunately, our memories of the events connected with the erection of the Berlin Wall almost preclude our thinking about a wall rationally. At our most restrained we murmur Robert Frost's line, "Something there is that doesn't love a wall." Experience indicates that fences are more acceptable to most people than walls, though even fences evoke some distaste. Better than a visible steel fence is an invisible electronic one. Good surveillance requires a corridor clear of surface encumbrances for a hundred meters or so. This presents no problem for most of the Mexican-American border, which is rather barren desert, but in border cities modifications would have to be made. In any case, the warnings given by electronic devices must be backed up by the prompt movement of personnel to the point of entry. Personnel must be paid for—and this Congress has been unwilling to do on any adequate scale (so the rest of the problem falls into the political category, to be taken up presently). But the technical problem of the border can be solved.

The technical problem inside the border also has a solution. This is the problem of identifying people in the United States so that we know whether they are native-born, naturalized immigrants, or illegals. By comparison with Europe, America has the slackest of identification systems. Our principal card of identity is the social security card, which is printed on cheap pasteboard. It can be counterfeited in the smallest job-printing shop. Worse, it is childishly easy to get an authentic social security card. There are people who make a good living furnishing them. Their technique depends on defects in the registration system.

When a child is born in the United States that fact is registered in the state of his birth; similarly when a person dies. There is no organizational mechanism for entering on the birth record the fact of subsequent death. Anyone who wants to get a certified copy of a birth certificate—which need not be his own—can do so by paying a small fee.

At this point the private enterpriser comes into the picture: he reads the death notices in newspapers, following up the ones that give the place of birth. If John Smith, born in 1955 in Oskaloosa, Iowa, dies, the enterpriser writes to the appropriate city or state official asking for a copy of his birth certificate, enclosing money for the fee. He can even have several copies if he wishes, with no questions asked as long as he pays for them. With birth certificates in hand, the enterpriser can guarantee to furnish anybody who wants it an official social security card based on a birth certificate. It's just a matter of matching the sex and approximate age of immigrant with that of the birth certificate.

The fee for a fabricated identity is fifty dollars and up. Putting an end to this fraud is not impossible, but it would take political action to do it. Since mobile Americans are inclined to die in a state other than the one they were born in, the bureaucracies of different states would have to be made to cooperate—a difficult task in a nation made up of fifty states that jealously protect what they regard as "states' rights," which include the right to be noncooperative.

It should be apparent by this time that the major problems are not technological but political. This means that human nature must be taken into account. Unfortunately, to date, those who want to sabotage the system of immigration control have shown the greater cleverness in manipulating the legislative process. The Immigration and Nationality Act of 1952 (the "McCarran-Walter Act") specified that the employers of illegal aliens could *not* be penalized—though the aliens themselves could be deported. This gave employers who paid substandard wages a weapon to use against their workers, namely the threat (implied or explicit) of informing the INS if the worker complained or made trouble. This astonishing piece of legislation was called the "Texas Proviso" because it was put in at the behest of agricultural interests in Texas. The successful proposers of the Proviso showed a real understanding of human nature.

Our hearts are touched by the apprehension and deportation of each illegal alien, whom we perceive as a powerless pawn in a game planned by others. It seems somehow unfair to penalize him. But an employer who is merely trying to hold his expenses down does not touch our hearts much, partly because we suspect he could survive even if he were forced to pay higher wages, the cost of which could be passed on to consumers. Making it legal to hire an illegal immigrant makes a mockery of the intention of immigration laws.

Polls show that the public is willing to impose responsibility on employers. For many sessions Congressman Peter Rodino worked on legislation that would invert the Texas Proviso, imposing sanctions on erring employers. He was successful in the House of Representatives, but none of his bills surmounted the necessary second hurdle—passage by the Senate. Senator Eastland, the chairman of the Senate Subcommittee on Immigration and Naturalization, did not call a meeting of his group from 1965 to 1975, during which time he collected 2 million dollars for expenses. There is no suspicion of embezzlement; the chairman merely diverted the money to defray the expenses of other committees that he regarded as more important. Finally, under pressure, Senator Eastland did call a meeting in 1976, but nothing came of it.

Eastland, who was from Mississippi, had many friends with large plantations on which illegals worked. Their stand was backed up by the owners of hotels and restaurants in the big cities. Despite their frequently expressed devotion to the free enterprise system, these people apparently felt that their businesses could not survive if they were required to pay legal wages. The pressure a few large business enterprisers can exert on Congress is greater than that of millions of plain citizens. This fact is not peculiar to the immigration problem; it is a general problem of representative government. Private interest groups with concentrated power can easily override a much greater but more diffuse public interest.

What countervailing forces can be mustered against such a concentration of political power? The most hopeful forces in sight are the labor unions. At the present time the total number of illegals in the country is estimated to be about the same as the total number of the unemployed—about 8 million. The equality of these figures may be coincidental, but there must be some causal connection between the two. Laborers should be able to see that any addition to the labor force weakens their bargaining power vis-a-vis management. This is true whether the additions are legal or illegal in origin, though illegals constitute the greater threat.

Unfortunately, the interest of the rank and file of the labor unions is generally opposed by the interest of the heads of the labor unions. Like all bureaucrats these men gain power from a large constituency. Consequently, labor leaders tend to favor more immigrants, regarding them as eventual members. It is not easy for the true interest of the rank and file to make itself felt, unless the press helps out (which it does not in the case of immigration).

The behavior of the United Farm Workers (UMF) under Cesar Chavez is worth mentioning. The UMF is made up largely of Mexican-Americans working the farms and ranches of the southwest. Most of them are migrant laborers, following the harvesting season northward during the year. For a variety of reasons, organizational and psychological, migrant workers always have more trouble achieving their ends than do workers who stay in one place. Chavez has repeatedly pleaded with Congress to put an end to illegal immigration so that the low wages illegals are forced to accept will not depress all wages.

But Chavez is caught in a dilemma. Though an American, he is part of the Mexican culture, and every Mexican-American has cousins he would like to see enter the country. The more thoughtful Mexican-Americans recognize that if all their cousins enter—and worse, if all the cousins' cousins enter *ad infinitum*—the overloaded commons will ultimately ruin them all. But first, the hyphenated American suggests, let's admit *my* cousins before we close the door. Chavez, subjected to conflicting pressures, is inconsistent in his public statements. This weakens his effectiveness as a countervailing force to big business. Compassion cooperates with the profit motive to create more grief for the compassionate.

No significant change can be made in immigration laws without substantial cooperation from those who control the "media"—television, radio, and the press. The year 1976 saw a considerable increase in attention given to immigration by the media, but it is not obvious that it had much effect on public opinion. People seem to be apathetic about this problem, and the writers for the media tend to use flabby rhetoric in discussing the subject. There are reasons for this state of affairs.

First, there is the great force of tradition. Of all the literature of the past three centuries the phrases that ring most in the mind are ones that are predominantly oriented around the plight of the individual, universalized in its implications. "No man is an island," said John Donne in the seventeenth century, "Every man is a piece of the continent, a part of the main . . . any man's death diminishes me." Better known to Americans are the lines of Emma Lazarus written in 1883 and inscribed on the Statue of Liberty twenty years later (and reinscribed on the Kennedy International Airport after another sixty years):

> *Give me your tired, your poor*
> *Your huddled masses, yearning to be free,*

*The wretched refuse of your teeming shore,*
*Send these, the homeless, tempest-tossed, to me:*
*I lift my lamp beside the golden door!*

A century after these lines were written foreign shores are teeming more than ever, while the gilt is flaking off our door. Americans don't really live by Lazarus' advice—if we did, we would remove all impediments to immigration. But any attempt to increase legal restrictions, or even to conscientiously enforce the ones we have, is sure to activate a talented cartoonist to limn a lachrymose Liberty.

"Poets are the unacknowledged legislators of the world," said Shelley; were he alive today he would surely include cartoonists, columnists, and the warblers of popular songs. Many of these are admirably acute in their perception of the sorrows of the individual, but lamentably obtuse in seeing that an aggregation of individually compassionate actions can add up to disaster for the populace as a whole.

Listen to Shelley again:

*Most wretched men*
*Are cradled into poetry by wrong:*
*They learn in suffering what they teach in song.*

The trouble is, the masters of the media have not suffered enough—not in a way that is relevant to the immigration problem. Chavez's people lose jobs to, and have their wages beaten down by, a tidal wave of immigrants. This never happens to the media people—*and never will*. The reason is quite simple: language skills are virtually untransferable from one country to another. There are a few contradictory examples to this statement, of course: Joseph Conrad (Polish), Vladimir Nabokov (Russian), and Arthur Koestler (Hungarian) come to mind. But who else? That's just about the roster.

One might postulate that literary ability of a lesser order would be transferable from one language to another, but the evidence points in the opposite direction. The ordinary journalist or TV writer may not produce Literature with a capital L, but he does know his idioms, and must, to hold his job. It is his idiomatic control of language that protects the rice bowl of the native journalist. The migrant farm worker can never escape the anxiety that a fresh horde of new workers from over the border may take his job away; in contrast, new immigrants pose no threat to men and women whose craft is language.

Drawing only on his limited personal experience, a journalist can be led to express the cruelist sentiments. In June of 1976 an editorial in the *Wall Street Journal* was entitled "The Illegal Alien Non-Problem." The anonymous writer had a simple solution to this "non-problem": simply declare all illegals to be legal. Since he did not say otherwise, one would assume he meant we should follow this policy in perpetuity—that is, that we should create a commons. One is reminded of the character in William Saroyan's *The Human Comedy* who had a recipe for putting an end to thievery: "If you give to a thief he cannot steal from you." True: and if we declare all immigrants legal we put an end to illegal immigration. But what will stop the suffering of Chavez's people? What would happen to all of us if we literally obeyed the injunction on the Statue of Liberty?

Compassionate impulses are commendable, but we will be ruined if we have not the imagination to see their consequences. If we build policy on the doctrine that the *need* of people bred in another culture confers on them the *right* to be supported in ours, we will soon find that their vast numbers—millions and millions—will overwhelm our support system. It takes imagination to see what is required to survive in even minimally prosperous conditions. Journalists have an opportunity to help Americans develop this imagination. This means they must downplay the vignettes (photographic and verbal) of the present suffering of poor illegals who are the victims of a social system that has, in their native country, allowed population to outrun resources.

Immigration has its population roots outside our nation. The poor of the world increase in numbers by 50 million a year. Perhaps the majority of these would, if they could, move into a rich country like the United States (if they felt assured of compassionate treatment once they got here). Of course, most of them can't afford the fare; but if we really believed in the sentiment on the Statue of Liberty we should say, "Send these, the homeless, tempest tossed, to us—*and here is the money to pay their fare.*" But we don't, nor should we.

It is discouraging to note that half of the yearly increase in the American population comes from uncontrolled immigration, and that this fraction is rising. At the least, this is an inefficient way to run a country, and it certainly makes the preservation of native traditions more difficult. But discouraging though the present is, there are encouraging signs that the tide is changing. This change is part of a larger shift in public opinion, which, under the stimulus of necessity, is reactivating a recognition of the importance of responsibility in the design of social and political systems, making people realize that actions originating in a commendable compassion for the individual must be informed by the interests of the larger group. The larger group includes our posterity to whom we pass on the national resources for which we are the trustees.

We will be doing well if we succeed in solving our own population problem and save something for our own posterity. National sovereignty permits this; what may be lacking is the will. But it would be quixotic to tackle the world population problem hoping to serve all posterity everywhere. There is no supranational sovereignty, and *without global sovereignty there can be no global solution to population problems.*

Adherents to the philosophy of zero population growth ask Americans to reject the individualistic bias which implies that "The size family that is individually best for me is also best for the group." Those who reject this individualistic bias and who make their personal actions consistent with their new-found wisdom thereby make personal sacrifices for the good of the group. It is intolerable if such sacrifices are to be rendered worthless by a conversion of the national domain into a world commons that will be overwhelmed by immigrants from other countries (where no such personal sacrifices for the sake of the group are made).

How we are to control our own population by acceptable means is still not clear, but of this we can be sure: population control is impossible without immigration control.

# 3

## *Smokescreens and Evasions*

Though insisting on their commitment to democracy, most Americans conveniently close their eyes to two facts. First, ours is not a democracy in the original Greek sense but a representative government in which the many vote for a few and then the few make the laws that govern all. The consequences of this arrangement have never been fully worked out in political theory. Particularly—and this brings us to the second aspect of our willful blindness—it should be noted that very frequently the will of the majority can be thwarted for a long time by the normal working of the machinery of representation. This fact deserves the closest study by those who want the will of the majority to prevail.

A clear instance of the frustration of the majority's will is found in the management (more exactly, the *non*management) of immigration. In the summer of 1977 the Roper organization took a reading of public opinion in this area. Ninety-one percent of the sample agreed that we should make an all-out effort to stop the illegal entry of approximately

1.5 million foreigners each year. In commenting on this finding, Burns Roper remarked, "It is rare on any poll question to find such a lopsided result."

Two years later the Roper poll repeated the question and got exactly the same result—91 percent. Probably, 91 percent is as close to unanimity as national opinion can reach.

It cannot be successfully maintained that this near-unanimity is the result of media indoctrination. Until the summer of 1976 the media had little to say about immigration, though the Immigration and Naturalization Service repeatedly called attention to the rapid increase in illegal entries. Residents of cities near the Mexican border had enough personal experience to be willing to bet that the situation was getting worse. Even many people in manufacturing centers in the Midwest and Northeast began to suspect what was happening. Hard data are hard to come by, but the INS, under the direction of General Leonard F. Chapman, raised its estimate of illegal immigration to 1.7 million during the last year of the Ford administration.

Of course the figures for any illegal activity are necessarily imprecise, a fact that can be used to thwart any attempt to institute corrective action. It seems so scientific to say, "Let's find out the *exact* facts before we act," but in the real world, action often cannot wait for precision (which may never come). Since time has no stop, not to act is to act. As Robert Allen said, "If you jump out of an airplane you are better off with a parachute than an altimeter." Obstructionists insist that we should take an altimeter reading before we buy a parachute—and then they throw sand in the altimeter. When Jimmy Carter became President, he replaced General Chapman with Leonel J. Castillo, a politician from the Mexican-American community. One of Commissioner Castillo's first acts was to clamp a secrecy lid on all estimates of illegal immigration.

The label "liberal" has been much overused, but I think most people feel that allowing immigrants in is a liberal sort of thing to do, and that keeping them out is illiberal. Some might argue that the Roper polls merely revealed how bigoted Americans are. This is the sort of arrogance that periodically leads "intellectuals" to say "Everybody's out of step but me." Unfortunately, "intellectuals" are the ones who run most of the media; the 91 percent is a rather silent majority—or has been silent until quite recently.

No responsible agency has asserted that the right to migrate *into* a country is a fundamental human right, though the opposite right is proclaimed in Article 13, Section 2 of the United Nations Universal Declaration on Human Rights: "Everyone has the right *to leave* any country, including his own, and *to return to his country*" (italics added). To assert a person's right to enter a country not his own would be tantamount to claiming the right of invasion. That the invasion might be gradual and peaceful is only secondarily relevant to the moral question.

Let us begin by sweeping several red herrings off the path. First, I do not assert that immigrants are inferior to citizens. The problem of innate quality is so complicated (and perhaps insoluble) that it is operationally wise to assume an innate equality between immigrants and longtime occupants of the land. The issue discussed here will be concerned with quantity only, not quality.

Second, I know of no thoughtful person who would (if he could) stop *all* immigration. The benefits of variety, of periodic fresh infusions of new peoples and new ideas are real. No adventurous, lively nation wants to forego them. But how many immigrants are needed to secure these benefits? A thousand per year? Ten thousand? Surely no more. Moreover, *if* the seasoning of variety is what we desire to secure by immigration, we should discriminate among immigrants, preferentially admitting those who personally embody more of the culture of their homeland rather than those who carry a lesser load; bluntly, we should discriminate in favor of the talented and highly trained against the untrained and incompetent. (This would, of course, raise another difficult moral issue, that of the "brain drain," which harms the country of origin.)

Adding legal immigrants to the illegals, it appears that the United States is now being invaded by approximately 2 million immigrants per year. Of all the other sovereign countries in the United Nations, not one is subject to anything like such an invasion. In fact, the annual immigration into the United States exceeds the immigration into all other 150-odd nations combined. To reduce the U.S. immigration rate to a fraction of its present value (as desired by more than three-quarters of our citizens) would merely be to bring our country in line with international norms. Entry is rigidly and narrowly rationed by almost all other countries.

We need to take the word "development" seriously. The development of every organism includes a juvenile period when growth is very rapid, followed by an adult period (often quite prolonged in time) during which *no* growth takes place. (Normally, that is: a cancerous tissue may continue the juvenile rate of growth indefinitely in the adult years, in the absence of surgical intervention.) The development of nations also has its juvenile and mature phases. The United States is surely in the mature phase now. There is no rational excuse for encouraging an immigration rate that was appropriate to, and beneficial in, our juvenile phase. Large numbers of immigrants, particularly if unskilled and ill-trained, cannot be acculturated rapidly. They undermine the shared culture. They erode national unity.

Vietnam and Watergate had a destabilizing effect on our national psyche. Perhaps it is a national identity crisis that explains our reluctance to take the steps needed to conserve our national culture, but this is a poor excuse. Our psychological uncertainty makes it all the more necessary that we closely control the inflow of immigrants while we work through our problems.

There is no clearer indication of our psychological insecurity than the 1975 extension of the U.S. Voting Rights Act which decreed that ballots must be provided in the language of any foreign-language group that exceeds 5 percent of the voters in a district. The expense of voting—a necessary expense in a democracy—is escalating in area after area. In San Francisco, instructional material and ballots are now being printed in English, Spanish, Chinese, Korean, and Tagalog. (Tagalog, in case you don't know, is one of the many languages spoken in the Philippines.)

The good intentions underlying this law are obvious and praiseworthy: they are to make minorities feel more welcome, to help them preserve their familiar and comforting subcultures. But of this well-intentioned act, as of all good intentions, we must ask the ecologist's question, "And then what?" As we continue to pursue this policy, what will the ultimate consequences be? Plainly Babel, against which the Bible warns us. How can we achieve anything like national unity if we lack the courage to insist that the language of the majority—the vast majority be it noted—must be the only language for exercising the franchise of citizenship? We have become a passel of poltroons who quail at the word "minority." We have lost our common sense.

The desire to encourage widespread knowledge of other cultures is, of course, a worthy one, but it can be better served by other means. We must distinguish between two meanings of the word "culture." As the anthropologist uses the word, every people, no matter how poor or uneducated, has a culture—call it the A-culture. The humanist, however, uses the word in a more value-laden sense to include knowledge and love of the arts, the literature, and the history of a particular people. Call this the H-culture. It is a degree of pluralism in H-cultures that we want to encourage. Immigrants who come here to escape grinding poverty bring (by definition) a standard load of A-culture, but most of them (in fact) bring precious little H-culture. Such immigrants should not be blamed: their deficiency is just one of the consequences of poverty. But how much will the immigrant's retention of their H-culture, or their acquisition of a new H-culture, be furthered by excusing them from learning English? Certainly the native majority receives little benefit from the expense of the Voting Rights Act.

If we are serious about diminishing the provincialism of the native majority, let us make a working knowledge of at least one foreign language a requirement of citizenship for all. Immigrants should be able to fulfill this requirement more easily than natives. For both groups, language education should be continued until the associated H-culture can be comprehended. Without doubt, such a proposal would be dismissed as utopian.

"The road to Hell is paved with good intentions." No more telling example of this truth can be found than the Voting Rights Act of 1975 and the subsequent legal compulsion to institute "bilingual" education in the public schools. The taxpayers of California, perhaps the most affected of all the states, were paying for instructors in 79 different languages as of 1981. Of the state's four million students about one million were Hispanic, with a similar number divided among the other 78 language groups. One can hardly be called an alarmist if he worries about the eventual consequences of the Voting Rights Act and "bilingual" education. To encourage the retention of multiple languages, as (in practice) "bilingual" education does, is to encourage the growth of tribalism in a nation. In the not too distant future we may face the task of welding together a multitude of feuding tribes to form, once more, a single nation. The second time may not be as easy as the first—which was something of a miracle.

Immigration can be understood only in the framework of population theory. The most basic fact for population policy is that ours is a finite world. The rapid growth of world population during the past two decades—nearly 2 percent per year—has befuddled our minds. For the past million years (including the past two decades) the *average* rate of growth of the human population has been but two-thousandths of 1 percent per year—scarcely more than zero. Realistically, the most optimistic accomplishment of the near future (i.e., during the next century) will be a reestablishment of zero population growth. At least as realistic, and far more pessimistic, is the possibility of a harrowing negative population growth rate.

Deliberate population control is the greatest need facing every nation today, and it cannot be solved by emigration. When we make it possible for another nation to get rid of its excess population by shipping it to us, we merely encourage the leaders of that nation to evade the hard problem of population control. Through emigration an overpopulated country can export its problems to any country that is foolish enough to permit uncontrolled immigration.

Massive immigration damages the receiving nation even in the near term. Every new baby or new immigrant imposes acculturation costs—both monetary and other—on the nurturant nation. Unless the utter disruption of the native H-culture is regarded as a matter of no moment, the public costs of acculturating immigrants and the children of immigrants is much greater than the public costs of acculturating the children of longtime residents. The present U.S. population of 235 million, with a fertility rate of fifteen per thousand, produces 3.5 million children in a year. If the year's inflow of immigrants (legal and illegal) is 2 million, this means that the load of immigrants to be acculturated is

57 percent as great as the acculturation load of new babies. This underestimates the load because many of the new babies are born into immigrant homes. Next year there will be a new wave of fertile immigrants.

The total costs of acculturation imposed by immigrants is difficult to determine, but with rising immigration and falling native fertility these costs must be increasing. To survive as a people, every nation must produce and acculturate the next generation, but accomplishing this largely by immigration is not the most economic way, whether one understands economics in a broad sense or a narrow. Who would propose, as a matter of policy, that immigration be the preferred way for producing the next generation?

From the point of view of welfare economics, illuminated by human ecological insights, the case against unrestricted immigration in a crowded world is overwhelming. The common folk who live outside idealistic and bemused Academia understand this perfectly well, and always have. Unfortunately, those who dominate the American media are more influenced by Academia than by the common folk. "Intellectuals"—more accurately described as "verbals"—are reluctant to reexamine old cliches. "A nation of immigrants," "the open door policy," "my brother's keeper," "fortress America," "isolationism," "bigotry," "for whom the bell tolls"—these are only a few of the verbal blockages to independent thought.

No discussion of immigration is complete if we neglect to deal with this argument: "Immigrants will do the work Americans are unwilling to do. Therefore they do not displace Americans, and they are good for the economy." It is undoubtedly true that the newest immigrants will work harder for less money at unpleasant jobs than will Americans. To the employer who pays only for the daily work, immigrants may be a bargain. Service jobs in restaurants and hotels have long been held by the latest wave of immigrants; employers maintain they could not stay in business if they had to depend on native labor. In the short run they may be right.

If we were honest with ourselves we would see that our attitude toward immigration reveals the hypocrisy in our praise of the economic dogma of "the market." In a true market economy the price of a product should reflect all the costs, including labor, that go into it. If the price is high, economic demand will be less. The true cost may be greater than anyone is willing to pay, in which case the product "prices itself out of the market." (How long has it been since you bought a jar of pheasants' tongues in the supermarket?)

Growers of California lettuce long maintained they could stay in business only if they had available low-priced "stoop labor"—illegal immigrants or "green card" holders (temporary guest workers). But there are other possibilities: the price of the product could be raised to reflect higher labor costs; in that case New Yorkers would either eat higher-priced lettuce or do without. In the latter event, lettuce farms could be devoted to growing something else.

Cheap labor, like cheap manufacturing processes, fails to internalize all the costs. The owner of a smoky factory produces a cheap product because he imposes external costs on the community at large, which must pay the bills for cleaning clothes and buildings. Air pollution can increase medical costs also: lung diseases don't come cheap. *The public interest dictates that all costs be internalized.* In a total accounting a clean factory is generally more economical than a smoky one—but it often takes public action to internalize all the costs.

What is the true cost of labor? It is not only the cost of food to fuel a laborer's muscles; it is also the cost of clothing, housing, and a modicum of luxuries—automobiles, TV sets, public parks, etc. More important, since labor will not settle for an unalterable second-class citizenship, the true cost of labor includes whatever it takes to bring the laborer and his children ultimately into a condition of full membership in the community. Many of these costs are mostly externalized as far as the employer is concerned: schools, health services, welfare payments.

It takes a tremendous community investment—during one or more generations—to bring the immigrant and his family fully into the community. Employers pay few of these external costs. Most are paid by the citizens at large. It takes a lot of money to turn new immigrants into fully acculturated citizens. The nominal low cost of immigrant labor is an illusion; but without community action—the passage and enforcement of laws—individual business enterprisers will continue to benefit from a dishonest accounting system.

At first glance one might expect strong opposition to immigration from individual laborers, if not from their leaders. But times have changed. In the days before the welfare state, if a laborer had no job he and his family were in danger of starving. No longer is this true. The welfare state has created a domestic commons into which unemployed laborers can dip. Life on unemployment and welfare payments is not as plush as it is on a weekly paycheck—reality does not yet quite live up to the Marxian ideal of "to each according to his need"—but the living is good enough to weaken the springs of action of any worker who might perceive a causal connection between immigration and unemployment. Conviction and vigor are needed to fight against the ever-recurring threat of making our territory a part of a global commons. The creation of the domestic commons of the welfare state has debilitated the forces that otherwise might be fighting for survival.

The interests of the whole community, though great, are diffuse. I know that I lose every time one more immigrant comes across the border. To acculturate fully one more immigrant and his family may cost my nation $80,000. But that cost (whatever its true magnitude) is divided among some 80 million taxpayers: my proportionate share is a tenth of a cent. The cost of a million immigrants is, of course, much more—a thousand dollars per taxpayer. But this cost is invisibly spread over several decades. Only insightful intellectual analysis enables us to see that immigrants do not come cheap. Our direct, "intuitive" appreciation of this reality is almost nil.

*It takes imagination to see the truth.*

At the present time no constituency in the United States is sufficiently informed and powerful to secure the end desired by the vast majority, namely a sharp curtailment of immigration. We suspect that democracy may be in jeopardy because of its apparent inability to meet the first test of any system—survival. The constituency opposed to community control of population growth has a pretty tight control of the media.

As the proportion of recent immigrants increases, their political power will increase proportionately. We already see signs of this in the growing intransigence of "Chicano" leaders, the younger generation of Mexican-Americans. At some level of population—five percent of the total population? ten percent?—the recent immigrants may well reach a "critical mass" (to borrow a concept from nuclear physics) whose power the more comfortable and passive multitude of longtime residents will find irresistible. As militant immigrants fight to keep the borders open, they will be aided by native political activists, left over from the 1960s, who seek new worlds to conquer. When the political power of this coalition becomes irresistible, the United States will have lost control of its destiny. Hoping to diminish world poverty by neglecting to control movements across our borders, the nation will merely have become sucked into a global commons that universalizes poverty.

# 4

# Thinking Hearts Are Better Than Bleeding

## Act I: Vietnam, 1979

Many Americans were horror struck when Malaysia announced that she would not only repel additional boat people but also would expel the 70,000 Vietnamese refugees already within her borders, putting them out to sea in boats to seek refuge elsewhere—or to die. What inhumanity! As in a movie, our minds evoked a vivid scene of the suffering of homeless, unwelcome men, women, and children perishing on the high seas. How could anyone be so heartless?

The government of Malaysia later softened its stand somewhat, no doubt because of criticism by countries that were comfortably distant from the problem. But Malaysia's hard-nosed decision was not unique. Thailand and Indonesia, also close to the problem, said that they too would accept no more refugees. Macao, the Philippines, Singapore, and Japan had long followed exclusionary policies.

Meanwhile, the United States at first admitted 7,000 Asian refugees a month. This was later increased to 14,000.

What do Asian countries know that we don't?

Just this: That the population problem is serious. Disguising it as a political problem—calling surplus people "refugees"—doesn't solve the population problem, unless you can fool other nations.

It is almost impossible for Americans to imagine what poverty coupled with overpopulation feels like. Observant tourists in India and Bangladesh have some knowledge; so also do many men who saw service in Vietnam. Nowhere in the United States can one find poverty like that in Asia.

Consider some statistics. The populations of Vietnam, Malaysia, Indonesia, and Thailand will double in about 29 years (as opposed to 117 years for the United States, if we ignore immigration). Except for Thailand, these Asian countries have to import grain for food. Some 38 percent of the Malaysian diet is made up of imported food, and 22 percent of Vietnam's.

If you were a Malaysian politician, how could you justify accepting refugees when 38 percent of your people have to be kept alive with imported food? If you were a Vietnamese politician, would you not like to reduce the percentage of your people who are dependent on outside food? Shipping people out is one way to do it.

Energy poverty, though not as lethal as food poverty, is even more severe in Southeast Asia. These countries get by on about one-fortieth as much energy per person as America does. We riot at filling stations when our rich energy budget is cut even a little bit. Why should we be surprised or indignant when Asians, having to get by on so much less energy, refuse to share with the boat people?

Massive immigration can stretch the fabric of a society to the breaking point. This is no condemnation of immigrants as people (nor of residents): it is just a fact about invasion, peaceful though it may be. We used to think of America as a melting pot in which cultural differences melted away painlessly. That was in the pioneer days when there was lots of room. No longer. Now our elbows dig into each other's ribs. Think how much worse it must be in the much more crowded and multicultural Asiatic countries.

Asians are closing their doors: Should we call them hardhearted or realistic? They *know* they live in a severely limited world. Why should they take on other people's problems?

As Singapore's Prime Minister Lee Kuan Yew said, "If you don't have callouses on your heart, you will bleed to death."

"Callouses" is perhaps too brutal a word; I prefer the image of a "thinking heart." Bleeding hearts do nobody any good, thinking hearts may.

A hastily adopted U.S. policy of generosity toward the boat people can all too easily lead to disillusionment later when we learn all the facts. Let's look at the facts first. The United States places legal limits on immigration, but we admit "political refugees" outside the limits. Our policy creates an obvious opportunity for Machiavellian politicians anxious to get rid of some of their people. All they have to do is mistreat them so that they will qualify as "political refugees," then we will feel morally bound to take them in.

The Machiavellian thinkers in Vietnam are even cleverer than that. They fleece the refugees before they go, making them pay up to $3,000 for the privilege of leaving. Quite a money-machine, this "political refugee" racket! Vietnam reduces its population, gets rid of "undesirables," and makes money at the same time. This racket, so long as it continues, frees Vietnamese politicians from seeking other, more humane solutions to their domestic problems.

Will Vietnam be the last country to play the "political refugee" game with us? Not if we continue to do what Vietnam wants. Every year there are 50 million more desperately poor people in the world. There is enough raw material to keep this game going forever, if we encourage it.

But, an unthinking heart may say, "America is rich—surely we can afford the game!" But are we that rich?

In America, as everywhere else, the rich and well-established have more power to determine policy than the poor. Before we are too generous in giving to the poor of other nations, should we not consult our own poor—who will pay the cost of our generosity? Let us remember the advice of ethicist Joseph Fletcher: "Give if it helps, but not if it hurts." Let us ask: Helps whom? Hurts whom?

Now, as always, millions of human beings are in desperate need. Being human, we would like to help all of them. But in this limited, interconnected world we can never do merely one thing. Helping one person, we may harm others. Before we go all out trying to relieve the suffering of the nearly 2 million people Vietnam wants to get rid of, we had better ask some hard questions.

As we accept more and more refugees, will our per capita income rise?

Will the supply of petroleum per person increase?

Will our unemployment rate decline?

Will the poor already in our midst be better taken care of?

Will an increase in the number of languages spoken here create more national unity?

Will the social friction between groups be lessened by having more, and larger, minority groups?

Will our children, and our children's children, bless us for mortgaging the property we pass on to them? Posterity is part of the "whom" we should be concerned about.

We generally call a deed "good" if its first, and intended, effect is good. But every "good deed" has side effects, and it is this fact of life that leads us to say that "Nature never forgives a good deed." We are justified in performing a "good deed" only if the totality of its effects is positively good. The genuinely good deed must not leave posterity out of the accounting.

The actions of the leaders of Malaysia are those one would expect of people who are concerned about their own posterity. Can the same be said of American actions? Our hearts bleed; can they also think?

## Act II: Cuba, 1980

No humane person can hear the stories of the incoming refugees without wanting to help them. The courage these people show in the face of nearly overwhelming disaster makes us proud of the human race.

Yet it is not enough to look just at the sorrow of the moment. Actions become precedents, so we must ask what policy we propose for the future. When the Vietnamese sought refuge by the hundreds of thousands in 1979, a few commentators raised the policy issue. But more Americans pretended not to hear or understand what is meant by "policy" as they sought to ease their consciences in the short term. With the coming of another hundred thousand "political refugees" from Cuba in 1980, the policy issue was raised once more.

We are only 5 percent of the world's population, and this percentage is decreasing. Our population grows only one-third as fast as the population of poor countries. Compassionate people often turn aside from such data, saying, "That's just a numbers game!" *Precisely*: It is the numbers that make the problem, not the individual case.

The immigrant named Manuel Estrada, educated in the school of adversity, is an admirable person. So is Hee Hong Lee, and Lam Van Sing, but what are we to do with millions of Estradas, Lees, and Van Sings? The number that will try to migrate into the United States tomorrow depends on what we do today.

The Cuban problem is not solely political. Basically it is a problem of too many people. Their number has exceeded the carrying capacity of the island. Before Fidel Castro took over, the United States kept this population afloat with generous subsidies to its sugar industry. Under Castro, excess young men (politically always the most dangerous group) were sent off as mercenary soldiers to serve the Soviets in Africa.

Now, plant diseases have created new stresses. If Cuba were underpopulated, these stresses could be endured. Castro is "generously" allowing some of the excess to come to the United States. Naturally, most of the migrants are politically opposed to Castro, but does that make the basic problem a political one?

Many Americans see Castro's actions as those of a latter-day Machiavelli who, until the latest episode at least, has manipulated an appreciable fraction of American opinion with skill. Even as the "Freedom Flotilla" was bringing thousands of Cubans to Florida to be met by an increasing chorus of opposition here, a prominent long-time Cuban exile, the banker Carlos J. Arboleya, accused the Carter administration of "playing politics" when it showed signs of bowing to public opinion polls which showed that the majority of Americans opposed the invasion.

Momentarily, we could cut Cuba's problem in half by taking in 5 million refugees. But the Cubans who remained there would, at the present rate of population growth, bring the number of inhabitants back up to 10 million in 58 years. (Perhaps, feeling less stress, they would do it sooner.) The question is: Can external generosity solve an internal population problem?

The candidates for our benevolence are almost beyond numbering. There are 6 million Haitians, most of them desperately poor. Cambodia, even after massive genocide, still has several million people who would jump at a chance to leave. A fair share of Vietnam's 52 million would like to emigrate, too. It is reported that 50 percent of the 40 million South Koreans also want to come to the United States.

Somalia has 1.3 million homeless refugees. International agencies estimate the world's total of displaced refugees at 9 to 16 million. Should we take them all in?

All told, there are some 800 million people in the world who are desperately poor, and their numbers are increasing by 25 million per year. Can we rescue them all? Most of them are having political problems: Is that relevant?

Consider the five most serious kinds of burdens immigrants place on us: food, housing, jobs, energy, and public services.

At first glance, it looks as if we have plenty of food. Americans produce twice as much grain as they consume. We could share the extra food with another 235 million people. Unfortunately, the sale of grain is our principal source of foreign exchange—which we need to buy oil to fuel up our tractors to grow next year's crops and to drive to work to earn the money needed to buy food.

Housing? Are we so awash in adequate housing that we can share with others? And who will do the sharing—our rich or our poor?

Jobs? Secretary of Labor F. Ray Marshall says we could reduce unemployment (now at 7 percent and expected to rise to 9 percent) to less than 4 percent, if there were no illegal immigrants in the country. Some college professors maintain that immigrants do not take jobs from citizens. It is quite true that they take few, if any, professors' jobs, and they do not take jobs from newspapermen. But what about the jobs that could be filled by the currently unemployed?

Energy? No immigrant brings any energy with him. Arrived here he must supply his energy needs from America's present energy stores and energy income. The more people, the less energy per person—or the faster the supply diminishes.

The burden of public services is a complex one, made up in part of schooling, health services, and police protection. Immigrants increase the variety of our society, and variety is a good thing; but they increase the burden of public services. It is possible to have too much of a good thing.

Bilingual education is already a headache. And now bilingualism is changing to polylingualism. If we admit every new unfortunate group as it surfaces, we may end up like India with 14 major languages and more than 100 dialects. Can democracy survive that much variety?

We are a compassionate people. When others knock at our door, we want to share. But at some point in the escalation of charity, we should think of our children. Do we have the right to give away the resources they will need to live? For that matter, are we adequately providing for the poor who are already with us? And how well are we treating our most recent immigrants and their children?

Our hearts bleed at the thought of the hundreds of millions of needy in the world, but bleeding solves no problems. Our hearts need to think too. There are limits to the amounts of good we can do. If we try to do too much, we will end up doing harm. It is time to admit that there are limits. We must do this not so much for the sake of those who are well off in America now, as for the sake of our poor and all of our children.

## Act III: Who Next? And When?

Haiti?
El Salvador?
Guatemala?
Mexico?
Costa Rica, Honduras, Nicaragua, Bahamas, Barbados, Dominican Republic, Ecuador, Peru, Paraguay, Bolivia?
Albania?
Portugal?
Sudan, Gambia, Ghana, Liberia, Mali, Niger, Nigeria, Senegal, Togo, Upper Volta?
Ethiopia?
Kenya?
Malawi, Mauritius, Mozambique, Rwanda, Somalia, Uganda, Zambia, Angola, Zaire, Chad?

Botswana?
Lesotho?
Namibia?
Iraq, Jordan, Lebanon, Syria, Turkey, Yemen, Afghanistan, Bangladesh, India, Pakistan?
Israel?
Northern Ireland?
Poland?

# 5

## *Throwing Facts in the Jurymen's Eyes*

"Immigrants," says economist Julian Simon, "contribute more in taxes than they use in services," adding that this is especially true ("to an indecent extent") of illegal immigrants. Simon and a few other social scientists think that immigrants are a bargain; we should stop complaining about our leaky borders. Simon's statement comes from his 1981 book, *The Ultimate Resource*, and is based, he says, on the findings of David North and Marion Houstoun published five years earlier. Let's take a look at this study.

What North and Houstoun found was that *in a particular group* of illegal immigrants 77 percent had social security taxes withheld from their pay and passed on to the government, while 73 percent had income taxes withheld. In the same group only 4 percent received unemployment insurance payments, and only 0.5 percent received welfare payments. Clearly *these* people were (at the moment) putting more money into the community pot than they were taking out. Such is the basis of Simon's claim.

But North and Houstoun themselves reached no such conclusion. On the contrary, they called attention to the very special character of the sample studied. Their immigrants were healthy young men who had been employed for two or more weeks in the immediate past. What else would you expect of such a population, immigrant or native? North and Houstoun identified the bias of their sample, but special pleaders for the immigrants have carefully failed to report the bias ever since. Professor Simon follows this tradition: though he cites the North and Houstoun study in his bibliography, he carefully reports only the facts that serve his purpose.

As compared with the natural sciences, the social sciences are poor in theory and rich in facts. Several evils arise from this. First, the poverty of social theory selects for practitioners who resist thinking in theoretical terms. "Facts" seem so scientific! Even the word "theory" is often a pejorative in nonscientific discourse: it implies something that might possibly be true, but probably is not. To scientists, "theory" means primarily a set of fundamental concepts woven into a structured and intricate web that is more beautiful and meaningful than the facts it embraces.

Mere facts minus theory—or worse, facts flying in the face of theory —are the stock in trade of the professional obfuscator. To such, the most delicious of all facts are statistics which, as R. W. Revans has said, "like bikini swimming suits, reveal those parts of the subject that are interesting while concealing those that are vital." The frequently exercised talent of social scientists to clothe their subjects in bikinis leads the common man to distrust statistics generally. John Q. Citizen recalls the old gibe, "There are three kinds of lies: lies, damned lies, and statistics."

On the theoretical level it is difficult to see how a nation that has some 8 million unemployed can be benefitted by the in-migration of several million more people looking for jobs. Immigrants may benefit employers, and consumers may be pleased with the resulting low price of manufactured goods. But if our unemployed are kept alive at public expense, someone has to pay the bill. And there is no assurance that some of the new immigrants, and their families, will not eventually end up on the public dole.

The recently employed immigrants of North and Houstoun's study were not publicly supported. Those without recent employment are another matter. In 1979, in Los Angeles County, welfare was denied to 17,684 applicants who were identified as illegals. The welfare they would have received had they not been so identified would have amounted to $3,325 per person per year, or a total of $58,799,300 annually. It takes a lot of taxes to make up such a sum. And the County authorities did not know how many illegals had slipped through their net.

Some more facts, again from Los Angeles, are also enlightening. The county has sued the federal government for $89 million to pay for medical services given to illegals who would not have turned up at the county hospital had the federal government not failed in its function of keeping illegal immigrants out of the country. The claimed sum is to cover the expenses of 1978 only. If the county succeeds in this suit it will then sue for 1979, 1980, and subsequent years when the expenses rose to even greater heights.

Impressive as these facts are they are not decisive because life is complex and there are always other facts around the corner. Live current controversies can seldom be neatly laid to rest with a complete rundown of the facts. We need an approach that bypasses the limitations of a recital of facts. Fortunately, such an approach exists.

When a ridiculous assertion is advanced, grant its truth (for the sake of argument) and then *insist that its implications be fully worked out.* If it is indeed true that immigrants are always a net economic gain to the nation, then we must conclude that the more immigrants admitted the better. In 1980 the United States probably took in a total of two million immigrants. Would we have been made even richer by 10 million? Still richer by 50 million? Or perhaps the entire 800 million estimated by the World Health Organization as the population of the malnourished of the world?

At this point special pleaders will no doubt protest: "Don't be ridiculous. Any course of action, carried to the extreme, produces bad results."

*Precisely*: but what is "extreme"? Evidently not *all* immigration is good; there must be a point on the curve at which the benefit of immigration to the country turns downward. It might be at 2,000,000 per year; or 100,000 per year; or maybe at only 1,000 per year. Who knows? Here is where we must relate facts to a theoretical idea of deep significance.

We need to know what the carrying capacity of the country is. Carrying capacity is inversely related to the quality of life (in its materialistic aspects). To enjoy the scale of living we have become accustomed to, it is possible that our population has already reached the carrying capacity of our land.

Or—who knows?—perhaps we have already gone considerably beyond the optimum point. Those who think about population problems should turn their attention to the admittedly difficult problem of determining carrying capacity, which means reaching agreement on values. It's time to stop throwing statistical dust in the public's eyes.

# 6

# *Immigrants and Oil*

When it became apparent in 1977 that Mexico had found vast new supplies of petroleum, the connection of this fact with the immigration problem was soon made. To judge from the number of letters appearing in newspapers and magazines, thousands of people must have realized the relevance of the two factors. Many of the writers evidently belonged to that guilt-driven contingent who see little that is good in America, readily finding excuses for the anti-American activities of other nations. This stance is the opposite of ethnocentrism (which these people denounce) and deserves a name of its own: "ethnofugalism" will do. Learning of the new Mexican oil, the ethnofugalists promptly demanded that the United States graciously admit unlimited numbers of Mexican immigrants in the hope that Mexico might then condescend to let us have some of her oil.

Missing in this proposal is any understanding of international economics. No country "lets" another have its exports; it *sells* them. Mexico wants to sell her oil. To help dispose of the surplus people she produces Mexico might insist on a package deal, and if we refused to take the immigrants she could then refuse to sell us her oil. And then what? The result is easy to predict. The United States would buy oil from other countries which would erase their deficits by purchasing an equivalent amount from Mexico: a game of musical chairs. Mexico would get rid of its oil, and we would get what we want. The principal effect of such an embargo would be to enrich the third parties that acted as go-betweens in the transfer of oil.

This scenario is not manufactured out of the whole cloth. In the days before the nation of Zimbabwe was brought into being, the treatment of blacks by the ruling whites in the predecessor-nation, Rhodesia, moved our Congress to pass a law forbidding the purchase of chromium from Rhodesia. The result? Rhodesia sold its high-grade ores to Russia while Russia sold her low-grade ores to the United States. Rhodesia's export business was unharmed, the United States was made poorer, and Russia was made richer. So much for good intentions.

Some of the commentators supporting an oil + immigrant package defended it from a purely patriotic standpoint. Realizing that each new immigrant would make new demands on our energy sources, members of this group suggested that we follow the policy of quid pro quo, seeing to it that the privilege of immigration was paid for in oil. The cartoonist Herblock depicted a strategy meeting in the White House at which one of the participants asked, "What if we ask each illegal immigrant to roll a barrel of oil in with him?" This was a good insight, but the quantity was way off. The data in the accompanying table show that as of 1977 the daily consumption of all forms of nonagriculturally derived energy, stated in terms of barrels of oil, amounted to some 36.7 millions of barrels of oil-equivalent per day. The U.S. Census Bureau tells us that there were 224 million Americans at midyear in 1977. This means that the consumption of energy by Americans averaged 60 barrels of oil-equivalent per person per year. An immigrant crossing the border, bringing in one barrel of oil, as Herblock recommended, would bring in only six days' supply of energy, if he used energy as lavishly as the average American. Of course the poor immigrant would not be so extravagant, but it is doubtful if his barrel of oil would last more than a few weeks. After that, as far as energy is concerned, he would be living at the expense of the rest of America.

## U.S. Energy Consumption, 1977

| Source | Daily Consumption in Terms of Millions of Barrels of Oil-Equivalent | Percentage of Total |
|---|---|---|
| Petroleum | 18.4 | 50 |
| Natural gas | 9.2 | 25 |
| Coal | 6.7 | 18 |
| Nuclear | 1.3 | 4 |
| Hydro | 1.1 | 3 |
| Food energy (Food crops) | Not included | Excluded |
| Organic fuel energy (Principally wood) | Not included | Excluded |
| Total | 36.7 | 100 |

But, someone may object, the immigrant is working, he is producing energy! Not so: *No human being has ever produced an erg of energy since the world began.* No human being can produce energy. Neither can any other animal or plant. We are deceived by language.

A business analyst waxes eloquent over the number of millions of barrels of oil that we "produced" last year. This is utterly false. We never produce oil—all we can do is extract it from the ground and destroy it under circumstances that ensure that we benefit from the energy released from the oil. The faster we extract oil—not "produce" it—the sooner the supply will be exhausted.

With the exception of nuclear energy (to which I shall return in a moment) all of our energy comes from the sun. The second law of thermodynamics simply means that the energy cascades down from a high level to successively lower levels until finally there is no useful energy— "negentropy," to be exact—left to run our machines and keep organisms going. One can think of the steps in this cascade as so many parallel terraces down which a waterfall splashes on its way to the sea (useless energy or maximum entropy). Human beings (and all other organisms) manage to place themselves on these terraces and enjoy the degradation of energy as it takes place. We cannot prevent the degradation; all we can do is try to increase the efficiency with which we exploit the degradation as it takes place. When we eat this year's potatoes, or burn the alcohol derived from them, we are using the energy captured from this year's sunshine. When we burn firewood we are restarting the cascade of energy that was interrupted when the tree laid down its cellulose, perhaps fifty years ago. But whether solar energy is used promptly, or is delayed in use, we never create or produce energy: we merely release it and take advantage of the release. The energy of petroleum or coal was captured by plants hundreds of millions of years ago and stored until burning released the "fossil sunlight."

What about nuclear energy? By his cleverness man can put certain kinds of atoms in such a relation with each other that they release the energy that is stored internally, a store of energy that does not derive from the sun. Again, strictly speaking, men do not produce this energy; but from a certain practical point of view (since the quantity of energy per atom is so tremendous) it is almost as if human beings produced this energy. Before we become too optimistic about this situation we must take into account a number of unwelcome facts. For one thing, it takes the massive and complicated technological machinery of a large nuclear plant to release the energy of the atom in a manner that allows us to make use of it. The energetic costs of producing a nuclear plant, mining and transporting the required ores, fashioning the metals into the proper shape, safely disposing of the dangerous products after the nuclear reaction, and distributing the electrical energy to where it is needed are considerable. For more than a decade after we began on our nuclear energy program the energy going into the system was greater than the energy coming out. Now the balance is more favorable, but today we face a new set of problems, the solutions of which cannot be technological. These are the problems of reliably operating the entire nuclear establishment, from uranium mine to nuclear graveyard, with satisfactory safety despite the inherent unreliability of human beings and the periodic determination of one group or another to exploit the dangerous potentialities of the atom. Sabotage is the ugly name for such activity, and the problem it presents is more than technological. No one can confidently assert that he has the final answer to sabotage and carelessness. For this reason many thoughtful people question whether atomic energy will ever significantly modify policies worked out on the assumption of no atomic energy. In any case, for several decades to come, nuclear power will not be a large portion of our energy budget. Since the problems raised by immigration are with us now, and escalating more rapidly than is production of nuclear energy, a conservative approach is to simply ignore nuclear aspects of the energy problem.

You may have noted that the table does not include the amount of energy derived from agriculture. One could maintain that an immigrant, by his labor, could increase the energy "production" from this source. This is true, but the effect of this "production" on the national economy is problematical. Immigrants do not increase the number of acres of American land exposed to the sunshine, though they may help bring new land under cultivation. This apology for immigration would be more convincing were we short of idle hands among our own people, but with some 8 to 10 million pairs of idle hands, the possessors of which must be fed and clothed whether they work or not, the argument for importing more energy-consuming bodies is weak. If it is objected that our own unemployed are unwilling to work at certain jobs, this merely defines another problem, that of matching people to the work that needs doing, which presupposes persuading workers to be content in the work they must do.

Each new immigrant constitutes a drain on our supplies of energy and a continuing demand levied against our energy income. How much of a demand? An American, on the average, uses 60 barrels of oil-equivalent per year. An immigrant certainly will not live this well, energetically speaking. Suppose we assume that he uses half as much energy per year, and that he comes into the country at age 20, surviving to age 70. He will, then, use $30 \times 50 = 1,500$ barrels of oil-equivalent before he dies. The immigrant brings no acres of land with him, and no sunshine. The only thing he might bring in to pay for his maintenance would be some energy-containing material, of which petroleum is a most convenient form. To correct Mr. Herblock's picture we would have to depict each new immigrant pulling a large trailer behind him in which there were 1,500 barrels of oil. Only by bringing in such a load might an immigrant pay his way.

Even this discouraging picture is not pessimistic enough. If the immigrant male later brings in a wife—which is not improbable—and if the two of them have children—which is also not improbable—the burden incurred by the first admission rises further. Nor does it stop with one generation. The employers of immigrant labor—hotel operators, agribusiness, small manufacturers, taxicab companies, and countless others—may each be able to demonstrate from his individual account books that he has benefitted economically from uncontrolled immigration. Such accounting does not include the total economic costs to the nation. With total accounting, the ratio of benefits to costs is less than unity, even on the conservative assumption of 1,500 barrels of oil-equivalent per year as the cost to the nation of each immigrant admitted. Those who defend uncontrolled immigration must find some other justification for their position.

# EVOLUTION

# 7

# *"Scientific Creationism"—*
# *Marketing Deception as Truth*

The seven-part TV series *The Voyage of Charles Darwin* ended in a reenactment of the 1860 Huxley-Wilberforce debate, in which Dr. Samuel Wilberforce, bishop of Oxford, attacked Thomas Henry Huxley for upholding Darwin's views but was thoroughly trounced. A television viewer might well have concluded that Darwinism had triumphed. How wrong he would have been!

Among scientists, it is true, the Darwinian theory did pass from triumph to triumph in the years after the debate to become the only view seriously entertained by professional biologists. The idea of natural selection now suffuses every branch of biology. There, Darwin has won.

But in the public arena, things are quite otherwise. Sixty-five years after Huxley-Wilberforce, the trial of John T. Scopes, a high school teacher, revealed an enormous resistance to Darwin's ideas among Fundamentalist Protestants. To the dismay of both parties in the dispute, this celebrated 1925 "monkey trial," in which Scopes was accused of teaching the theory of evolution in Dayton, Tennessee, was ultimately decided on purely technical grounds. Scopes was first convicted and fined $100, but on appeal he was acquitted on the technicality that the fine had been excessive. Within a few years, other trials around the country determined that state laws could not mandate the teaching of the biblical story of creation nor forbid the teaching of evolution in the public schools. Both violated the First Amendment of the Constitution, which established the separation of church and state.

In the 1860 debate, evolutionists won the battle; in the following century, they nearly lost the war. By the time of the centenary of the *Origin of Species*, in 1959, the vast majority of high school biology texts had resolved the dispute simply by suppressing both special creation and evolution. The word "evolution" was usually omitted, with the flabby word "development" standing in its place. Natural selection was scarcely touched upon. A high school student in 1960 would generally have had no inkling of the importance of Darwin in the intellectual history of humanity.

The public resurrection of Darwinism came, curiously, from space. In October 1957, the Soviet Union launched *Sputnik I*, the first artificial earth satellite. By beating us out in the race to space, the Soviets shattered American complacency about our technological superiority. There arose an immediate outcry for greater emphasis on the teaching of science in the high schools. As biologists took up their portion of the educational burden, they became aware of how disastrously school administrators and textbook publishers had sabotaged biology. A feisty geneticist, Nobel Prize winner H. J. Muller, protested in an article entitled "One Hundred Years Without Darwin Is Enough." In response, the Biological Sciences Curriculum Study (BSCS), the official arm of the biology teaching profession, put out three different high school textbooks, each of them assigning a major role to evolution and natural selection. When the state board of education in Texas asked for a special edition that would mitigate these frightening ideas, BSCS refused to compromise.

In human affairs as in Newtonian physics, action provokes reaction. Within a few years, Fundamentalists had developed a new attack, which ran around the end of the First Amendment. Knowing that they could not insert an explicitly religious view into the school curricula, they called their view scientific, christening it "scientific creationism." Their plea that it be included in the curricula had a surface plausibility. No human being *was* present at the origin of life on earth, nor did anyone actually observe and record the evolution of one species into another millions of years ago. Therefore (said the creationists), it is just as scientific to believe that all existing species were created in an instant in exactly the same forms that they now appear as it is to suppose that they evolved. Scientific creationists do not ask that their theory displace Darwin's in the schools. They ask only for equal time.

Are scientific creationists concerned primarily with science or with religion? In a presentation to the California Board of Education, one of their spokesmen said, "Creation in scientific terms is *not* a religious or philosophical belief." At the same time, an appeal for funds made by the Creation Science Research Center, in San Diego, bragged that it intended "to take advantage of the tremendous opportunity that God has given us . . . to reach the 63 million children in the United States with the scientific teaching of Biblical creationism." Note that the spokesman unconsciously let the veil fall when he dropped "scientific" and reverted to "Biblical" in finishing his sentence. An astute opposing attorney would not let this lapse to truth pass without comment.

Even at the religious level the creationist view is a biased one. The only creation story they mention is the one in Genesis (in which there are actually two stories—the version in the first chapter being so different from that in the second chapter that biblical scholars believe they were written hundreds of years apart). Why do they not mention the belief of Hindus that the world began with the creation of the cosmic egg? What about the Babylonians' belief that there was not a single creationist god but two cosmic parents?

Many outsiders see the creationists' call for fair play as little more than a legal ploy. A close reading of Fundamentalist literature by social scientist Dorothy Nelkin, of Cornell University, led her to believe that these earnest people are most deeply disturbed by what they regard as the moral disintegration of our society—rising crime rates, profligate sexuality, breakdown of the family, undermining of authority, and so on. Darwin may be only the scapegoat.

Because many of the views of Fundamentalists are widely shared, creationists have considerable support among those who couldn't care less about the creation-versus-evolution argument. During the past generation, Americans have become ever more concerned about fair play toward minorities. Protecting minorities increases diversity, which is regarded as a positive good. Scientists have long insisted that truth cannot be determined by majority vote: Galileo, after all, was in his day a minority—or "a majority of one," to use Thoreau's inspired phrase. We worship fair play; we are intolerant of dogmatism.

So in town meetings and in public debates, scientific creationists have proved formidable opponents. Scientists have not found it easy to explain to creationist supporters why a view held by a sizable minority should be forcibly excluded from the public schools.

To see what is involved, let us adopt a tactic discovered long ago by the mathematicians: When one question stumps you, ask another. That is, ask a related question whose answer throws light on the first.

Let our other question be this: Why don't we teach astrology in the schools? Astrology holds that the course of each human life is determined to a considerable degree by the position of the stars in the sky at the exact moment of the individual's birth. Belief in it, in one variant or another, has probably been held by most of the people on earth. Even today, some universities in India offer degrees in the subject. Yet American believers do not pressure boards of education to add their subject to the curriculum. If believers in astrology became as well organized as the creationists, it is hard to see how their demands could be withstood. Our emotions concerning this issue have not been aroused; we can objectively examine the issues. On what grounds might scientists object to the inclusion of astrology in the public schools?

The reason for not calling astrology a science is simple: Its assertions cannot be proved false.

There is a widespread belief among the public that the statements of science are *provable*. Scientists and philosophers now agree this is wrong. No scientific statement is ever fully proved. Science is made up of statements that are vulnerable to falsification but which have not (so far) been proven false by the most rigorous tests scientists (or their opponents) could think of. A statement that is not falsifiable is a *waterproof hypothesis*; it is beyond the pale of science.

Let's see why astrology is not science. Over 1,500 years ago, Saint Augustine cited what he regarded as a definitive disproof of astrology. He knew of two babies who were born at the same time, one to a wealthy couple and the other to a slave woman. When these babies grew up—surprise!—the child born to wealth became wealthy, and the slave's child became a slave. Since they had been born at the same instant, it was obvious, said Saint Augustine, that the astrological hypothesis was nonsense.

Did Saint Augustine prevail? He did not. Astrologers had a very simple response to his "disproof," which they continue to repeat to the present day. It is this: No two babies are ever born at *exactly* the same instant. Therefore, their astrological signs are different, and their futures must differ as well. Insistence on the word "exactly" converts the astrological position into a waterproof hypothesis.

Should astrology be taught in public schools? Not as science. On this scientists must be adamant. The total exclusion of doctrines based on waterproof statements is one of the few dogmas of science. If the public wants to have astrology taught as part of some other course—history? sociology?—that is a matter about which a scientist, *as a scientist*, has nothing to say.

Having shown that astrology is not scientific, we can return to our principal question: Is scientific creationism scientific? Curiously, a complete answer to this question was worked out more than a century ago in a brief dispute that has, by a quirk of history, been almost completely forgotten. The idea of evolution is much older than Darwinism. What Darwin contributed was a believable mechanism to account for evolution. Fifteen years before the *Origin of Species*, an anonymous volume, *Vestiges of the Natural History of Creation*, espoused the evolutionary view. Scientifically, *Vestiges* was, in the opinion of scientists both then and now, a poor thing, but it was very popular; it went through ten editions before the *Origin of Species* was published.

Many religious people saw evolution as a threat to morality and religion. One of the most disturbed of these was Philip Gosse, a minister in the Fundamentalist group called the Plymouth Brethren. Gosse was not only a minister but also a naturalist (a common combination in Victorian England). During the 1850s, Darwin consulted him on many matters, though without ever revealing the heretical trend of his thought.

Gosse, upset by *Vestiges*, set out to demolish completely all theories of evolution. He began with geology. Geologists explain the strata of the rocks by physical principles, deducing that it must have taken millions of years to deposit layer upon layer of sedimentary rocks. There is no way to reconcile this deduction with the religious belief that the world began in the year 4004 B.C., so proclaimed in the seventeenth century by James Ussher, archbishop of Armagh. But Gosse thought he had found a way. His book, published two years before the *Origin*, was entitled *Omphalos*. The name is significant: It is Greek for "belly button."

Consider Adam and Eve, said Gosse. Did they have navels? Since the navel is a vestige of the link between the fetus and the placenta, one could argue that they had no navels, since Adam was created from dust and Eve was created from Adam's rib. But one could also argue that the first human had to have a navel; it is inconceivable that God (a perfect being) would create imperfect creatures. Adam's and Eve's navels were not evidence of a preexisting being (namely a mother) but were merely what one would expect in God-created creatures.

Gosse explained the stratification of the rocks by the same logic. Strata are not evidence of processes occurring over millions of years; they are merely what one would expect to find in a perfect world. The strata and their fossils were all created on day three (see Genesis) as a materialization of God's thought. The fossils are merely artifacts that God was pleased to place among the strata when he created the world. The deductions of the geologist and the biologist fall to ground, and the Bible stands supreme as the revelation of truth. So said Gosse.

Gosse expected *Omphalos* to be attacked by scientists. It was. He was not prepared for the bitter denunciation by the religious community. Asked to write a review of *Omphalos*, his friend Charles Kingsley, a minister and the author of *Westward Ho!*, refused. He wrote a letter to Gosse explaining why.

"You have given," Kingsley said, "the 'vestiges of creation theory' the best shove forward which it has ever had. I have a special dislike for that book; but, honestly, I felt my heart melting towards it as I read *Omphalos*.

"Shall I tell you the truth? It is best. Your book is the first that ever made me doubt [the doctrine of absolute creation], and I fear it will make hundreds do so. Your book tends to prove this—that if we accept the fact of absolute creation, God becomes God-the-Sometime-Deceiver. I do not mean merely in the case of fossils which *pretend* to be the bones of dead animals; but in . . . your newly created Adam's navel, you make God tell a lie. It is not my reason, but my *conscience* which revolts here. . . . I cannot . . . believe that God has written on the rocks one enormous and superfluous lie for all mankind.

"To this painful dilemma you have brought me, and will, I fear, bring hundreds. It will not make me throw away my Bible. I trust and hope. I know in whom I have believed, and can trust Him to bring my faith safe through this puzzle, as He has through others; but for the young I do fear. I would not for a thousand pounds put your book into my children's hands."

Gosse, abandoned by churchmen, gave up theorizing and returned to merely observing nature. As a popularizer of nature, his position in science education is an honorable one. His *Evenings at the Microscope* persuaded many an English gentleman to take up the microscope as a hobby.

Returning to the present we note that the waterproof argument for creation has not disappeared. Since Gosse's time physicists have developed the ingenious "radioactive clock" which biologists have used to date strata and fossils. Creationists have explained the findings away as easily as Adam's belly button. If an Archeozoic crystal has more lead and less uranium than one formed during the Cenozoic era, it is merely because God set the two clocks at different times when he started both of them ticking in 4004 B.C. So say the creationists.

Neither scientist nor scientific creationist can suggest any deduction from the creation hypothesis that can be proved false, now or in the future. But the hypothesis of evolution *is* falsifiable by a thousand conceivable observations, for example, finding *Australopithecus* bones in strata from the Mesozoic era. Evolution, therefore, might be a false hypothesis. But creationism can never be proved false.

The Reverend Charles Kingsley was closer to the truth than perhaps he knew when he said it was not his reason but his conscience that made him reject the waterproof belly button argument. In some abstract sense, science may (as some claim) be value free, but the practitioners of science often become very emotional when they are confronted with waterproof hypotheses. They exhibit what can only be called moral indignation—or the sort of contemptuousness a professional gambler would express if he were asked to play poker with twos, threes, fours, fives, and one-eyed jacks wild. Grown men don't play such games.

There is a paradox in the present Mexican standoff between scientists and scientific creationists. Bible supporters want Genesis taught because (they say) it is scientific; evolutionists want waterproof hypotheses excluded because (they feel) they are intellectually immoral. With Bible-idolaters claiming to be scientists and scientists preaching morality, it is small wonder that the general public is confused.

Actually, all the *arguments* given here could be presented in the public schools without creating any legal problems or disturbing scientists. The educational benefit would be enormous. That the arguments are not presented has many explanations. The principal one is no doubt this: It is always easier to teach facts than arguments. It is particularly difficult to *examine* for an understanding of arguments. Teachers—some of them—are lazy. So are some students. Classes—most of them—are large; this militates against teaching subtle arguments. A pluralistic society like ours makes it easier to run away from a controversy than to deal with it fairly and openly.

One wonders: When the second centenary of the *Origin of Species* rolls around, in the year 2059, will the theory of evolution through natural selection be universally accepted? Evidences of natural selection are everywhere: in the unwanted appearance of DDT-resistant insects and antibiotic-resistant disease germs as well as in the wanted development of domestic plant and animal varieties in response to breeding programs in which man defines the selective criteria. But these evidences are nothing to a person who does not reject waterproof hypotheses.

Our social world is a chaotic one. It is understandable that many sincere people should seek emotional refuge in a waterproof hypothesis like that of instantaneous creation. Broadening the support for Darwin's view depends not so much on accumulating more scientific evidence as it does on getting more people to understand the nature of science itself.

# 8

# Sociobiology—Aesop With Teeth

The interest of the general public in the human implications of biology increased enormously following the publication of Edward O. Wilson's *Sociobiology*. This is a monumental work in more than one sense. Over 90 percent of the 575 pages of text proper is a noncontroversial summary of social behavior among animals. This portion has been universally praised. It is unlikely that it will be supplanted in our generation. Research in this field is being so vigorously pursued (partly as a result of Wilson's book) that the eventual successor of this volume will no doubt have many authors and less artistic unity.

The bulk of the book deserves the title and the unqualified praise. It is a minor proportion, principally the first and last chapters, that has stirred up a tempest and needs to be discussed separately (so far as that is possible). The material in these chapters should really be called *bio-sociology*—sociology erected on a foundation of biology. However, it is too late to make the change.

Calling Wilson's work monumental is apt in another sense. Monuments attract graffiti: already this one has been defaced with the epithets *racist, sexist, elitist, biological determinist, social Darwinist,* and *reductionist.* As Kenneth Boulding has said, "There is something in the 'ist' sound which conveys an almost snakelike hissing and venom." That this is the intention of Wilson's detractors is evident in such a work as Marshall Sahlins's book-length review *The Use and Abuse of Biology.* With a few conspicuous exceptions, anthropologists and sociologists have not welcomed the incursion of a zoologist into the realm of human behavior.

To take the long view we might say that Wilson is continuing in the tradition of the legendary Aesop. Aesop, of course, did not pretend to be a zoologist: he merely used the animal world as a refracting lens to transmit his view of human nature. Aesop's *Fables* are not research protocols. Fables (like humor, negation, and symbols) are, as Freud has taught us, a way of getting repressed thoughts admitted to the conscious mind. At the moment of reception all such prosthetic devices become ambivalent. The audience will be appropriately educated only if it sees through the disguise; but if the insight is too sudden, too clear, the conventional mind's defenses will be mobilized in a personal attack against the seer. According to the legend the citizens of Delphi turned on Aesop, hurling him to his death from the cliffs of Mount Parnassus. (Legend also has it that his crime was the vulgar one of embezzlement. This is not surprising: the hoi polloi cannot admit that they have killed a soothsayer for the noble crime of speaking the truth; a base excuse must be found.)

Going beyond Aesop, contemporary students of ethology take animals seriously, seeing in their behavior hints—and sometimes more than hints—of the human condition. Seeing, however, is not a purely passive act, and therein lies the potentiality of error. "I am," said Charles Darwin, "a firm believer that without speculation there is no good and original observation." Darwin's followers, who have not hesitated to speculate, have found that speculating about the causes of human behavior is no less perilous today than it was in Aesop's time. It is no longer fashionable to hurl prophets from cliffs, but many of the defenders of the conventional wisdom are perfectly willing to destroy a man's reputation with polemics. Pejorative labels substitute for the objective examination of evidence.

The pursuit of knowledge about human behavior is not a safe occupation. The passions of the defenders of the intellectual status quo are kept at hair-trigger readiness and can be released not only by the assertions of ethologists, but even by mere questions. Defenders may even infer questions where none are implied.

The battle for free speech and freedom of inquiry begun so nobly three centuries ago by John Milton with his *Areopagitica* is never decisively won. "Let Truth and Falsehood grapple:" said Milton, "who ever knew Truth put to the worse in a free and open encounter?" This calm faith is not shared by those who in our day are members of an organization bearing the righteous name, "Science for the People." At a symposium on sociobiology held in San Francisco in June 1977, the meeting was disrupted by political activists who chanted for more than two minutes (by actual measurement), "No free speech for racists! No free speech for racists!" Their exhortation was grossly redundant: once the first three words were said all else was otiose. One felt like crying with Wordsworth, "Milton! thou should'st be living at this hour: the world hath need of thee."

Are the races equal? Are the sexes equal? Is there a hereditary component to human behavior? These are questions a right-thinking person never asks unless he immediately makes it clear that the answers are (in the same order): *Yes, Yes,* and *No.* It is the misfortune of sociobiologists that its detractors have inferred from their writings the opposite answers and so have sought to excommunicate sociobiologists from the scientific, and indeed from the larger, community. For their anxiety to shield the public from the knowledge that the three questions listed above even exist, the detractors deserve to be called the New Puritans. Actually, the first two questions are scarcely raised in any of the sociobiological literature, though they have received the lion's share of attention by indignant political activists. The third question, however, occupies a central position in sociobiological thinking about human affairs.

One of the joint productions of the Cambridge-Boston caucus of "Science for the People" is entitled "Sociobiology—Another Biological Determinism," and begins with this sentence: "Biological determinism represents the claim that the present states of human societies are the specific result of biological forces and the biological 'nature' of the human species." This is an interesting sentence. The meaning of the adjective "specific" is not clear, but I think it is a fair inference that the caucus maintains that the position of a determinist is that the form of human society is rigidly and uniquely determined—by something. One can hardly dispute a definition, but we should ask whether the class of determinists, so defined, has any members? Marx was an economic determinist of a sort, but we must doubt that even he regarded political organization as rigidly and uniquely determined by economics: otherwise, why go to all the trouble of writing the *Communist Manifesto* and *Das Kapital?*

As for biological determinism, I know of no one who fits the caricature attacked by the Scientists for the People. A thoughtful biologist maintains that our nature—no need of derogatory quotation marks—has something to do with social organizations and social problems (which problems are the consequences of our variable nature not fitting the straitjacket we call social organization). If human beings had the pituitary-adrenocortical-gonadal system of domestic sheep our social problems would surely be different; so also if we had the endocrine system of weasels or shrews. The characteristics of these endocrine systems are inherited, and what is inherited has social consequences. This is not to say that genes rigidly determine the social order: even populations of housemice develop social differences due to what can only be called historical accidents. How much more important the accidents of human history are hardly needs arguing. "Biological determinism" with its implications of absolute rigidity is a straw man set up for the convenience of polemicists; we would do well to ignore it. Determinism, like racism, sexism, and social Darwinism, is less a definable formal intellectual position than it is a pejorative used to tar an opponent.

The opposite of complete determinism is complete indeterminism. Do the critics of biosociology assert that inheritable behavior is completely indeterministic of the social order? It is hard to see any other interpretation of this assertion by Richard Lewontin: "Nothing we can know about the genetics of human behavior can have any implications for human society." Lewontin is a brilliant theoretician; it would help us all if he would enrich this *ex cathedra* statement with a mathematical demonstration that social organization is utterly independent of individual behavior (which is necessarily affected by individual variations).

The argument over heredity versus environment (or nature versus nurture) is as rancorous today as it was a century ago. It has frequently and truly been pointed out that both heredity and environment are important, because the end result (the phenotype) is produced by genes interacting with each other in a given environment. In principle, the end result can be changed by varying either heredity or environment (though producing one kind of variation is often practically more feasible than producing the other). Biologists and sociologists both pay lip service to these general statements—and then generally go their separate ways. Their positions polarize. As a biologist I will not claim to be objectively neutral, but I do want to point out some subtleties of the problem that I think are not adequately considered by sociologists (or even by some biologists like Lewontin).

The first point—and this is an extension of a point made earlier—is that *determination*, with all its cognates, is an unfortunate term. *Influence* is far better: it implies a weak rather than strong relationship of behavior to social structure, and of heredity with behavior. With respect to the latter association, one of the major contributions of R. A. Fisher half a century ago was the demonstration that even the weakest of heredity is adequate to produce evolutionary effects in the long run. Probably wisely, we regard the weakness of a hereditary factor as relevant to problems of ethnic stereotyping and social justice; but the weakness scarcely matters in the evolutionary process (assuming the mode of selection remains the same). By habitually speaking of influence rather than determination we should be less tempted to indulge in rhetorical bombast. The practical question this approach leads to is this: How much influence? And, if controllable, controllable at what cost? (Cost must be understood in the widest sense as comprising psychological, social, and political costs as well as the merely economic.)

The nature-nurture problem has a further subtlety that is insufficiently appreciated: the connection between heredity and environment is one of circular causation. This idea has been independently rediscovered (or at any rate, independently reemphasized) by several people over the past century, under several terms, of which the Baldwin effect and genetic assimilation are best known. The gist of the idea may be put in folksy terms: "First we select the environment and then the environment selects us." This important principle can be illustrated by taking a new look at a classic popularization of anthropology, Benedict's *Patterns of Culture*.

Ruth Benedict (1887–1948), a student of Franz Boas (1858–1942), was committed to the view that culture was nearly all, heredity next to nothing. Comparing the life of different North American Indians, she divided their cultures into Apollonian and Dionysian. In the former the model person was restrained, low key; the latter greatly honored individuals who were given to visions and trances. Each generation learns from the preceding; culture is self-perpetuating. Environmentarians denigrate genetics as a cause of ethnic differences on two grounds: (1) it is an unnecessary hypothesis, and (2) the genetic mechanism works too slowly to account for the rapid cultural changes that occur when people are transferred from one culture to another.

Curiously, biologists grant the validity of both points and yet dispute the conclusion that there cannot be statistically relevant genetic differences between the people of two cultures. Theoretically the matter could be settled by identical twin experiments—separating many pairs of identical twins and having the members of each pair raised in contrasting cultures. For the results to be decisive the experimental design should be that of a "double-blind test," that is, the exchange of children should be so surreptitiously made in the hospital that the parents, knowing nothing of it, could not influence, through their expectations, the way in which their children were raised. The logic of the double-blind experiment was not made explicit until 1937, by which time the evolution of the idea of individual and civil rights had proceeded so far as to make such an experiment culturally impossible in the European community. Since the decisive experiment cannot be performed, the heredity-environment question cannot be decisively settled for the species *Homo sapiens*. In the eyes of environmentarians, the burden of proof that genetics is of even the slightest importance falls on hereditarians; since the decisive experiment cannot be performed, they say, we must dismiss the idea of a genetic component in culture.

Hereditarians would put the burden of proof on the other side, for reasons that are basically Darwinian. In all animals but man the necessary decisive tests can be made, and in those species that have been adequately tested the following facts have been found to be invariably true. There is always variation; the variation always has a genetic component;

there is a genetic component to behavior; and different environments select for different behaviors, hence (ultimately) for different genetic types.

The relation between genetic attributes and behavioral opportunities or demands is not a simple one. Dogs of two different breeds *may* be trainable to follow the same behavioral path but the cost—to the trainer and to the dog—may be exorbitant in some cases. If you don't believe that, just try to train a cocker spaniel to catch rats the way a wire-haired terrier naturally does; or a terrier to round up sheep as a border collie does; or a dachshund to "point" game. A professional dog trainer who ignored heredity would lose his shirt.

It is a long way from simple behavior reactions to human culture, but the logical distance is a continuum. Genetically identifiable units are involved in the behavioral traits of all other animals. To suppose that human behavior is uninfluenced by heredity is to say that man is not part of nature. The Darwinian assumption is that he is; Darwinians insist that the burden of proof falls on those who assert the contrary.

The differences between Benedict's Apollonians and Dionysians are certainly behavioral: can they be exclusively cultural? The Darwinian would say not. Generously he can grant that at the outset such a difference *may* be exclusively cultural: "some mute, inglorious Milton," persuasive above all others for unknown but purely idiosyncratic reasons, may persuade his tribesmen that the ways of Apollo (or Dionysius) are best and succeed in creating a new culture. But culture, once created, is a sieve by which all future individuals will be tested. In an Apollonian culture little honor will accrue to Dionysians, and the reverse will hold in the Dionysian culture. On the basis of what we know of other animals, it is inconceivable that the sort of nervous temperaments that we call by these two names could have no genetic component whatever. Even the slightest genetic difference will, as Fisher has taught us, lead to differential survival—to natural selection, and a change in gene frequency in subsequent generations. First we select our culture, then our culture selects us.

*What we are, we become.* This, in brief, is the essence of the "Baldwin effect." Nonbiologists have occasionally glimpsed some such ideas, through a glass darkly. I have been told that Hegel once said: "Man, in so far as he acts on nature to change it, changes his own nature." And from Sartre we have the aphorism: "Man makes himself."

The traits a culture honors will, in time, be supported by hereditary tendencies that facilitate the acquisition of those traits. An important qualification of this statement must be made, a qualification that revolves around the verb "honors." For the statement to be true, the honoring must have differential reproductive consequences, that is, those who are honored must leave behind more children (on the average) than do those who are not so honored.

For an example in which this condition was not met, consider clerical celibacy. Assume that Christians regard the estate of priesthood as an honorable one (as they generally do); and that there are statistical, genetic differences between those who willingly take a vow of chastity and those who do not; and that priests, though they may sometimes violate their vow, still have fewer children than laymen—if all this is true there is a self-destructive element in the system that honors priestly qualities by exacting a vow of chastity from those who become priests. The system is counter-selective with respect to its ideals.

The term "social Darwinism" was popularized by Richard Hofstadter. It has become a term of social opprobrium; should it be? It depends on what is meant by it. When it is ostensively defined, it is usually by this quotation from John D. Rockefeller: "The growth of a large business is merely a survival of the fittest. . . . The American Beauty rose can be produced in the splendor and fragrance which bring cheer to its beholder only by sacrificing the early buds which grow up around it. This is not an evil tendency in business. It is merely the working-out of a law of nature and a law of God."

When this is identified (as it commonly is) as an example of the application of the idea of natural selection to the human condition, confusion is compounded. In the first place, Mr. Rockefeller's example has absolutely nothing to do with natural selection, as that term is used in biology: the multiple buds of a single rose plant are genetically identical. Selecting among them has absolutely no selective consequences. ("Selective consequences" means genetically differential consequences.) If you feed a child (or a rosebud) well, it will grow bigger than it will if you don't—but that's the end of the matter.

In the second place (to come closer, no doubt, to the intention of the speaker), if the prospering of a business means the prospering of its managers, then selection is possible. But we must not assume the possible is the actual: the winning managers may, like the leader of a wolf pack, have more offspring than the losers; on the other hand, they may, like Christian priests, have fewer. In the first instance the system will select for whatever heritable qualities contribute to the rise to leadership; in the second the system will select against these qualities. Very seldom do we have sound statistical knowledge of the biological selection associated with social selection or social honoring.

Third—and this is the most important point of all—there is nothing "natural" about the criterion for selection in a culture (if one makes the useful distinction between nature and culture). Man makes himself, as Sartre said; human beings can determine what is selected for by the rules they establish in their culture. In principle, every cultural rule must have some selective effect, however slight. This must be so even though we are usually ignorant of what the effect is. Consideration of the possible selective effects of a proposed change in the rules is seldom a part of the debate when a social change is proposed. But the power of selection is in no way diminished by our nearly universal ignorance of its reality. This is the frontier between knowledge and ignorance that our society seems unwilling to approach.

The simplest summary of Darwinism is perhaps this: *we get what we select for*. This is almost tautological: it must be true. How could the world be otherwise? The question is, what are we selecting for? More importantly, what do we want to select for? The choice is ours. Natural selection is not (as many anthropologists assert) something that human culture has escaped from; on the contrary, like it or not (acknowledge it or not), we are now our own selectors. It is quite understandable that the realization of this fact sometimes creates panic—and even a call for an end to free speech.

The application of Darwinian reasoning to social problems is a necessity. Logically, *this* could be called social Darwinism. But this term, used pejoratively from the date of its coinage, has been utterly spoiled by being identified with nonsense like Mr. Rockefeller's. There's no saving the good in it; we must let it rest as a pure pejorative. What is true and defensible in the application of Darwinian reasoning to social problems deserves a new name: "sociobiology" will do. I do not know whether or not Wilson followed this line of reasoning in choosing the term, but his description of its content is compatible with this approach:

> Sociobiology is defined as the systematic study of the biological basis of all social behavior. . . . Taxonomy and ecology . . . have been reshaped entirely during the past forty years by integration into neo-Darwinist evolutionary theory—the "Modern Synthesis," as it is often called—in which each phenomenon is weighed for its adaptive significance and then related to the basic principles of population genetics. It may not be too much to say that sociology and the other social sciences, as well as the humanities, are the last branches of biology waiting to be included in the Modern Synthesis. One of the functions of sociobiology, then, is to reformulate the foundations of the social sciences in a way that draws these subjects into the Modern Synthesis.

To sociobiologists and humanists Wilson is saying: we are going to biologize your subject. However much these scholars may reject the application of the zoological concept of territoriality to human affairs, we can now expect—indeed we have already seen—a most vigorous territorial behavior on the part of the present professional occupants of the field of human sociology.

# 9

## *Ethics for Birds (And Vice Versa)*

Toward the end of the strange twentieth century, philosophers, ever eager to expand a logical lemma, developed the idea that animals had rights just like human beings. A historical trend was viewed as both destiny and decree. In the earliest days only the elite had rights; then the bourgeoisie; then all free men; then, as slavery was made a null class, all men. Caught in their own net, philosophers—men only at that time—somewhat reluctantly had to admit that women were men too (in the generic sense) and must be accorded the same rights.

At this point something like panic swept over the philosophers. Some, aping Alexander, wept because there were no more worlds to conquer. Others, more creative, turned their attention to the animal world.

"Look!" they said, "We've neglected the beasts. Darwin proved that all living things spring from a common ancestor. All animals are our brothers, if we interpret 'brother' to signify any degree of kinship. When we ask 'How should we treat animals?,' we are really asking

'How should we treat our brothers?' Identical origin implies identical nature. Shared genes necessitates sharing of rights."

Vegetarianism was first encouraged and then made mandatory. Not only was killing of animals outlawed, but it was presently made a crime even to allow them to die. The right to food proclaimed for human beings by the United Nations was extended to all other animals. (Does the spirochaete that causes sleeping sickness have a right to its food, namely human beings? Awkward cases like this were quietly ignored.) Laws forbidding the bringing of dogs into restaurants were declared unconstitutional. Restrooms were opened up to all who could walk, hop, jump, or crawl into them. Universal brotherhood had arrived.

Rights imply responsibilities. As the Animal-Righters won their battles people began to question whether the righted animals were behaving responsibly. The more bizarre forms of animal behavior, previously known only to zoologists, now became matters of hot debate. Does a male walrus have a right to a harem? (Doesn't the female walrus have a right to monogamy?) What right does a black widow spider have to eat her mate after fornication? And the several species of spiders in which the mother allows herself to be eaten by her young raised the serious question of whether this was not going too far with Juvenile Liberation. Surely maternal anthropophagy should be outlawed for all animals, anthropos or not?

The unification of ethics came to a head when zoologists called moralists' attention to the behavior of *Apus apus*, a swift. The food of this skillfully-flying bird is insects caught on the wing. In cool, overcast weather there is not much food to be had. If a swift has nestlings at such a time it will have a hard time catching enough food for itself and its young. Cool days do not occur at random but tend to occur in runs. Through evolution the species has adapted to this reality in the following way. Suppose a bird has a nest with three eggs at the time bad weather begins. After a few days it tips one of the eggs out of the nest. After a few more bad days it destroys a second egg. If the bad weather still doesn't let up it destroys the last egg. Then when the weather turns fair again it lays more eggs and tries again to raise a family. Given the pattern of European weather the swift's behavior is clearly such as to maximize the number of its descendants. To augment life, it kills life.

By the close of the century the principle of the "sanctity of life" had been recognized in law. Parliaments and congresses had agreed that the legal existence of the individual began when the sperm entered the egg. If it was so for human beings, so also must it be for other animals in the reign of Animal Liberation. The infanticide—or was it abortion?—carried out by swift mothers was particularly abhorrent to Mariolaters, who, despite all the progress of the Women's Liberation Movement, still thought of mothers as something very special. Volunteers set up a Swift Watch to prevent swift infanticide, and bills were introduced into legislatures to establish agencies to grow and distribute fresh insects to nestlings born in unfavorable times. Criminal sanctions were sought against infanticidal mothers of all species.

At this point the American Civil Liberties Union stepped in to object that it was unconstitutional to punish any person (read, *animal*) until it had had a chance to defend itself in court. But how could a court hear the testimony of an animal that speaks no human language? Impasse.

Philosophers despaired, but not Hermann K. Leibnitz, the leading scientific practitioner of Providentialism. "It is part of the plan of nature," he said, "that demand creates supply. Look at the history of energy. First man ran out of wood for fuel; but just in time, we discovered coal. Then coal became terribly expensive; but just in time, we discovered petroleum. In turn, petroleum began to run out. Again (just in time) we developed fission energy. And after that fusion. *Just in time* is the greatest of all guiding and conserving principles. Necessity breeds creativity. Now that we really need to converse with animals we will learn how to. This is a necessary truth."

And so it turned out. A pan-animal electronic translator was invented, and it worked beautifully. One of the first animals to be interrogated was a female swift. The interrogator was one of the leaders in the Right-to-Life movement, which had succeeded in outlawing all forms of abortion among human beings.

*Right-to-Lifer*: I won't try to conceal from you our horror at your actions. When you push your fertile eggs out of the nest I don't know whether to call it infanticide or abortion. Certainly it is murder of the worst sort, murder for selfish reasons. You aren't willing to exert yourself extra hard in bad weather to feed your children.

*Mother Bird*: You've obviously missed the point. I cherish motherhood—successful motherhood. At the end of my life I want to know that I have the largest number of living descendants I possibly could. I kill embryos to save children.

*Right-to-Lifer*: On the contrary, you rape language to save your conscience. Embryos have the same genes as adults, therefore there is no moral difference between embryo and adult. Murder is murder.

*Mother Bird*: Let's try to get out of this thicket of words. Let's look at consequences. What would happen if I did *not* selectively kill embryos? In cool weather I can hardly catch enough insects to stoke my own metabolic fires much less feed any children. If I don't survive in vigorous health my children will die. If I failed to push out the eggs of doomed offspring I would lose part of the precious breeding season as I futilely attempted to feed young who had been hatched at the wrong time.

What would you think of a businessman who refused to "take" an obvious loss, who insisted on investing in failure? Predicting the outcome of a particular experience is always chancy, but what should be our policy? Is investing in probable failure a good policy?

*Right-to-Lifer*: We must do what is right, always. That is our moral and religious obligation.

*Mother Bird*: If it's religion you want to talk, let me remind you what your Bible says. "To everything there is a season, and a time to every purpose under the heaven: A time to be born, and a time to die; a time to plant, and a time to pluck up that which is planted; a time to kill and a time to heal."

The Preacher had it just right. When the parents' best estimate of the future is that they will not be able to take care of the children now in embryo, then it is time "to pluck up that which is planted." That is the moral justification for abortion among humans and pushing eggs out of the nest among birds.

*Right-to-Lifer*: How dreadful! What you are saying is this: the end justifies the means.

*Mother Bird*: If the end does not justify the means, what does?

*Right-to-Lifer*: Anathema! The Bible says, "Thou shalt not kill."

*Mother Bird*: No, it doesn't. I suppose you think God spoke in English? The English language did not exist, even in embryo, when the Old and New Testaments were written. What you've just given me is the English version from the King James Bible. Since that was published more careful translations have rendered the sixth commandment thus: "You must not murder." Killing is just a fact; murder is an interpretation, a value judgment. When the season is not favorable for motherhood, the loving would-be mother compassionately kills embryos because she loves babies.

Legislators who forbid compassionate killing force people to invest in failure and thus increase suffering in the world.

What irony! Concern for the rights of animals forced philosophers to consider their responsibilities; then when the animals were allowed to speak for themselves they cast serious doubts on the legitimacy of some of the human versions of rights and responsibilities. This is not what the Animal Liberationists had in mind when they began their campaign.

Economists were equally disturbed by the turn of events. The investing in failure called for by human welfare and health legislation had already diminished the treasury enough. Proposals to save every animal life in the name of animal rights and to forbid sterilization of animals (on the grounds that it would violate the right of parenthood) threatened to complete the bankruptcy. The most thorough analysis of the problem by Gerhardt Garton von und zu Esels resulted in this four-word conclusion: "Animals are not people." For this Esels was awarded the Nobel Prize in economics.

When news of the award reached a village store in Appalachia Jed McCoy remarked: "Shucks, I've known that all my life. There's a lot of fools in them big cities." Jed puckered his lips and spat out a stream of tobacco juice that caught the old tomcat right in the eye.

What the cat thought about it all is not recorded.

# 10

## *The Moral Threat of Personal Medicine*

When we use the word "medicine" we usually mean personal medicine, medicine aimed at alleviating the problems of the individual. In the Hippocratic Oath there is no mention of the interests of society as a whole or of posterity. This systematic blindness has been reinforced by the rise of radical individualism in the western world in recent centuries. The thrust of this movement can be summed up in one crude sentence: "Whatever is best for the individual is, ipso facto, best for society." In truth, however, it is easy to show that personal medicine, pursued without restraint in a society that commonizes the costs, actually works against the interests of society, which means it works against the individual interests of all its members. In the relief of hereditary defects personal medicine can work against the interests of posterity. The justification of this statement is simply made.

The mutation process is unstoppable, and most new mutations are harmful. Good mutations are almost as rare as hen's teeth. Under natural conditions bad mutations are eliminated by the process we call natural selection. The effect of medical measures is to diminish the force of natural selection, thereby increasing the genetic load in the next generation. This effect was fully appreciated by Darwin more than a hundred years ago.

Since perception of the genetic effect of personal medicine has led to no public action, a critic might well ask, "But does it really matter? After all, medicine treats the person by diminishing the phenotypic effects of his genes, whatever they are. If the phenotypic bad effects of genes are diminished, why worry about the partially hidden genes themselves? Aren't medical prosthetics just as good as the real thing?"

The answer is *No*, for several reasons. In the first place, almost every prosthetic device has what one might call a "simple" defect. Poor eyesight we remedy with eye glasses; this works pretty well, but just ask anyone who wears glasses if he functions as well as somebody who doesn't. If nothing else, when he gets out in the rain, he wishes his glasses had windshield wipers. That's the sort of thing I mean by a "simple" defect.

More complicated defects are what we might call cybernetic defects—lack of sophistication in design to take care of many different circumstances. For example, crutches (which I can speak about from experience) suffer from the great defect of having no knees. Just try to walk on ice without bending your knees! Of course, we might engineer some knees into the crutches, together with the necessary feedbacks. What would this cost? Ten thousand dollars? Would the result ever be as good as real knees? Artificial cybernetic systems are both expensive and prone to malfunction.

Hormone therapy also fails to be completely satisfactory. It lacks sophisticated and sensitive feedbacks. Ask anyone who is "on thyroid." It is hard to match ingestion with unpredictable and varying needs which express themselves after a considerable time delay.

Consider phenylketonuria (PKU), a hereditary metabolic abnormality in which an excess of ketones in the blood evidently causes the brain to develop abnormally, resulting in a mentally deficient child. We try to minimize the damage by restricting the intake of phenylalanine. This amino acid is both indispensable and dangerous to PKU youngsters; trying to ingest the right amount is like trying to balance oneself on a knife edge. It is hell for the families that have to monitor the life of a PKU child. There is a regrettable lack of candor in medical reporting of the "successes" of diet control in PKU: the psychological trauma is usually swept under the rug. Think of having a PKU child in the family and having to watch it every moment of the day every day of the year; having (in effect) to be the child's jailer, having to inhibit all the child's spontaneity in eating. Even if we grant that PKU can be controlled by diet—and it is not completely clear that it can—the resultant anticybernetic life with its attendant psychological stresses is a mighty poor way to live. But in their published accounts, physicians, like the spectators in Anderson's *The Emperor's New Clothes*, report seeing only what they are supposed to see. Optimism is obligatory.

The financial cost of prosthetics is often great. There are signs that the public is waking up to this. You have heard that it takes $25,000 a year to keep a Tay-Sachs child alive, for the tragic few years of its existence. According to a news report the best treatment of hemophiliacs, involving frequent transfusions of the missing factors from the blood of normal people, costs some $22,000 a year. There are about 25,000 hemophiliacs in the United States. This means that giving the best possible treatment to American hemophiliacs would cost about half a billion dollars per year. This is only the directly identifiable medical expenses: and hemophilia is only one of a long list of hereditary diseases.

Prosthetics should never be regarded as a complete substitute for the real thing. They are always second best. And we shouldn't pride ourselves too much on how much we can do with prosthetics. We must not forget the genetic malfunctions that made prosthetics necessary.

The gravest danger arises when the use of prosthetics in personal medicine increases the number of children produced by the bearers of hereditary defects over what it would be if prosthetics were not used. Personal medicine is then in conflict with community medicine. The increase in genetic load is slow, but it is inexorable if personal medicine is not coupled with some control of breeding.

Perhaps an analogy will help. The reproduction of genetic material has some points of resemblance to the printing of a book. But whereas thousands or even millions of books can be printed from one typesetting, each genetic "setting" is used only for a few replications. The analogy would be closer if the first printing of a book were used as the model to set up type for the second copy, which was used as the model for setting up type for the third copy, and so on. Each replication of the genetic "type" brings a fresh exposure to the risk of making "typographical errors," i.e., mutations.

Under natural conditions, natural selection is the proofreader that eliminates "typographical errors." Whenever our humanitarian impulses lead us to employ personal medicine to protect individuals against the proofreader, the ultimate effect of our good intentions is to increase the number of errors as the mutation process continues to add new errors to the old ones already protected. In the genetic process, errors are copied just as faithfully as correct readings. Of course a second error at the same place in the text *might* correct the first, but probability is against it. (Who would rely on the unguided carelessness of typesetters to correct a text rich in "typos"?)

Let's return to the problem of hemophilia with its potential societal cost of half a billion dollars a year. Not too long ago four hemophiliacs brought a class action suit in one of the eastern federal courts to compel the U.S. Department of Health, Education, and Welfare to give the best medical treatment known free to all hemophiliacs in the United States. The plaintiffs argued that such treatment is a human *right*. Since the "best treatment" would require a generosity in the giving of blood by normal people that may not exist, it is likely that the hemophiliacs' demand cannot be met in any case. But (for the sake of argument) let us put this objection aside and ask if their demand is the sort that society *should* accede to? Half a billion dollars is a lot of money; and hemophilia is only the tip of the iceberg of hereditary defects.

For the courts to establish a new right to the best personal medicine for all citizens, for all diseases, would be to establish a devastating drain on the economy of the country—which would adversely affect the welfare of all citizens, whatever their genetic constitution.

One way to look at problems like this is in terms of that much abused word *responsibility*. We must admit that if there is one thing a person is not responsible for, it is the genes that were passed on to him. No one has the opportunity to pick his parents. One can sympathize with hemophiliacs and, indeed, with the bearers of all hereditary genetic errors. But that is literally *each* of us, as Bentley Glass has pointed out:

every one of us bears (in all probability) at least one hereditary error, great or small—and these errors were not of our choosing. We are not responsible as the recipients of errors.

But should we not be responsible as the transmitters of errors? If there are some people in society who refuse to take such responsibility, who say *No* for whatever reason, refusing to inhibit their own breeding in spite of the fact they are passing on genes known to be undesirable genes, does not then the issue of responsibility arise in a very acute form? Consider the case of a hemophiliac (almost invariably a male). His children, with rare exceptions, will all be asymptomatic. But his daughters will have one dose of the gene. When it comes time for them to reproduce, half of the sons of the daughters will (on the average) be hemophiliacs. With a delay of one generation the hemophiliac who insists on reproducing is saddling posterity with his problem.

Should individual freedom extend so far? Should individual freedom include the freedom to impose upon society costs that society does not want? This is the issue all of us must face. When such costs are very slight, we might avoid the issue by saying that the law is not concerned with trifles. But hemophilia, Tay-Sachs, sickle-cell anemia, and PKU are not trifles.

We must recognize that this is a finite world. The money we spend for one purpose, we cannot spend on another. If we spend all our income on the phenotypic correction of genetic defects, there will be none left for preserving an adequate equality of life.

This is one of mankind's major problems. It doesn't require an immediate solution; but let us keep the issues clearly in mind so that we do not lightly assert such a thing as a right to breed under any and all circumstances, regardless of the consequences.

What I have been discussing, of course, is eugenics. The practice of eugenics is often divided into two classes: negative and positive. By negative eugenics, we mean the taking of such measures as will diminish the genetic load in later generations. By positive eugenics, we mean taking measures that might in a positive way improve the quality of human life for future generations. We can do this by encouraging the breeding of people who are unusually low in genetic defects, and perhaps unusually well-endowed with desirable human "talents."

In all of the years of its very checkered career, eugenics has had its only successes (and they haven't been many) in gaining the assent of society to the practice of negative eugenics. The reason for this, I think, is quite clear: negative eugenics is the only form that is easily reconcilable with the universal human phenomenon of envy.

Each of us can comparatively easily agree to the institution of negative eugenic measures because he can say to himself: "Well, I am essentially OK. As for this small minority of other people who aren't OK, I am perfectly willing to admit they are my inferiors, so I will accept infringements of their liberty. Negative eugenics doesn't threaten *me*."

Positive eugenics is another matter. To single out a few people as being unusually superior and ensuring that they have more children than the average does threaten me because I will probably be left out of this select group. Envious, I will say, "How come they are better than I am?" or I might try to base my objection on general principles: "We should never make invidious comparisons."

The adjective "invidious," I would remind you, is derived from the Latin word for envy. It means provoking envy. Because of envy, positive eugenic measures are not, I think, a possibility for the near future. The most we can hope for, for a long time, is negative eugenics. And there's not much hope for that.

The cost of negative eugenics is dependent upon the stage at which we employ selection. Should we eliminate unsatisfactory gametes; or unsatisfactory embryos; or unsatisfactory newborn babies; or unsatisfactory adults? Clearly, without developing the full argument here, we should be able to agree that the earlier the stage at which we make the elimination, the more acceptable it is for everybody. The purpose of prenatal diagnosis is to identify defective individuals before they are born, while the cost of selection is *comparatively* little. We are less unwilling to sacrifice embryos than we are to sacrifice newborn children.

As far as the genetic effect is concerned, it is precisely the same whether we sacrifice a gamete, an embryo, a newborn child, or an adult before reproduction. But the human costs, in terms of both ordinary economic costs and the more subtle emotional costs, are clearly less the earlier the sacrifice is made. The aim of eugenics is to identify a defect at the earliest possible stage so as to eliminate it before the individual and society have made any appreciable investment in the unwanted genotype.

I take issue with those who promote surgery on embryos *in utero*. This seems to me to be an unwise goal to pursue because such surgery is exceedingly expensive and exceedingly difficult under the best of circumstances. Let me be blunt. In terms of both money and emotions an early embryo (say a 12-week fetus) has had so little invested in it that the loss from aborting it is certainly much less than the financial cost of heroic fetal surgery, and (I maintain) less than the emotional cost to the parents anxiously awaiting the outcome for another 28 weeks. I frankly think that the goal of fetal surgery principally serves the ego of surgeons and is destructive of the even more valid ego needs of parents. My heart is with the parents. That is where the interests of economics and eugenics lie also.

# 11

## *In Praise of Waste*

Darwin changed our view of the origin of living things, but more important still, he changed our attitude toward waste. Before Darwin, the adaptedness of species was explained by William Paley as an example of "design in nature"—a design that existed in the mind of a Creator Who then fashioned nature in accordance with His blueprint; only so, said Paley, could such a marvelously adapted structure as the eye have been produced.

Not at all, said Darwin. It is not necessary that there exist in some mind the idea of a beautifully adapted machine in order that this machine may come into existence. It is enough if nature be permitted to try countless experiments—"mutations" we now call them—among which a tiny percentage produces good results. Each such successful experiment is saved by natural selection and used as a base for further experimentation and natural selection. Mutation occurs at random and entails enormous waste, but natural selection acts like a ratchet to preserve each tiny element of progress; thus do nature's beautifully adapted machines come into being. There need be no blueprint for design to emerge; trial and error suffice. Something of this sort must have been meant by the poet William Blake who said, "To be an error and to be cast out is a part of God's design."

Design can emerge from blind waste. How old is this thought? Who can trace the earliest embryological stages of so tenuous an entity as an idea? Perhaps it is centuries old, but certainly its form was not unambiguously clear until Robert Malthus wrote his *Essay on Population* in 1798. This much-misunderstood work, yearly buried by liberal critics and yearly resurrected by its own vigor, has, entangled in its many errors, a correct view of stability achieved through waste—the Malthusian dynamic scheme of population. From the superabundant vitality of nature comes the ever-present threat of geometric increase, but this is opposed by the limitations set by the environment. The result is an equilibrium achieved through waste, an equilibrium that may, it is true, be subject to temporal shifts, but an equilibrium nonetheless. Forethought, planning, and charity are either of secondary importance or are self-defeating in such a system.

This mode of thought met with immediate favor when it was put forward by Malthus, but within a very few years it was vigorously opposed by another idea of independent birth and apparently contradictory implications—the idea of cruelty, *i.e.*, the idea that cruelty is something to be abhorred rather than enjoyed. Strange as it may seem, this idea is a rather young idea as far as the bulk of mankind is concerned. In the distant past, the gentle Jesus was a conspicuous exception among men. It is only within comparatively recent times that many Christians have become Christian.

The Christianization of Christians was made possible by a change in perspective. In the Middle Ages it was common for the population of a city to be lowered as much as 10 percent in a single year by disease or famine; even a 25 percent loss was not unknown. In a world so filled with suffering not caused by humans, it would seem to some rather out of perspective to complain of a little human fun—like the Spanish Inquisition, say. As suffering and death from seemingly divinely caused diseases decreased—as it did even before Pasteur and bacteriology—man's view of his own cruelties changed, perhaps because they loomed proportionately larger. Cruel fate was becoming reformed; cruel man

now looked crueler. Tender-minded poets and novelists were determined that he, too, should reform, and quickly.

Into this world of tender intentions burst Malthus, asserting that suffering was inevitable, simply because population had the capability of
increasing more rapidly than the means of subsistence. A reasonable
balance between population and subsistence—a decent scale of living
for some—could be maintained only if others suffered from insufficient
means of subsistence. Nor would it be a true solution for the haves to
divide their means with the have-nots—this would merely encourage
the production of more have-nots. Such a sentiment provoked a storm
of protest from the literati, who were now making the cause of the poor
and the unfortunate their cause. The wealthy Percy Shelley saw a great
social threat in "sophisms like those of Mr. Malthus, calculated to lull
the oppressors of mankind into a security of everlasting triumph." The
poet's friend William Hazlitt asserted that "Mr. Malthus' gospel is
preached only to the poor."

This is not the place to examine Malthus' thesis—or rather, his
theses, for there were several. We need only point out that the early
decades of the nineteenth century saw an establishment of sharp lines of
battle between—shall we say—humanitarians and analysts; it is difficult to name the factions without arousing prejudice. It must not be
supposed that men like Malthus were inhumane; in his personal relations with family and friends, Malthus was the kindest and most con-
siderate of men. But in his public statements he insisted on the primacy
of analysis in the attack on social problems, whereas his opponents insisted on the humanitarian treatment of all existing people—particularly the poor and unfortunate—in the hope, or belief, that future generations would present no problem. The here and now is much more
real than the there and tomorrow. The humanitarians won the minds of
common men—who are, in the nature of things, the majority.

What Malthus was trying to get at in his bumbling way, and all-
unconscious of what he was doing, was what we now call the impotence
principles of science and logic. The trisection of an angle with ruler and
compass alone is impossible—this is an impotence principle. So also is
the principle of the conservation of matter and mass, and the finite ve-
locity of the speed of light. Impotence principles tell us what cannot be
done and for that reason are inacceptable to immature minds. Angle tri-

sectors, circle squarers, and inventors of perpetual-motion machines we will always have with us. What these men fail to realize is that impotence principles are not only restrictive but also permissive. *Only if some things are impossible can other things be.* The second law of thermodynamics not only tells us to stop looking for a perpetual-motion machine but also tells us how to improve the machines already invented.

One of the impotence principles of biology is this—waste is inevitable. Waste, in the Darwinian scheme, not only produces progress but also conserves the advances already made. There is no heredity without its tax of mutation; most mutations are bad; their production and elimination are a kind of waste. The sentimentalist who seeks to eliminate the waste in a species by preserving all mutants and breeding equally of all genetic types ultimately brings about the extinction of the entire species. It is a throwing of good money after bad. It is the saving of pawns and losing the game.

One of the most surprising things about science is the way it begins as common sense, and ends up with most uncommon-sensical statements to which, nevertheless, common sense must give its assent once it has examined the evidence. The curvature of space is such an idea in astronomy. In biology we have the astonishing conclusion of the Haldane-Muller principle which says: In a state of nature, all bad mutations are, in their cumulative, ultimate effects, equally bad. How can this be true? To say that a gene that is only mildly harmful to the individual is just as harmful to the race as is one that is completely lethal to the individual seems to be flying in the face of reason. But it is true.

When we say, "Gene A is not as bad as gene B," what do we mean? How do we measure "badness" in nature? The only acceptable way, in an evolutionary sense, is by the gene's effect on success in leaving progeny. The "worse" the gene is, the greater the diminution in progeny it causes in early generations; and consequently, the sooner the gene is completely eliminated. A gene that causes only slight damage in each generation does so for many generations. These two factors—damage in one generation, and the number of generations sustaining damage—bear a reciprocal relation to each other. As a result, the total damage of a gene, over all generations, is a fixed quantity, the same for all deleterious genes.

The preceding discussion presupposes a species living "in a state of nature." The meaning and the reason for the qualification should be fairly clear—the principle applies directly only to organisms other than man, organisms that do not consciously control their breeding. Man, if he controls his breeding, may be said, in some sense, not to be living in a state of nature—in which case the losses exacted by mutation need to be examined all over again. Can man alter these losses?

Certainly he can increase them. In fact, he is increasing them now deliberately, though not intentionally, by increasing the general radiation level through medical X rays, atomic bombs, and atomic-energy installations. How much he is increasing the mutational losses through his present actions we do not yet know; nor do we know how much he will increase the general radiation level in the future. We play with atoms because we believe there are benefits to be gained from our play. We know there are losses. Ethics is not so well-developed a science that it can tell us how to balance possible profits and certain losses. At the present time, unavoidable mutations cause the production of about 2 million defective babies per year throughout the world. Suppose we increase radiation to such a level that it brings about an ultimate increase in the number of defective babies produced each year by 200,000. Is this a trivial addition or not? Is it small in comparison to the gains brought by atomic energy? How can we say? It is a small wonder that men of equal intelligence and Christianity come up with opposing answers.

Another of the impotence principles of biology, and of sociology, is this—*competition is inescapable*. The form of competition and the participants may change; but it is always with us. A species that is not numerous competes principally against other species; as it increases in numbers, the situation changes. The "successful" species ends by becoming its own principal competitor. So it is with man, now. The world, in spite of comic-strip science, is a limited one. Man, freed of the population-controlling factors of predators and disease organisms, must—willy-nilly, like it or not—control his own numbers by competition with his own kind. By taking thought, he can elect the kind of competition he employs; but he cannot escape all kinds. This is not to imply that the election is a trivial matter. Surely there are few who would not prefer the endemic celibacy of the Irish to the ritual blood sacrifices of the Aztecs, who, at the dedication of the temple of Huitzilopochtli in 1486, slaughtered at least 20,000 victims—by the most conservative accounts—tearing the hearts out of the living bodies. There surely can be no serious question as to which behavior is preferable, but we should note that, though both practices have a religious "reason," both are, in the eyes of a biologist, competitive techniques associated with the threat of overpopulation, however unconscious of that threat the practitioners may be. The question is not whether competitive techniques shall be employed, but what techniques and by whom.

The game must go on; that is nature's command. But it is up to man to determine the ground rules and the teams. The determination of the rules is principally the responsibility of the specialist in ethics. The delineation of the teams—well, that is a task for which many disciplines are needed. It may be that no synthesis of all the relevant considerations is yet possible. But such a synthesis is one that we must work toward. The biologist, with the wisdom gained from a century's preoccupation with evolution, has some things to say about the choosing of the teams.

Any species that becomes one big melting pot of genes puts—to mix metaphors—all its eggs in one basket. If circumstances change rapidly, it may be unable to adapt, and so will perish. Conspicuous success in evolution, as in human affairs, is all too likely to be the prelude to extinction. That the dinosaurs should have become extinct at the end of the Mesozoic era is no cause for wonder; what needs explaining is how such highly successful forms lasted so long.

It is not that the relatively unsuccessful have a better chance of survival because of their deficiencies. Rather, their advantage comes when their lack of success results in the species being broken up into many separate breeding populations, among which there is very little interchange of genes. Under these conditions, there is a great increase in variety within the species, each isolated population necessarily differentiating into a different race; how different will depend on many factors, including the extent of environmental differences. With a greater variety of harmonious genotypes in existence, the species is better adapted to face a varying and unpredictable future. Not all of its breeding populations may survive a change; but the chance that at least some will is greater than the chance of survival of a single, large population. And those races that survive a change can then repopulate regions left vacant by those that have succumbed.

Such is the picture presented to us by a spelling out of the consequences of biological inheritance. But man is subject also to a kind of inheritance that we may call cultural. Will this alter the picture? We don't know. The Gregor Mendel of cultural inheritance has not yet appeared. But there are strong intuitive reasons for believing that the mechanism of cultural inheritance will, if anything, merely increase the contrast in the picture. The loss of adaptability of a species is the result of the inevitable tendency of a breeding population to become genetically uniform. Surely we have seen enough of social power to realize that the pressure toward uniformity is even greater in the cultural realm than in the biological.

To the biologist it is clear that the best chances for man's long-time survival depend on the fragmentation of the species into well-separated populations. But it would be foolhardy to say what form the separation should take. It might be a matter of nations, as we know them; or some sort of caste system that would permit genetic isolation with geographic unity; or—far more likely—some new kind of communities: neither nation nor caste nor anything yet conceived.

In postulating a new world are we adding but one more "utopia" to library shelves that are already too well stocked with these childish wish fulfillments? I think not, for what we have just suggested differs in significant ways from the classical utopias. These dream worlds, however much they vary, agree in two characteristics. The societies they sketch have a high degree of rigidity and finality; and they seek to eliminate all waste, which is variously conceived in terms of economic waste, human suffering, or moral turpitude. The student of biological evolution cannot accept a utopia that embodies either of these features. Evolution is an unending process, in which waste plays an indispensable role. Until proof to the contrary is forthcoming, the evolutionist must assume that man is a part of nature. The biologist sees no end-state for man and his society, which must continue evolving until the day of his extinction. Noone has conceived any substitute for the mechanism of evolution (whether biological or social) that does not necessarily involve variation and selection—that is to say, waste. Man, the slender reed that thinks, can alter the force and direction of natural forces somewhat, but only within limits. The wisdom of so doing is always questionable. Who is so wise as to descry the lineaments of man 1,000 millenniums from now, using these visions as guides for consciously warping the course of human evolution? And as for waste, the more we try to eliminate it, the more we are impressed with its protean changeability and elusiveness. The time-study man who saves 1,000 man-hours by altering work procedures, may be astonished to find himself faced with a sitdown strike that costs 1,000,000 man-hours. Reducing the waste of walking to work by inventing horseless carriages may ultimately double the time wasted in transportation by making possible the modern city and its congestion. And so it goes. We do not yet have a scientific theory of waste, but all men of experience recognize its ubiquity and its inevitability. We can often exchange one kind of waste for another; and we can sometimes— though not as often as we like—decrease it somewhat in amount. But always we must live with it. If we are wise, we even make waste work for us a bit.

But though we may never be able to get rid of waste entirely, it is only natural—or rather, human—that we should try to diminish it as much as possible. Spontaneous mutations entail waste; can we do anything about this? In one sense we cannot. The Haldane-Muller principle tells us that each gene mutation must be paid for by one gene elimination— "genetic death," Muller calls it. Genetic death—which is not really death—is a subdivisible quantity; it may occur by degrees and over many generations. A lethal gene kills at one fell stroke—this is death as we ordinarily conceive it. But a gene that has a selective worth of only 90 percent (as compared with a normal gene) diminishes the reproductivity of every individual in which it shows by 10 percent. If we multiply the fraction of the population that suffers this loss by the amount of loss each individual suffers, we come out with the number 1, no matter what the selective worth. This means that each new, bad mutation is ultimately eliminated completely, and that it "kills" a total of one individual, which it may do by "killing" fractions of several individuals. But it does not follow from this that there is nothing that can be done to diminish the loss to human beings. To say that nothing can be done is to assert that death is the only form of human waste, a thesis that surely few would hold. The sublethal gene does not merely diminish the reproductivity of its possessor, it also diminishes his vigor, his health, his *joie de vivre*. We would be little concerned if genetic death were the only consequence of Huntington's chorea, Mongolism, phenylketonuria, pyloric stenosis, or fibrocystic disease of the pancreas. But these conditions cause other losses that we state in terms of human suffering. These losses can be reduced.

Until very recent times, the only method of attacking the problem of suffering was by medicine. Medicine is surely one of the glories of mankind, but we are now perceiving its limitations. For a disease in which it is accurate to say that the hereditary component is negligible—say, for smallpox—medicine has been an unalloyed blessing. But where the hereditary component is great—for instance, in hemophilia—we have our doubts. In such conditions recourse to somatic medicine only delays genetic death while increasing human suffering. Hemophiliacs are now kept alive by frequent, sometimes daily, blood transfusions. We can, if we wish, encourage them to have children. Suppose we saw to it that hemophiliacs had, on the average, precisely as many children as normal people; what would be the result? Genetic death would thus be completely eliminated, but the cost in suffering would be established as a perpetual and continuing cost, a kind of overhead of misery. However small the cost might be per generation, it would increase without limit as time went on. Every bad mutation is a sort of fine levied against mankind. We can either pay the fine promptly, or we can delay or avoid payment altogether—by paying in another way.

We are in the position of the traffic violator who either can pay a fifty-dollar fine once in court or can pay one-dollar hush money every week to a dishonest officer to keep from having the violation reported. In the long run, even the cheapest blackmail charge mounts up to more than the most expensive fine. In the long run, unobstructed genetic death is the cheapest way to pay for the unavoidable misfortune of mutation.

Mutation is a form of waste which, manage it though we will, we must in some sense accept. It is inevitable. It is the stuff from which are fashioned new adaptations to the world. In this realization we are brought back to an insight that is old, very old; much older than the theory of evolution. When we come to think of it, we realize that what we call charity owes its origin at least in part to a subconscious realization of the value of waste. Most interesting of early prescriptions for charity is the Jewish "law of the corner," which is given thus in Leviticus 19:9–10: "And when ye reap the harvest of your land, thou shalt not wholly reap the corners of thy field, neither shalt thou gather the gleanings of thy harvest. And thou shalt not glean thy vineyard, neither shalt thou gather every grape of thy vineyard; thou shalt leave them for the poor and stranger. . . ." Such a directive sprang, no doubt, in part from a tender heart; but it may also have indicated an embryonic recognition of the danger of an unmodified competition in human affairs—a recognition that if competition were pure and unbridled, the more efficient man (the landowner) would starve out him who was less so (the poor and the stranger). Coupled with this was a surmise that perhaps complete efficiency might not always be best or right.

In Deuteronomy 24:19, there is a further injunction: "When thou cuttest down thine harvest in thy field, and hast forgot a sheaf in the field, thou shalt not go again to fetch it: it shall be for the stranger, for the fatherless, and for the widow. . . ." Thus there came into being that curious entity of Jewish practice known as "that-which-is-left-through-forgetfulness," which belongs to the poor. The devout were urged always to see to it that something was left through forgetfulness. It is certainly difficult to remember to forget. It is no wonder that the principle of the deliberate tithe—one-tenth of one's income given to charity—later replaced so operationally difficult a procedure as deliberate forgetfulness.

Post-Darwinian developments in the theory of evolution, principally at the hands of Sewall Wright and R. A. Fisher, have shown that evolution also proceeds most effectively when competitive pressures are mitigated somewhat. It is highly probable that the same principle applies to progressive change in the human social realm. A country that is "crowded to the gills" is unlikely to produce much pure science. Before 1000 A.D. at least as much ingenious technology came out of China as out of Europe; but the explosive growth of pure science in Europe following the Renaissance found no echo in crowded China. Pure science is, in its inception, pure waste. An item of information in pure science "pays off" in a practical way only after it has long been in existence and has been combined with other items of pure science. We are reminded of the new mutation, which is almost always bad, but which—if protected somewhat—may eventually be able to combine with other and similarly "wasteful" genes to produce a new and superior constellation of genes. Prosperity is the great protector of novel thought. A people whose nose is constantly to the grindstone of poverty cannot look up to see the world as it is; all that exists is the nose and the grindstone. A people living under completely Malthusian conditions cannot discover even so much as the Malthusian principle. Science is not produced by eternally busy, wretched people. The flowering of science in the western world in the last four centuries paralleled the increase in prosperity. Cause? Effect? Both. However the new science got started—prosperity was only a necessary condition, not a sufficient one—once started, it produced more prosperity as an effect which fed back into the system as a cause. Science and technology make a circular system that produces wealth and material progress.

Can this system go on forever? Who can say? It is not without its enemies, and among the most important of these today we must count the ever-increasing population of mankind and the "other-directed" men that crowding produces. An other-directed man—we use David Riesman's phrase—is an animal who tends to be intolerant of the independence of thought that is indispensable for the advancement of science. But other-directed men may be rational, and if rational, may be convinced of the necessity of cherishing those not of their own kind. The inner-directed man, he who is answerable only to his own conscience, is always a thorny tablemate, doubly so when nature's board is crowded. To ask that all men be inner-directed would be quixotic in the extreme; but it is not unreasonable to ask that other-directed men add the care and nurture of a small corps of inner-directed men to their tithing duties. It is not planning that is needed here, and certainly not organization. It is, rather, a systematic allowance for waste, for heterodoxy, for the unforeseeable. It is, perhaps, not even understanding that is demanded—that would be asking too much of other-directed man—but something in the nature of faith. Faith in the future, and faith in the fruitfulness of waste, properly allowed for.

Those who have painted pictures of an organized heaven have, implicitly or otherwise, appealed to the aesthetic sense in man to try to gain assent to their plans. We know now that a completely planned heaven is either impossible or unbearable. We know that it is not true that design can come only out of planning. Out of luxuriant waste, winnowed by selection, come designs more beautiful and in greater variety than ever man could plan. This is the lesson of nature that Darwin has spelled out for us. Man, now that he makes himself, cannot do better than to emulate nature's example in allowing for waste and encouraging novelty. There is grandeur in this view of life as a complex of adjustive systems that produce adaptedness without foresight, design without planning, and progress without dictation. From the simplest means, man, now master of his own fate, may evolve societies of a variety and novelty—yes, and even of a beauty—that no man living can now foresee.

# 12

## An Evolutionist Looks at Computers

A little more than a hundred years ago we abolished slavery—and now we are the greatest slave owners in the history of the world. But our slaves are not alive; they are machines. And that makes a world of difference.

How many slaves does each of us have at his command? The easiest way to calculate this is in terms of energy. The average American consumes about 3,000 calories of energy a day in the form of food. But he uses about 150,000 calories of energy for other purposes, that is, for running tractors, automobiles, trucks, and refrigerating equipment and for all his manufacturing processes. If we figure that 3,000 calories worth of work each day is equivalent to one slave then the average American owns the equivalent of fifty slaves.

Even this large figure underestimates our wealth. No longer are our slaves merely energy-slaves; we have information-slaves as well. Unfortunately, it is hard to devise a metric for measuring their importance.

It would be easy to estimate the work of a cash register in terms of human work. But how would you measure the slave-equivalent of a long-distance telephone conversation? Would it be a marathon runner? How would you express the human equivalent of the automatic space assignment system of an airline? Such a function could not even exist in the absence of modern information-processing systems. Our information-slaves are probably already more numerous than our energy-slaves, and daily are growing more important.

We are all slave owners—and we love it! However, the fact that a slave owner loves his privilege does not prove that the privilege is, in the long run, good for him. One of the annoying characteristics of biologists is that they insist on asking questions about "the long run." By temperament, biologists are not satisfied with the mere appearance of stability. They suspect short-run peace—and even a human lifetime is only a short run in the eyes of biologists.

As a biologist, I cannot help but wonder: is slavery good in the long run? Classical slavery was not without its distinguished defenders. St. Thomas Aquinas defended it as being part of the natural order decreed by God. Friedrich Engels, a somewhat less saintly character, in his *Anti-Dühring* (1877) said: "Without slavery there would have been no Grecian state, no Grecian art and science, and no Roman empire . . . no modern Europe . . . [and, at last getting down to his favorite subject,] no modern Socialism." At about the same time Alexander Herzen stated the same point more operationally: "Slavery is the first step towards civilization. In order to develop, it is necessary that things should be much better for some and much worse for others; then those who are better off can develop at the expense of the others."

Put another way, no community in which the average income is little above the subsistence level can afford to develop the arts and sciences if it insists that all must share the poverty equally. Whether pleasing or not, this analysis gives a sort of historical justification for slavery and other inequities. Does "the end justify the means"? Take your choice.

However we may feel about flesh-and-blood slaves, we all believe that the "exploitation" of inanimate slaves is perfectly justified. Inanimate slaves also can make possible a higher development of the arts and sciences. Inanimate slavery furnishes a necessary but not a sufficient condition for the flowering of a civilization.

Are there any bad "side effects" to slavery? With inanimate slaves we don't worry about cruelty to the slave; we want to know what are the effects of slavery on the slave owners. Back in the days of human slaves many critics pointed out the deleterious effects of slavery on the masters. In various ways slavery corrupts the owners. Most obviously, it tends to make them physically soft. When all the hard work is done by slaves, and none by the slave owners, then given even reasonably good food at the slaves' mess, middle-aged slaves will be much healthier animals than their middle-aged masters.

In addition, the ability to summon slave labor at the snap of the fingers does not tend to develop intellectual ingenuity in the owners. Why develop a labor-saving machine when labor is all around you to be had for the asking? For more than 2,000 years horse-loving knights-errant, surrounded by slave labor, did not have the wit to invent a horse collar. Why should they? It was easier to harness up a man than a horse. It was not until about 1000 A.D. that the horse collar was invented, probably by nonslave-owning medieval peasants. This invention made a work horse—for the first time—worth more than a man. With the appearance of the horse collar one of the principal economic bases for slavery was destroyed.

When it comes to the causes of the downfall of the Roman Empire, every man is his own historian. But among the multiple causes most people would include the physical softness and intellectual laziness concentrated in the ruling classes of Rome by slavery and other social arrangements for "letting George do it." In its last days the Empire was overrun by barbarians, and even by slaves who had not enjoyed the benefits of degeneration through prosperity. Though an exact assignment of blame for the downfall of any institution is hardly possible, still it would be difficult to defend human slavery as the bulwark of any long-lasting society.

But what if the slaves are inhuman? What if they are automobiles and machine tools and computers? To understand the long-term effects of inanimate slavery we need to put human inventions into an evolutionary framework.

In imagination let's go back about 100,000 years to the time when man made one of his first inventions, a sharp knife-edge of flint or volcanic glass. With this simple tool he could skin an animal he had perhaps killed with a stone. If you don't have such a knife-edge you have a hard time getting at the meat. You have to grab the fur between your teeth and rip. About the biggest game an effete modern man can handle in this way is a rabbit. Prehistoric man, with his much more powerful jaws, may have been able to deal with a small antelope.

But it was hard work. A stone knife-edge for making the first incision was a marvellous invention. It opened up a whole new world of food to man, the hunter; and it started his jaw on the road to degeneration.

An unused structure necessarily degenerates; a partially used structure partially degenerates. The reasons for this generalization are technical and somewhat involved; I don't want to go into them here. But please take it as gospel.

The invention of the cutting knife caused the partial degeneration of the human jaw. Was this bad or good? When you receive the dentist bills for a large family you may feel that we have paid a pretty high price for the knife; but aside from that we've gotten along very well.

The invention of the knife caused no *overall* loss of function. The function was merely moved (in part) from inside the man's skin to the outside; from his jaw, which is part of him, to his knife, which is not. The knife is one of a large class of devices to which a wise old evolutionist named A. J. Lotka gave the name *exosomatic* adaptations— "outside the body" adaptations. Teeth are endosomatic, knives are exosomatic. In a sense, both are produced by evolution, and both have evolutionary consequences.

Every exosomatic adaptation tends to bring about the degeneration of its endosomatic precursor. This sound generalization has ethical implications. Whenever we move an adaptive mechanism from inside the skin of man to the outside, we affect man's position in the universe in two important ways. First, we increase the selective value of the intelligence needed to manufacture the exosomatic adaptation—for the species as a whole, if not for the individual. Secondly, we make the species vulnerable to the consequences of accidental loss of the exosomatic adaptive ability.

Our dependence on exosomatic knives is not a very serious matter. Even if our civilization were utterly destroyed, leaving only a few million people scratching for a living in a new Stone Age, the knife would not disappear. It is a simple concept. New knives would soon be made.

But we've made other exosomatic inventions that are not so simple.

Consider the exosomatic heart pacemaker; and the exosomatic artificial kidney. Suppose everyone were dependent on these outside-the-skin adaptations. What would happen then if civilization were destroyed? Very likely the species *Homo sapiens* would disappear also. Very few people have the knowledge, or even the intelligence, required to manufacture pacemakers and artificial kidneys.

Of course very few people need them now (fortunately). But if we keep on supplying them, more and more people eventually will. There's not much danger when we equip a sixty-year-old man with either of these exosomatic devices. He's nearly past the breeding age and hence what happens to him from now on has little selective effect.

But evolutionists look with horror at pictures of ten-year-old children equipped with pacemakers or artificial kidneys. If their deficiencies are even in part genetically caused (which they probably are) and if they insist on having children later (which they probably will), the long-term effect of equipping them with these exosomatic adaptations will be to move the adaptive function from inside the skin to outside—and to make the species more vulnerable to accidents, which we have no assured way of preventing.

I am worried about the evolutionary consequences of that grand class of exosomatic adaptations we summarize in the phrase "the computer." We are moving the calculating functions from inside our heads to machines outside. Desirable and necessary as this shift may be, I think it also brings grave dangers with it. Let me illustrate my point with a story.

When I was young I used to accompany my father to the grocery store. As we stood at the counter waiting for the clerk to add up the items on the cash register, it was my father's delight to add them up in his head and arrive at the answer sooner than the clerk. My father never went to college. In fact he never finished high school. However, his interest and ability in mental arithmetic was, I believe, not exceptional for one of his generation. It was just assumed that any ordinarily intelligent person could add up a long column of figures in his head and get the right answer.

What do we see now? Certainly not customers adding up figures in their heads for the pleasure of it. Nobody adds anymore. In fact, the clerk at the cash register no longer even has to make change. At the punch of a button, the machine does it for her. On the rare occasions when a machine fails, we frequently discover that the clerk can add up the figures neither in her head nor with a pencil and paper. It is as though 3,000 years of development in mathematics had never taken place.

This is no isolated instance. This is the trend of evolution in a computer-centered society. Human thinking functions, disused, have been set on the road toward degeneration.

Of course, someone has to design and manufacture the computers. This is a bright spot in the picture, but it is a very small bright spot. Only a minority of a minority of the population are subject to selection for this sort of intelligence. With every advance in computer technology the great bulk of the population is increasingly free from selection pressure favoring any thinking at all of a mathematical sort. A rift is being created in the species. This is dangerous.

H. G. Wells partly foresaw the possibility of such a rift in the human species. In *The Time Machine*, you may remember, he told of a visit to a future world in which there was a rigid bifurcation of society into two groups, groups so different that they could rightly be called different species, though they had had a common origin in the author's time. The Upper World people, called the Eloi, were the beautiful people. They were the Haves of the future world and the descendants of the Capitalists of Wells' day. Below the Eloi—literally below them, permanently confined to underground caverns—were the Have-nots: hideous, subhuman, revolting Workers; they were called Morlocks. The Morlocks owned nothing and did nothing but work all the time. The Eloi owned everything and did nothing but play and make love all day long. For the Eloi life was pleasant—but unquestionably precarious. They were living on borrowed time.

Was that *our* world that Wells prophesied? Yes and no; even the best of prophesies is always subtly wrong. But the best—or luckiest—prophets make us see things about our world that we might otherwise miss.

We can see a good beginning—I mean a *bad* beginning—of the bifurcation of the population that Wells foresaw. We can call our disjoined
groups the Eloi and the Morlocks, for want of better names. But the
separation of functions between these two groups is perversely different
than from that which H. G. Wells foresaw. Because of labor-saving machinery we are moving into a world in which *no* Morlocks will be
needed for labor. Because of thought-saving machinery, no Morlocks
will be needed either for routine calculations and "thought" at the
lower levels. In fact, no Morlocks will be needed at all—but it looks
like we are going to have them.

Our Eloi work. Look around you at a computer conference—our
Eloi are working very hard and having a hell of a fine time doing it. But
what are our Morlocks doing? Increasingly, they are doing nothing at
all. This is not because they choose to do nothing. It is because society
deprives them of the opportunity of doing anything.

I exaggerate somewhat in describing the present, but what of the future? Is not this the direction in which the evolution of society is moving? With the Morlocks doing little but spinning their wheels, can there
be a stable society? Wells' Morlocks were decently working underground, out of sight, out of communication with the Eloi. Ours are
aboveground, and very much in sight. Deprived of the meaningful
work that is the natural delight of man, they threaten society with other
activities for which the computers of our clever Eloi have no answer.

What are we to do? I don't know. Let me describe various possibilities and see what you think of them. See how you like them.

First of all—and this is easiest—we can just do nothing, that is, continue thoughtlessly doing what we are doing now to bring about an un-
planned evolution. It is probable that our Morlocks will continue to
breed, without being asked to; in fact, having little else that is meaningful to do, they may even breed faster than the Eloi. What will such a
differential in reproduction do to society if it is continued generation
after generation?

The tremendous disproportion in numbers may eventually result in
some sort of a revolution, of an unimaginable sort with hardly desirable
consequences. The bases of an exosomatically dependent civilization
may be destroyed. Or possibly the vastly outnumbered Eloi (of whom

so few are needed to keep the computers going) may eventually become slaves of the Morlocks who haven't the foggiest notion of how to make or service a computer. This would be a strange reverse twist to H. G. Wells' fable!

Another possibility: by chance or by design the Morlocks might be inveigled into breeding less rapidly than the Eloi. It is taboo to discuss such a possibility; I only mention it. If it came to pass, the problem would eventually solve itself.

At the moment there is no sign that the problem is solving itself. There is little sign of the solidarity among the Eloi that would have to exist if a solution were to be found. In fact—and this is the most frightening aspect—children of the Eloi in large numbers are leaving the parental society and joining the Morlocks. This has the good effect of lessening the rift between the classes, but it leaves the support for the ideals of the Eloi dangerously eroded.

In looking around for measures we might take to offset these present tendencies, one of the few possibilities I see is in education. I wonder if we might not, in intellectual matters, take a hint from athletics. The original Marathon race was run for a real purpose—to carry a needed message as fast as possible. This function of running no longer exists, but our people still enthusiastically run marathons and enthusiastically watch others run them.

We pursue most athletics for what we can properly call *transcendental* reasons—reasons that transcend simple necessity. We know this, and it does not lessen our respect for, or our participation in, athletics. We dimly recognize that, in the long run, we will be badly off if we do not continue to honor and encourage physical prowess.

Are we not close enough to a possible downfall of the computer-based world to see that we must similarly encourage intellectual athletics? Simple necessity requires only a dangerously small minority of Eloi to keep the world going, so few in number that they may be overwhelmed by the Morlocks. To create a broad base of public support do we not need an explicit glorification of the transcendental values of thinking?

To maintain such a transcendental value system in the intellectual realm, we will have to defend the relevance of intellectual training in a world that may become increasingly dominated by mental Morlocks.

We will also have to see to it that the genetic ability to be so trained is nurtured and even multiplied relative to the rest of society. It goes without saying that this will be no easy task.

Computers are part of the authentic evolutionary trend of man. They are exosomatic devices the invention and multiplication of which is made possible by endosomatic intellectual abilities. The computer men who have developed these exosomatic devices are themselves agents of man's evolution now and extending into the future. If man is to survive, these agents must become conscious of the evolutionary implications of their actions.

# 13

## *Discriminating Altruisms*

The failure of genetic knowledge to make its way into eugenic policy is a fascinating and deep problem. As far back as the sixth century B.C., the Attic poet Theognis commented on the paradox that we use intelligence in breeding our domestic animals, but not in producing the next generation of human beings. Perhaps we should not; perhaps, as Darwin's grandson Charles Galton Darwin said in *The Next Million Years*, man is a wild animal, resistant to domestication. Perhaps we human beings prefer to remain so. Be that as it may, it is clear that one of the rocks on which the ship of eugenics foundered was the rock of radical individualism. Why, asks the individual, should I forego or limit the pleasure of breeding and raising a family for the sake of the larger community? Why should I be altruistic? What's in it for me?

Eugenics, for all practical purposes, is a dead issue at the present time, but the controversy over the reality and nature of altruism has erupted with new fury since the sociobiologists have taken the stage.

Darwinian reasoning has thrown new light on the problem and raised new and more profound questions.

According to the *Oxford English Dictionary* the word "altruism" (Latin *alter* = other) was first used in 1853, following the introduction in 1722 of the word "egoism" (Latin *ego* = I). Does this mean that people were unable to discuss motivation and the consequences of human actions before these nouns were coined? Certainly not: contrasting adjectives ("generous" and "selfish") and their related verbs ("to give" and "to take") sufficed to deal with the contrasting phenomena of social life. But the creation of the nouns—substantives—moved the discussion to another plane by suggesting that there was a thing, a substance as it were, behind each kind of action. In the Indo-European languages (and many others) nouns imply a reality that is greater (more *substantial*) than that suggested by verbs and adjectives. Once a substantive is created it is all too easy to assume a substantial reality behind the word. An unsophisticated public is inclined to put the burden of proof on the iconoclast who doubts the substantive. This stance is 180° wrong. Nonetheless, in the case of the substantive "altruism," biologists have accepted the burden and have shown that, strictly speaking, altruism does not exist; or, to put the matter more exactly, altruism, though it may *exist* discontinuously in space and momentarily in time, cannot *persist*, expand, and displace the natural egoism of a species.

Many people find this disturbing news. Fortunately we need not give up "altruism" altogether. Colloquially, we use many words that are, from a strictly scientific point of view, indefensible. For example, we speak of the "cold" of a winter's day (note the substantive), though physicists have convinced us that there is no such *thing* as cold, only degrees of heat. Instead of complaining of the "cold" of $-13°$ Fahrenheit we should speak of the "heat" of $+248°$ Kelvin. But that is pedantry; not even physicists use such language in everyday life. When employed with sufficient care, inexact colloquial expressions do no harm. "Cold" is one such colloquialism, "altruism" (as we shall see) is another.

The sufficient care that we must exercise with "altruism" is this: we must modify the substantive "altruism" with the adjective "discriminating"—or use the noun in such a way that the audience infers the missing modifier. Pure altruism is so rare and unstable that policy need make little allowance for it; but impure forms of altruism—discriminating altruisms—are the very stuff of social life.

Before we comfort ourselves with the impure altruisms that can exist and persist, we need to accept this basic fact: *A species composed only of pure altruists is impossible.* The simple theoretical proof of this fundamental principle is found in the following "thought-experiment."

Let us suppose that I am God. I wish to construct a species of animal in which every individual is a pure altruist, i.e., a being that prefers serving others to serving itself. Put another way, when there is a conflict between serving others and serving self, the individual acts in such a way that the benefits of his actions accrue more to others than to himself. Since (by hypothesis) I am God, there is nothing to prevent my creating such a species. *But not even God can make altruism persist.*

Why not? At this point we depart from pure theory to commit ourselves to a single empirical fact, namely the inevitability of random mutations. ("Random" means random in terms of the species' need, not in terms of the chemistry of the genetic material.) In the language of the thought-experiment we assume that not even God can put an end to the mutation process. In creating the chemical elements with the properties they have, God committed the living world to change.

Those who like to reinterpret the story of Genesis in the light of new ideas and facts might note that the "firmament," which surely must include the elements of the periodic table, was created on the second day, but living things were created later, plants on the third day and animals on the fifth. The Fundamentalists' belief that God's creation was final and incorrigible implies that the dynamic, unstable characteristics of atoms and molecules were inherent from the beginning, leading inescapably to the instability of the genetic code of plants and animals. (This paradox needs to be called to the attention of Fundamentalists who rest their faith on the unchangeability of biological species.)

Once we recognize the inescapable fact of mutability, we must acknowledge that the hypothesized pure altruist cannot be what taxonomists call the "type" of any species. Whenever a mutant arises that is less than purely altruistic, the actions of this mutant necessarily benefit its possessor more than the actions of altruists benefit altruists. The egoistic mutant flourishes at the expense of the altruists. If the benefit is translatable into greater fertility (as it must be to make biological sense) then, as the generations pass, the descendants of the egoist will replace those of the altruists. Perhaps not completely—those familiar with genetics will think of the phenomenon of "balanced polymorphism"— but the egoists will become the "type" as altruists diminish in relative frequency, ending up as no more than rare variants in the population.

Mutation and selection, inescapable and ubiquitous, make pure altruism unstable. Our attention must, then, be turned to impure altruism, to the other-serving actions of an individual that in some way serve himself as well.

The best known other-serving action is parental care. That this is not pure altruism becomes obvious the moment we shift our focus from the individual to his or her genes. By caring for his young the parent increases the probability that his genes will survive to remote generations. This care may result in some loss to the parent, in some instances to the greatest loss imaginable, the loss of the parent's life. There is a species of cricket in which the mother permits her numerous brood of offspring to eat her up, thus getting a good start in life. At the individual level, her action is purely altruistic. At the genetic level, however, it is not at all altruistic. The mother cricket does not permit any young cricket that happens to be around to eat her. Those who eat her are her own children and carry her genes. The mother's self-sacrifice is not "for the good of the species"; rather, it serves the good of her germ line. The genes that cause her to behave in this way are, in a genetic sense, behaving selfishly. This is the insight that led Richard Dawkins to entitle his book, *The Selfish Gene*. Some people regard the term "selfish genes" as a perversion of language, but significant new insights often put old language on the stretch.

It is an irony of history that the term "altruism" was no sooner coined than the pure form of it was shown to be nonexistent. Just six years later, in 1859 to be exact, Charles Darwin, discussing the possibility of one species acting altruistically toward another, wrote in his *Origin of Species*:

> Natural selection cannot possibly produce any modification in a species exclusively for the good of another species. . . . If it could be proved that any part of the structure of any one species had been

formed for the exclusive good of another species, it would annihilate my theory, for such could not have been produced through natural selection.

Persistent pure altruism is impossible not only between species, but also within a species, as the earlier thought-experiment showed. Darwin realized this, as is evident in scores of passages in both the *Origin* and *The Descent of Man*, though he nowhere expressed the point in a brief and quotable way. Nevertheless, it is not too much to say that the entire literature of sociobiology is an extended gloss on Darwin.

Sociobiology has been one of the stimulants to a revival of interests in altruism; another has been the concern for the "environment" which has burgeoned in the past two decades. The exact denotation of the word "environment" is often far from clear, but discussions of environmental problems seldom continue for long without demands that individuals set aside their selfish desires in favor of the needs of their contemporaries, posterity, or even of an ill-defined "environment."

In general, environmental goods and the costs of environmental abuses are shared by many people, usually without consent. Environment is a common good (or a common bad). Actions, however, have to be carried out by individuals. Proposing that the individual work for the common good raises old questions about the care and nature of altruism. Must the individual sometimes act against his own interests to achieve the common good? Or will self-serving actions suffice?

In the economic context Adam Smith is widely (though not correctly) thought to have answered *Yes* to the last question. His model of the "invisible hand" works well enough (in the absence of monopoly and collusion) to ensure that enterprisers sell at the lowest price: seeking their own interest they unintentionally serve the public interest. But Smith himself knew that the invisible hand sometimes fails. It fails, for example, to prevent ruinous soil erosion when each farmer seeks only his own (short-term) interest, as the history of America's "Dust Bowl" has shown. People often must act in concert (generally, though not necessarily, through government) to bias the free enterprise system so that self-interest becomes congruent with public interest. In general, environmental problems that have not yet been solved are ones that still await the political and social engineering needed to bring about such congruence. Willing assent to engineered changes in the political system requires that many egos be concerned with something other than their *immediate* self-interest. Putting the matter in personal terms, my long-term interest is an interest in my future self, a self who may never be because of intervening death. This future self is a sort of "other"; certainly its interests can conflict with those of my present self. Posterity is another sort of "other"; it too is often served only by some sacrifice of present interests. Concern for the environment cannot be separated from the problems of altruism.

At the most superficial level of analysis, the best of all conceivable worlds for a conscienceless egoist is one in which his egoistic impulses are allowed full reign while his associates are urged to behave altruistically. Unfortunately for the egoist's dreams, symmetry causes other actors to hold the same view. The resulting conflict threatens to produce a stalemate in a world made up of egoists only. . . . But *our* world is not in stalemate so it cannot be composed solely of wholly egoistical individuals. There is at least the appearance of a great deal of altruistic activity, and the appearance needs to be accounted for.

We easily make sense of other-serving actions once we abandon the search for pure altruism and look for modified or limited altruisms. A significant advance was made when the term "kin altruism" was coined as a name for gene-selfish, individually altruistic actions, like that of the mother cricket. The central characteristic of all forms of altruism is this: *discrimination is a necessary part of a persisting altruism*. A few examples, from among thousands that could be cited, will illustrate this point.

A bird does not take care of eggs until it has laid its own. Then it does not care for just any eggs but only for those in its own nest; and the nest has to be in the right place. If an experimenter moves the nest a few feet, even though the bird sees the action, it will not sit on its own eggs in its own nest once the total *Gestalt* fails to match that demanded by the genetic program in its brain. Caring *and* discrimination are both genetically programmed.

In some species the male helps in the feeding of the young. If the father is killed, the mother soon takes on a new consort. The new male ignores nestlings until (1) the offspring of his "wife" have grown up and left the nest and (2) he has had a chance to mate with the female, who then produces a new family. In human terms, the bird doesn't give a hoot for "his" stepchildren. Quite a few words are required to state the necessary discriminating characteristics, and our description is probably never complete, but heredity manages to "write" all these discriminations into the genetic code.

Language is treacherous. We are tempted to say that a bird is programmed to take care of "his" or "her" offspring. This would be strictly true only if the individual bird were miraculously capable of recognizing his or her offspring, an ability that technological man, with all his scientific instruments, still cannot do with certainty. What a parent recognizes is a complex sequence of phenomena that identifies, with nothing more than a high degree of probability, offspring that are probably his own.

That this is the correct interpretation of the facts is shown by the success of the cuckoo bird in exploiting the discrimination system of another species. A cuckoo lays its egg in a nest of the "host species," thus taking advantage of the fact that the host bird does not really recognize its own eggs, reacting merely to eggs of an appropriate size and appearance found in the proper place. When the young cuckoo hatches, it proves to be far from altruistic: it grows faster than the young of the host and soon pushes the host nestlings out of the nest, thus securing all the parental care for itself.

Is altruism inherited? Yes, but it must be analytically decomposed into inherited helping behavior and inherited ability to discriminate. Among nonhuman animals with limited intellect, analyzing altruism into these two components may seem rather academic, but for the human species this analysis is of the utmost importance.

Culture, a by-product of inherited intelligence, can modify the inherited rules of discrimination almost without limit. Culture is extragenetic: it is transmitted from generation to generation by tradition (principally through words). Culture mutates in ways that are quite different from the process of gene mutation.

A complete catalog of all the ways in which human beings have coupled discrimination with caring would be unwieldy. Nevertheless, we need some sort of map through the jungle. I present here a grouping of discriminating altruisms that includes the most important altruisms of our time (see Fig. 1).

Universalism   (Promiscuous altruism)
Patriotism
Tribalism
Cronyism        (Discriminating altruisms)
Familialism
Individualism
Egoism

Figure 1. Egoism and the varieties of altruism, arranged by size of group. In a rough way, the historical sequence is as given, with the older categories toward the bottom of the list.

The various behaviors are arranged in the order of their inclusiveness. At the bottom of the list is *egoism* of the purest sort, a nonaltruistic behavior in which the individual literally cares only for himself. In its pure form egoism is nonexistent. We are social animals of necessity. (If nothing else, parents must take care of children.) But the concept of pure egoism is a useful base for the assemblage of altruisms.

Immediately above egoism comes *individualism*. It may not be immediately evident that individualism differs from egoism, but individualism can be viewed as the most limited form of altruism. The individualistically oriented person *does* care for others, but mostly on a one-to-one basis. "Love thy neighbor as thyself" is the ideal of an individualistic altruist.

Dealing with his neighbors one-by-one, the individualist could theoretically include the entire world within the circle of his discrimination. In practice, the circle is far smaller, leading to the rhetoric of individual "rights," which often work against the common good. It takes cooperative action under a majority rule to provide for a national defense force, municipal sewers, and mandatory smog control devices. "Libertarians," the most extreme doctrinaire individualists of our time, have difficulty accepting the necessity of any altruism more inclusive than individualism.

*Familialism* is the term for the altruistic care that family members take of one another. Beyond parental care, familialism is not nearly as important in contemporary America as it is in other parts of the world. In India, for instance, the family is the greatest reality of social existence. In Indian competition strong family ties and obligations are a necessity for individual survival. Indians regard nepotism as perfectly normal and ethical behavior. They are not alone in this. Familialism is powerful in every poverty-stricken, socially chaotic society. So far have Americans departed from time-hallowed familial discrimination that we have even passed laws against nepotism. When the Italian-derived Mafia practices a strong form of extended familialism on American soil we regard this as distinctly unfair, even when their activities are perfectly legal *per se*.

*Cronyism* is a form of altruism in which discrimination is made on the basis of long association, regardless of genetic relationship. The word "crony" is derived from a Greek word for long-lasting. Cronyism is an adaptive response to the anxiety-creating question, "How can I trust the *other*?" The extensive literature on "The Prisoner's Dilemma" attests to the importance of this question. Because of the "egocentric predicament" *I* can never really know what goes on in the mind of the *other*. Siblings may grow up blessedly untroubled by mutual doubt, but strangers do not enjoy this luxury. Cooperative work, particularly when combined with suffering, creates trust. This is why battle-tested military squads are many times more valuable than green squads. Cronyism then approaches brotherhood; the discriminative delight of it is well expressed by Shakespeare's King Harry in *King Henry V*:

> *We few, we happy few, we band of brothers;*
> *For he that sheds his blood with me*
> *Shall be my brother.*

The perils of social and commercial life are different from those of the battlefield but they are just as real: they too nurture cronyism. Not only must cronies trust each other, but, in the disorderly maelstrom of civic competition, cronies must often stand together against the rest of society. The mutual loyalty of cronies in government bureaus and business enterprises can easily neutralize the public-spirited actions of "whistle-blowers" who seek to serve the common good by informing against work associates whose actions violate public laws. Expecting praise, whistle-blowers are more often rewarded with abuse and exile.

The crony-bias of adults has important roots in early childhood. We praise "good citizenship" to our children and proclaim the merits of serving the public; but at the same time we teach the young to detest, loathe, despise, abhor, and condemn the "snitch," the informer, the tattletale, the squealer, and the "stool pigeon." Where in all these condemnatory words is there a hint of the public interest? The two kinds of messages we give our children are incompatible. Faced with dissonant pressures in adult life the individual, more often than not, favors his cronies against the common good. Both biology and education are responsible for the resulting miscarriage of justice.

The way of the transgressor against cronyism is hard, as the following example shows. Beginning in 1966 officer Frank Serpico tried to reform his corrupt branch of the New York City police department from within. After four years of failure he took his story to the *New York Times*. Publication led to an official investigation and the resignation of many high-ranking officers. Serpico, regarded as a traitor by his fellow officers, was shot in the face and almost killed in a police raid. The circumstances of this event were highly suspicious. In 1972 Serpico went into voluntary exile in Europe and did not return until 1980.

Economic determinists might regard the loyalty of cronies in business as springing solely from mercenary motives. Economic self-interest certainly enters into the conscious or unconscious calculations of cronies, but it surely is not the sole motive. When the member of a business team voluntarily leaves to join another firm the severance is usually final. If he becomes disenchanted with his new position he knows, or is soon told, that he cannot resume his old position. Such is the case at least nine times out of ten. His defection is viewed as a rejection of shared values; his former cronies feel themselves spurned by his departure and find it hard to regenerate their old trust in him. The erstwhile crony is perceived as an apostate: the benefits that might come from reassociation seldom seem enough to take the risk. We will accept great objective losses before we will condone or forget apostasy. The spirit of revenge is sure evidence that human beings are far from being pure, or purely rational, egoists.

*Tribalism* is altruism operating within a tribe, a unit that defies easy definition. Tribal members need not be close kin, nor need they all know each other. They are usually of the same race, but need not be. They share common beliefs, particularly of the sort we call religious. They have the same enemies and react to the same threats. Almost always they speak the same language. They may share geographic territory with other tribes, but if they do they do so in a segregated way. Tribalism is the great reality that has interfered with the development of modern nations in Africa. Africans themselves are acutely aware of this, as one quickly learns by reading their newspapers.

Until recently tribalism has been a very minor kind of altruism in America, but some observers now see the rise of ethnicity and the insistent preservation of multilingualism as signs that America is moving into a tribalistic phase. The bloody conflict in Northern Ireland and the threat of national fission in Belgium are also viewed as tribalism on the rise. It should be noted that since the founding of the United Nations in 1945 there has been much fissioning of nations and no fusion. It would be naive to suppose that the days of tribalism are over.

*Patriotism* is nation-wide altruism. I prefer this term to "nationalism," the connotations of which are now so unfavorable as to discourage objective inquiry. Even "patriotism" is in some bad odor. Later I shall argue that patriotism can be a virtue. For the present, let us pass to the last and most inclusive altruism, namely universalism.

*Universalism* is altruism practiced *without discrimination* of kinship, acquaintanceship, shared values, or propinquity in time or space. It is perhaps shocking, but entirely accurate, to call it *promiscuous altruism.* Its goal was aptly expressed by a now unknown poet soon after the end of World War I:

> *Let us no more be true to boasted race or clan,*
> *But to our highest dream, the brotherhood of man.*

The roots of universalism are to be found in the writings of philosophers and religious leaders thousands of years ago, but the promiscuous ideal was given a great boost by the *generalized* idea of evolution in the nineteenth century. W. E. H. Lecky (1838–1903), in *The History of European Morals*, wrote: "At one time the benevolent affections embrace merely the family, soon the circle expanding includes first a class, then a nation, then a coalition of nations, then all humanity. . . ." From this passage the contemporary philosopher Peter Singer derived the title of his book, *The Expanding Circle*. Singer believes, of course, that total universalism is not only praiseworthy but possible—perhaps even inevitable.

Universalism is commonly coupled with the political ideal of a world state. The fatal weakness of this dream was pointed out by Bertrand Russell: "A world state, if it were firmly established, would have no enemies to fear, and would therefore be in danger of breaking down through lack of cohesive force." By his phrase "if it were firmly established" Russell indicates that he has carried out a thought-experiment of the sort described earlier in demonstrating that a universally altruistic species could not persist. Russell "pulls his punches" however in saying that a world state would merely be "in danger of breaking down." In fact, it would be certain to break down.

To people who accept the idea of biological evolution "from amoeba to man," the vision of social evolution "from egoism to universalism" may seem plausible. In fact, however, *the last step is impossible*. The forces that bring the earlier stages into being are impotent to bring about the last step. Let us see why.

In imagination, picture a world in which social evolution has gone no farther than egoism or individualism. When familialism appears on the scene, what accounts for its persistence? It must be that the costs of the sacrifices individuals make for their relatives are more than paid for by the gains realized through family solidarity. In the aggregate, individuals who practice familialism have a competitive advantage over those who do not. That is why the step from individualism to familialism is made.

The pattern of the argument just given is characteristically biological, but it is essential to realize that it does not depend on the genetic inheritance of differences in behavior. It assumes no other inheritance than that of the impulse to help and the ability to discriminate. Both impulses can be presumed to be nearly universal in the species. That inherited *differences* are not required by the argument is shown by the following thought-experiment.

Assume a random exchange of children resulting in all children being raised by foster parents. Culture alone can then be assumed to dictate who does, and who does not, behave familialistically. If familialism is competitively advantageous over the lesser form of altruism (individualism), then familialism will persist. Since biology need not be invoked to account for this cultural step there is no reason for antihereditarians to take umbrage at the thought that familialism confers a selective advantage to its practitioners ("selective" being understood in the broadest sense).

Note also that a "higher" grade of altruism does not necessarily extinguish the grades below it. The word "environment" is a singular noun, but the actual social environment in which people have their being is a mosaic of many microenvironments, complicated beyond the possibility of being captured in words. In some "spots" individualism will confer an advantage over familialism, in others the reverse is true. If this were not so, social life would not exhibit the mosaic of behaviors that it does.

The argument that accounts for the step to familialism serves equally well for each succeeding step—*except the last*. Why the difference? Because the One World created by universalism has—by definition—no competitive base to support it. Familialism is supported by the competition of families with each other (which favors those with the greater family loyalty) and by competition of families with simple individualists. Similarly, tribalism is supported by competition between tribes and by competition of tribal individuals with individuals who give their loyalty only to smaller, less powerful groups. But those who speak for One World speak against discrimination and for promiscuity: "Let us no more be true to boasted race or clan." What in the world could select for global promiscuity? Only—as science fiction writers have often pointed out—the enmity (competition) of people from Mars, from other worlds. And if the unifying factor of an external threat were to come into being, it is highly probable that the idealists who now speak out for One World would then agitate for One Universe. Evidently what these idealists dislike is discrimination of *any* sort. Unfortunately for their dreams, the promiscuity they hunger for cannot survive in competition with discrimination.

Universalism is truly the Grand Illusion of many in the community of "intellectuals" in our day. How did it get established? This is a fascinating subject for scholarly research. Let me contribute a few pages to the monumental work that needs to be written. One of the most significant short documents is a famous passage from John Donne that Ernest Hemingway drew on for the title of his novel, *For Whom the Bell Tolls*:

> No man is an island, entire of itself; every man is a piece of the continent, a part of the main. If a clod be washed away by the sea, Europe is the less, as well as if a promontory were, as well as if a manor of thy friends or of thine own were. Any man's death diminishes me, because I am involved in mankind, and therefore never send to know for whom the bell tolls—it tolls for thee.

This is beautiful rhetoric and clearly the work of an "intellectual," as we now use that term. But what is an "intellectual"? Alas, it is all too often a person skilled in words but deficient in the imagination required to see the reality behind verbal counters. Consider carefully the images Donne's writing calls forth in the attentive reader. Imagine a promontory, say a cliff at the edge of the sea. If the pounding waves wash away a whole cliff is the loss no greater than if a mere clod were to be washed away? Clod and cliff are equal? And is the loss *to you* the same in these four cases: your house is destroyed—your friend's house is destroyed—a cliff (without houses) is destroyed—a clod is destroyed? No man of common sense asserts such absurdities.

Donne's prose is a paeon to promiscuity; on this foundation is the dream of universalism built. Denied are all distinctions between large and small, near and far, mine and thine, friend and foe. Yet we must not forget this: for 3 billion years biological evolution has been powered by discrimination. Even mere survival in the absence of evolutionary change depends on discrimination. If universalists now have their way, discrimination will be abandoned. Even the most modest impulse toward conservatism should cause us to question the wisdom of abandoning a principle that has worked so well for billions of years. It is a tragic irony that discrimination has produced a species (*Homo sapiens*) that now proposes to abandon the principle responsible for its rise to greatness.

We can understand how this has come about if we divide the proficiencies that education produces into three categories: literacy, numeracy, and ecolacy. Extending the dictionary meaning somewhat, we may say that literacy is the ability to deal with words, whether written or spoken. John Donne was supremely literate: his evocation of man as a piece of the continent "mankind" at first compels our assent to the proposition that each person must be concerned with the welfare of every other person. In weaving his dialectical web the skilled but purely literate man constantly asks himself, "*What is the appropriate word?*"

The numerate man asks another sort of question: "*How much? How many?*" Numbers make a difference. If there were only one hungry human being in the world, who would doubt that we should feed him? But what if the number of malnourished people is 800 million (as it probably is)? And when the number grows to 2,000 million, what then? Is it a matter of indifference whether I give a bushel of wheat to my literal neighbor, or to an equally hungry man 12,000 miles away? (Remember, energy must be used to transport the wheat, energy which cannot then be used to drive a tractor to grow more wheat next year.) Quantities matter, distances matter, numbers matter.

The person whose education encompasses ecolacy is supremely sensitive to time and to the changes that come with time and repetition. The key question of the ecolate person is this: "*And then what?*"

"Ecolacy," derived from the word ecology, tries to take account of the total system in which reactions take place, including such phenomena as synergy, positive and negative feedback, thresholds, selection, and boomerang effects. Do pests threaten our crops? Then, says the nonecolate person, let us generously douse them with "pesticides." (Note the appropriateness of the word.) But ecolacy points out the error: pesticides select for pesticide-resistant pests. Such selection can ultimately defeat our intent and make the situation worse off than before. . . . Is there a housing shortage in our city? Then let us build more houses—surely this will cure the shortage? Not so, says ecolate man. The city is part of a larger system: building more houses will attract more house-dwellers to the city, leaving the housing situation as bad as ever, and making the traffic situation worse.

It becomes ever more apparent that the burning questions of our time need to be subjected to the discipline of the ecolate question, "And then what?" Unfortunately, this question is seen as threatening by many vested interests, none more than the philosophers who habitually deal with ethics in a purely literate way. Ethicists attempt the impossible when they try to solve ethical problems with such dull tools as sin, duty, right, and obligation—words that are all blind to number and time-related processes.

The plurality of altruisms breeds dilemmas. The character of a culture is revealed in the way it tries to resolve a dilemma. No characterization of our culture is complete without some discussion of a famous statement by the novelist E. M. Forster:

> I hate the idea of causes, and if I had to choose between betraying my country and betraying my friend, I hope I should have the guts to betray my country. Such a choice may scandalize the modern reader, and he may stretch out his patriotic hand to the telephone at once and ring for the police. It would not have shocked Dante, though. Dante places Brutus and Cassius in the lowest circle of hell because they had chosen to betray their friend Julius Caesar rather than their country Rome. . . . Love and loyalty can run counter to the claims of the state. When they do—down with the state, say I, which means that the state would down me.

Forster wrote this in 1939, just before the beginning of World War II. By this time many stories coming out of Nazi Germany told how patriotic Hitler Youth often informed on their own parents when the latter were heard to make statements about Der Fuehrer that were less than enthusiastic. Patriotism was given absolute precedence over familialism. The world was shocked.

As Forster's final sentence implies, patriotism is theoretically capable of overwhelming altruisms of lesser scope. Why does it not *always* do so? Forster said it was because "loyalty can run counter to the claims of the state." The matter can be put more strongly and in quasi-numerate terms: the power of loyalty is *inversely* proportional to the size of the altruistic group. In contrast, political power to control and repress is *directly* proportional to the size of the group. The opposition of the two powers is indicated in Figure 2.

The ineradicable opposition of small group loyalty to the sheer political power of large numbers confutes the supposed drive toward universalism. Because of the egocentric predicament the inference of sincerity in the "other" is always risky, and the greater the number of "others" in a group the greater the risk. The power of loyalty is deeply rooted in innate biological responses to propinquity and repeated association. The power of loyalty to the few constantly erodes the political power of the many. Patriotism depends more on intellectual arguments than does cronyism: this is a key weakness of patriotism. This inherent weakness helps explain the adaptive significance of the theocratic state which proclaims the "divine right of kings." Whenever the support of a state can be made a divine imperative, patriotic loyalty is removed from the realm of rational doubt and shielded from the corrosion of cronyism.

Do the opposing forces create an intermediate point of stability? This seems unlikely. The life histories of individuals vary immensely; the relative valence of political power and loyalty power in the character of each individual is determined by his particular experiences. A crude statistical average might be made for each culture, but there is no reason to think the average would be stable. History forever roils the social systems of the world. Compare the England of Rudyard Kipling with England in the 1930s with its pacifistic "Oxford Oath" taken by millions of young men. The Boer War and World War I moved the statistical balance point of the discriminations "downward" (on the list in Figure 2—no ethical interpretation is implied). Then when Germany invaded Poland in September of 1939 the Oxford Oath was abruptly jettisoned, and the balance point moved decisively "upward" toward patriotism. It has since fallen in England. In America it has fallen even more, as a result of the Vietnam war. The manifest dangers of nuclear war argue (to some) for a permanent abandonment of patriotism, but the argument is valid only if there are no reasons *other than war* for supporting discrimination at the national level. We will return to this point later.

"Liberalism" is an ill-defined term of constantly-changing meaning, yet (whatever its meaning) it is not far off the mark to say that liberalism

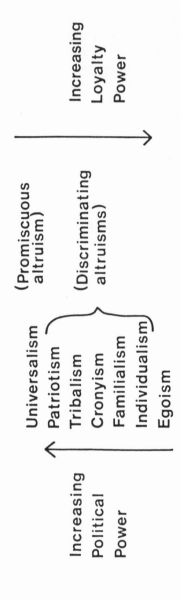

Figure 2. The conflict of powers that works against stabilization at any one level of altruism.

enjoyed more praise than power in the nineteenth century, whereas now it enjoys more power than praise. Hell, someone said, is when you get what you want. With power, self-doubts have come to the liberals. The fashionable journals of the literate world are now pulsating with liberal threnodies.

The political philosopher Michael Novak has put his finger on a key weakness of what is, in our time, called liberalism:

> The liberal personality tends to be atomic, rootless, mobile, and to imagine itself as "enlightened" in some superior and especially valid way. Ironically, its exaggerated individualism leads instantly to an exaggerated sense of universal community. The middle term between these two extremes, the term pointing to the finite human communities in which individuals live and have their being, is precisely the term that the liberal personality disvalues.

That liberals should regard themselves as elite—literally, "chosen"— means nothing more than that they are human. They enjoy an *esprit de corps*, a feeling which those outside a chosen circle identify as ethnocentrism (a sin, be it noted, especially deprecated by contemporary liberals). What needs explaining is the apparent paradox (irony, Novak calls it) of combining individualism and universalism in the liberal personality, with no "middle term."

In the assemblage presented in Figure 2, Novak's "middle term" is decomposed into four different altruisms. Of these, the most conspicuously lacking among contemporary liberals is patriotism. Forster's condemnation of this form of altruism could easily be matched by hundreds of other statements coming from the liberal, "intellectual," literate community. Patriotism has had a bad press ever since Dr. Johnson's offhand remark, "Patriotism is the last refuge of a scoundrel."

Never has the defense of individual "rights" been as strong as it is in our time. Why, then (to paraphrase Novak), does exaggerated individualism lead to exaggerated universalism? To a biologist this puzzle presents little difficulty. Among altruisms, individualism is clearly a borderline case; psychologically it is close to naked egoism. *Homo sapiens* is a social animal: his social appetite is not completely satisfied by an altruism that goes no farther than the *I-Thou* relationship of Martin Buber. Our groupish hungers are seldom completely satisfied by purely dyadic relationships. A significant fraction—perhaps even a large fraction—of humankind craves identification with groups larger than *I and Thou*.

Radical individualism is often linked to hedonism. One sees this clearly in the multitude of magazines in the *Playboy* mode. A practicing playboy is not a complete egoist because "it takes two to tango," but his individualism is of a low order, for the *other* is little more than a sex object. In the past, women (more than men) may have been the guardians of community values; now there is a *Playgirl* magazine that seeks to erase the difference. For Americans, the Declaration of Independence has supplied a banner for hedonism: "the pursuit of happiness."

Hedonists of both sexes should be informed of what the nineteenth-century philosopher Henry Sidgwick called the *Hedonistic Paradox*: those who most actively pursue pleasure as a primary goal are least likely to achieve it. Personal happiness is best gained by indirection, by serving some larger cause. I think this can be taken as an empirical fact. By way of theoretical explanation I would point to two factors.

First, since we are social animals who find pleasure working with others, the horizon of our attention must be broadened beyond the bounds of egoism; perhaps the greater the cause the greater the pleasure in serving it. Second, human beings find so much pleasure in overcoming difficulties that they even seek out difficulties to overcome. We climb mountains that stand not in our way—and thus discover new ways to happiness. Behavior that to a simple rationalist might seem perverse plainly has contributed to the success and progress of the human species. Progress has selected for temperaments that find the simple hedonism of unalloyed individualism too low a peak for complete satisfaction. Not all human beings transcend the demands of simple hedonism, but enough do to affect the course of history. To forego short-term hedonistic gain for a dream that may—only *may*—be realized in the future is to fall into a behavioral pattern that supports altruism.

The dreams of today's more far-seeing individualists are most commonly universalist dreams: One World, the Brotherhood of Man, and the like. Though universalists disparage the moral value of lesser groups, in furthering their cause they necessarily rely on cronyism. Ironically, cocktail parties to which liberals alone are invited are a great place to denounce elitism, the enemy of promiscuity. Thus is the cause of promiscuity advanced by discrimination.

All causes succeed through close-knit, small groups. The effectiveness of a great army, serving patriotic ends, is determined by the cronyism of multitudinous small squads (a fact long recognized by the military). Similarly, the effectiveness of liberals in pursuing universalist ends is determined by the cronyism developed in small groups. The grass roots of patriotism and universalism are the same, only the ends differ. Why has patriotism been rejected by contemporary liberals? It is to this that we must now turn our attention.

The universe may or may not be finite, but prudence demands that we assume that the portion *practically* available to humankind is finite. Technology effectively expands this portion somewhat, but at a rate that is less than the expansion of our expressed demands: hence, the unending complaints of "scarcity." The analytical model for productive economic thinking must be that of a "closed system," a system in which input matches output (diminished somewhat by entropic loss). The enduring task of political economy is the allocation of scarce resources.

No sizeable, prosperous society has been able to persist for long under a rule of equal distribution of income, wealth, or privilege. This empirical fact has not interfered with the persistence of the dream of distributing goods by the rule, "to each according to his needs"—to use Marx's language for an ideal furnished him by the religion he despised.

Empiricism is not enough: before we can assent to an apparent impossibility we must "understand" it, that is, we must find the theoretical "impotence principle" that sets the limits. Why won't a Marxian distribution work? To answer this we must ask, distribution of what? It makes a difference.

The "whats" of the world come in three varieties: matter, energy, and information. Every redistribution of matter and energy is in accordance with zero-sum principles: the gain to A is exactly matched by the loss to B. Equations must balance: the mass (or quantity of energy) on the left side must match that on the right. Matter is conserved. Energy is conserved. Matter and energy obey "conservation laws." Information is not conserved, as we shall see presently.

However great our social impulses, evolution has selected for an irreducible minimum of egoism. Any proposal to transfer the goods of matter and energy from B to A is likely to be resisted by B. Overpowering such resistance uses up "energy," either in the physicist's sense or in some other significant sense. It is highly doubtful that there ever was any "initial state" of equidistribution of human wealth or social power. Equidistribution, if possible at all, can be achieved only by some impoverishment of the group as a whole—in the case of violent revolution, by massive impoverishment (and an invariable failure to achieve the goal of the instigators). Violence, which accelerates the drive toward entropy, creates a negative-sum game. This is the consideration that moderates the enthusiasm of the prudent man for "distributive justice." Territorial behavior in other animals and property rights among human beings often serve the same cause—the cause of peace.

There are three basic politico-economic systems: privatism, socialism, and commonism. Privatism (under various names—"private enterprise," "capitalism," "free enterprise," etc.) never takes equidistribution as a goal, though apologists often assert that a "trickle-down effect" slowly works toward that end. Socialism and commonism, however, seem congenitally committed to the ideal of equidistribution. Under socialism, the major part of the community's wealth is kept as common property, which is managed (supposedly) for the good of all by managers appointed more or less directly by the community. Such property may be spoken of as a "managed commons."

Under commonism, however, the commons is unmanaged, being left available to all under the Marxist rule, "to each according to his needs." Under conditions of abundance, commonism may work very well. The hunting grounds of the pioneer days of America were a commons that worked. An unmanaged commons has the advantage that the cost of management is zero. But when people become crowded and resources scarce, an unmanaged commons does not work well because each individual is the judge of his own needs. With scarcity, commonism favors egoism over altruism. The would-be altruist, if he is to survive under scarcity, must become as egoistic as the worst. In the name of freedom and distributive justice, an unmanaged commons breeds harsh egoism, inequality, and injustice. So long as such a system endures, men of good will are powerless to change the results: such is the "tragedy of the commons."

The commons that led the obscure English mathematician W. F. Lloyd to deduce its analytical properties a hundred and fifty years ago is not very important now. This was the commons of English pasture land. But the commons of oceanic fisheries and the seabed (from which valuable minerals can be extracted) still exist and promise to create international trouble in the future. So too does the commons of the atmosphere, which serves as a sink for the "bads" of volatile pollutants.

Without being aware enough or honest enough to use the proper label we constantly create new commons. Insurance, which begins as a wager, tends toward a commons as the fraction of people insured approaches unity. Those who are insured pressure the system to make premiums equal while wanting payouts to be made according to unmonitored needs. To keep the costs of automobile accident insurance and fire insurance from ruinous escalation, there must be constant monitoring by managers alert to arson and fraudulent repair claims.

Universalism is the ideal of One World in which clod equals cliff: the "rights" of all are equal, whether friend or foe, native or foreigner, relative or stranger. A universalist is, whether he acknowledges it or not, a follower of Marx and a promoter of the tragedy of the commons. How, then, are we to account for Novak's observation that the liberals of our time. By words we convey information. Unlike matter and energy, *information is not subject to conservation laws.*

The answer is to be found in the peculiar nature of words, the medium of the merely literate intellectuals who are so influential in our time. By words we convey information. Unlike matter and energy, information is not subject to conservation laws.

Agent B, in the act of giving information to A, loses nothing. In fact, if A reworks the information into an improved form and passes it back to B, both gain. Far from being a zero-sum game, information-sharing can be a positive-sum game. When we deal with information there are strong reasons for sharing generously, even for maintaining a commons of information. Science could not have made its rapid progress had information been treated like a property subject to conservation laws. In espousing universalism professional literates are merely generalizing from their profession to the world at large, unaware of the significant difference between information on the one hand and matter and energy on the other.

What, then, accounts for the individualism of this group? This is no secret: "Shakespeare's plays could not have been written by a committee." Creativity at the highest level is inescapably individualistic. There is no "group mind" to carry out the decisive act of creation.

The One World that universalists dream of is clearly a world freed of many of the restraints of lesser political units, a free world ("to each according to his needs"). It is easy for a radical individualist to embrace universalism while rejecting all intermediate altruisms. The strengths of individualism are unaffected by this hybridization of ideals precisely because no real universalist world exists to act as a restraint on the individualist who worships it as an ideal. Were One World to come into being, and were it to acquire the sanctions that all lesser associations have taken unto themselves, the individualist would find himself unhappier than ever. There would then be no larger ideal for him to aspire to.

Universalism is attractive in large part because the ideal is used as a weapon to beat off the restraints necessarily imposed on individuals by family, tribe, and nation. In deciding how much support to give individualism we are well advised to examine the "track record" of individualism. Philosophers and historians are pretty well agreed on the meaning of the Greek experience:

> The greatness of the Greeks in individual achievement was, I think, intimately bound up with their political incompetence, for the strength of individual passion was the source both of individual achievement and of the failure to secure Greek unity. And so Greece fell under the domination, first of Macedonia, and then of Rome.—Bertrand Russell in *Authority and the Individual*.

> Individualism in the end destroys the group, but in the interim it stimulates personality, mental exploration, and artistic creation. Greek democracy was corrupt and incompetent, and had to die.— Will Durant in *The Life of Greece*.

It is exciting to live in a world of richly creative people, but the individualism that fosters creativity may, *unless it becomes self-conscious*, destroy the foundations of the society that supports it. "Becoming self-conscious" means that "intellectuals" must realize that the One-World commonism they aspire to is only a *natural, though fatal, inference from their craft*, which is the elaboration and distribution of ideas and information. Matter and energy, by contrast, must be distributed with discrimination—not promiscuously—else the tragedy of the commons will be set in train. "Intellectuals" must learn to praise virtues different from the ones that give them their craft-strength. The survival of a civilization in which intellectuals have great social power requires that this power be coupled with a degree of objectivity that is rare among men of all vocations.

Universalism is unattainable, and individualism is not enough—not in a competitive world where a larger group has the edge over smaller ones. The last remark is, of course, to be understood *ceteris paribus*; but the thrust of the argument pushes us toward the conclusion that there will always be an important role for the altruism that is only one step below universalism. That is the altruism we call "patriotism."

Many concerned people today find this conclusion hard to swallow. Patriotism, war, nuclear holocaust, destruction of civilization—this chain of ideas has led many to believe that patriotism must be expunged to save civilization. The establishment of One World is seen as a way to dismantle the armaments of nations. But promiscuous universalism would destroy the world too, though in a different way: in T. S. Eliot's prescient formula, "not with a bang, but a whimper."

The whimper has begun, but so far as I know, only one literary man has noticed the form it is taking: the French writer Raspail in his novel *The Camp of the Saints*. His argument is only implicit (as a good fiction writer's should be), but it is easy to translate it into explicit stages. The logical steps in the developing disaster are these:

1. By virtue of their craft, opinion-makers worship the ideal of promiscuous sharing: for them, patriotism is unthinkable.

2. "To each according to his needs" means that when immigrants from a poor country knock at the door of a rich country they must be admitted.

3. The process of moving from poor to rich will continue until wealth is equalized everywhere.

4. But since there is no group limitation on individual freedom to breed, it is not so much wealth that will be equalized as it is poverty—thus plunging everyone into the Malthusian depths.

Have we no choice other than between the whimper of common pauperization and the bang of thermonuclear destruction? I think we have. I am enough of an optimist to believe that we can create and sustain forms of patriotism based on national pride in the arts of peace—science, music, painting, sports, and other arts of living. Excellence in these accomplishments can be the occasion for community pride (hubris, if you will), which has its dangers but without which life is not fully lived. Accompanying all this there must be the patriotic will to protect what has been achieved against demands for a worldwide, promiscuous sharing. A community that renounces war as a means of settling international disputes still cannot survive without that discriminating form of altruism we call patriotism. It must defend the integrity of its borders or succumb into chaos.

## In Sum

The caring impulse, generalized without limit, produces universalism which, though desirable in the realm of information, is destructive when it comes to matter and energy because promiscuous sharing of limited physical resources leads to the tragedy of the commons. Some people have revived the old motto "All men are brothers" with the assertion that the pageant of Darwinian evolution gives it new meaning. Possibly so, but the conclusion that brotherhood requires us to perish in a commons is a *non sequitur*.

If biology is to be consulted for guidance we must take note of this supremely important fact: a species does not survive because its members act "for the good of the species," but because individuals act for the good of themselves, of their germ lines, or of reciprocity groups smaller than the total population. The survival of the species is, as it were, an accidental by-product of discriminating altruism. Biologists have known this more or less ever since Darwin, but it has become crystal clear only in the last two decades.

Completely promiscuous altruism in a species that has no important enemies would destroy both the species and its environment. A judicious mixture of discriminating altruisms is required for survival. The universalist's dream embodied in St. Augustine's *City of God* can be realized only in the realm of ideas, which, alone, can be promiscuously shared with safety. We must be chary of deducing any *material* consequences from the assertion that "All men are brothers." The pleasures of brotherhood are sweet, but only because they involve both caring *and* discrimination, as Proudhon realized a century ago: "If everyone is my brother, I have no brothers."

Brotherhood requires otherhood. Civilization has been built upon, and can only survive with, a changeable mixture of discriminating altruisms.

# HUMAN ECOLOGY

# 14

## *Biological Insights Into Abortion*

When the U.S. Supreme Court legalized early abortions (pregnancy termination during the first three months), many people thought this decision brought an end to a controversy that had flourished for the past decade. This turned out not to be the case. In a very few years a backlash from so-called Right-to-Life groups intensified public disagreement. Most Right-to-Life groups were "single-issue groups," that is groups which informed politicians up for election that they would support or oppose them on the basis of their position on this single issue. Poll after poll has shown that the majority of the electorate—65 to 90 percent, depending on how the question is worded—is in favor of a woman being allowed the freedom to continue her pregnancy or terminate it, as she wishes. Given this majority view, one might suppose legislators would not have to pay much attention to the wishes of the Right-to-Life minority. Not so. Many elections are won by only a few percentage points. When the majority of the populace considers many issues in reaching their voting decisions while a minority focuses on only a single issue, a determined minority can effectively coerce a candidate for election into supporting their cause. This will, of course, displease the majority. Thus is the politician placed in a quandary. Abortion is one of those "no win issues" that canny politicians sidestep whenever they can. They can hardly be blamed.

Silence easily leads to taboo, and eventually we may recreate a Naked Emperor that we thought we saw the end of in the 1960s. If that happens, biologists will be among those who have the best chance of keeping alive the necessary knowledge of the substantive facts. It is for this reason that this essay is addressed principally to biology teachers.

The controversy over abortion involves more than biology, and the biologist must be careful not to claim expertise in fields not his. However, if he treats the subject in a narrowly technical way he risks appearing insensitive to human values. Therefore, while emphasizing the biological side, he should show that he is aware of alternative approaches, without appearing to claim professional competence in other fields.

At the outset we need to ask, Why consider abortion at all? Isn't contraception preferable? Indeed it is, but a few rough calculations demonstrate the need for abortion.

What is the failure rate for contraception? It varies with the method used and the population using it. The data from the numerous studies are not very consistent, but seldom is the failure rate as low as 1 percent, i.e., one unwanted pregnancy per 100 women practicing contraception for an entire year. (Pregnancies followed by very early spontaneous abortions are not even counted in the failure rate.) In a U.S. population of 228 million about one-half are women, and one-half of these are between the ages of 15 and 45, the most fertile years. One-fourth of 228 million is 57 million.

Assume that the 3.5 million babies born in the year are all wanted babies (certainly not true). That leaves 53.5 million women exposed to the risk of pregnancy if they are all having intercourse (which is almost true). If this entire population uses the best method of contraception in a conscientious manner (far from true), then 535,000 of them will become pregnant against their will during the year. All things considered, this is a conservative figure.

Since these women will have taken proper precautions they will resent Nature's throw of the dice that made them pregnant. Some of them are against abortion and will do nothing to escape their fate. But none of them are really "for" abortion—just as no one is "for" appendectomies. Both men and women are against peritonitis (the alternative to a needed appendectomy), and women are against mandatory motherhood (the alternative to a desired abortion).

Perhaps the major nonscientific issue is that of women's rights. Should a woman have the right to determine how her body is used or not? The same issue does not arise for men. If copulation is sometimes a sin, it is one for which Nature punishes only the female. To use a current cliche, nature is "sexist." Those who favor abortion on request attempt to correct somewhat nature's sexism.

Economics is an important aspect of abortion. The figures vary a great deal from region to region, and inflation constantly pushes them upward, but the approximate economic costs of abortion and its alternative (bearing a child and rearing it to adulthood) are as follows. A normal childbirth costs about 10 times as much as an early abortion. Childbirth and raising the child to adulthood costs about 400 times as much as an early abortion. In figures valid at the beginning of the 1980s, T. J. Espenshade calculated that the choice is between $200 for an early abortion and some $80,000 (of which $2,000 is prenatal care and delivery) for bearing and rearing a child. If the parents are unwilling ones, the cost of bearing and rearing a child will be regarded as an unwelcome burden imposed by society. Resentment hardly makes for good citizenship or good parentage. If, however, the greater costs are assumed by society, danger of a different sort is raised, namely that of shared impoverishment through the commons of socialized medicine and social services.

The political danger raised by a law that prohibits abortion on request is that of any prohibition law. The consequences of alcohol prohibition by the Eighteenth Amendment of 1919 are well-known: it failed in its mission (it was repealed by the Twenty-First Amendment in 1933), and it created a powerful criminal establishment that is still with us. Those who propose to prohibit abortion should demonstrate that there is no danger of strengthening the criminal element of society.

Much nonproductive argument can be avoided if the correct historical and anthropological framework for abortion is set up to begin with.

Abortion-prohibitionists usually imply (if they do not explicitly say) that the practice of abortion has *always* been prohibited in decent societies. The opposite is true. Historical studies of N. E. Himes and an anthropological survey by George Devereux have shown that abortion has been practiced by almost all cultures throughout all time. Most experts agree with Ronald Freedman that "abortion—whether legal or illegal—is the most used *single* method of birth control today." We in the Anglo-American culture have an erroneous impression of the history of abortion because we are just emerging from an abortion-prohibition period that extended from about 1870 to 1970. A hundred years is about three generations. It is all too easy to assume that something that has existed as far back as you, your parents, and your grandparents can remember has existed for all time.

The historical puzzle is this: why was there that anomalous period in western civilization when abortion was prohibited? Abortion was neither prohibited nor abhorred by the great majority of women before then (and perhaps not by the men either, insofar as they thought about it). The circumstances leading to the rise of abortion-prohibition in the United States are detailed in James C. Mohr's excellent history, *Abortion in America.*

Of course the fact that the practice of abortion has been widespread in both space and time does not prove that it is morally "right." But it should suggest to the thoughtful that they ought to at least make a thorough inquiry into the facts associated with abortion before making up their minds.

It is my personal impression that biologists as a group are not drawn from a particularly argumentative segment of the population (as, for instance, lawyers are). Many professional biologists not only do not seek controversy, they will evade it if possible. It is quite understandable that many teachers of biology should avoid the subject of abortion. In so doing, however, they deprive themselves of a marvelous chance to develop some important biological concepts in a context that captures the students' attention.

The first great opportunity of the teacher is to get his students to recognize that scientific facts are relevant to decisions in moral matters. Few scientists can agree with the attitude expressed by Chief Justice

Warren Burger when he dissented from the Supreme Court decision of 22 January 1973 that legalized abortion: "I am somewhat troubled that the court has taken notice of various scientific and medical data in reaching its conclusion." The *exact* bearing of scientific facts upon ethical decisions is not always clear, but this is a matter for further thought. Let us see what some of these scientific facts are.

First, it must be emphasized that early abortion is *not* medically dangerous. Illegal abortions, carried out under grossly septic conditions, are dangerous—but this is because of the septic conditions. Very late abortions are also dangerous. But the women who want abortions want them early. When delay occurs it is usually because a time-consuming legal procedure is required to get permission. In such case, the danger is created by the law, not by medicine.

How do we decide when a health risk is "acceptable"? This question brings us to another principle of scientific analysis students need to know. *Never make a null-comparison when that is not a real option.* Do not compare the risk of abortion for a pregnant female with the normal risks of life for a nonpregnant female. The risk of abortion must be compared with the risk of its real alternative, namely childbirth. A woman already pregnant has to run one risk or the other. Under American conditions an early abortion is less than one-sixth as dangerous as a normal childbirth. If medically complicated deliveries are included, the comparative risk of early, medically supervised abortion is still less.

The psychological dangers of abortion are harder to evaluate (as all psychological phenomena are). At one time there was much talk of the guilt that women felt following induced abortion. This no longer seems a serious matter. Remember: women who are strongly opposed to abortion don't ask for abortions. Self-selection removes the principal group that might have guilt feelings. The suffering of women who have abortions must be weighed against the suffering of women who are denied them: "postpartum depression," a not uncommon sequel to normal childbirth; the rage of reluctant motherhood; and the heartbreak of bearing a child only to give it up for adoption.

One further misconception must be dispelled. Those who oppose abortion on request almost universally present their case as if there were only one ethical system of thought (just as there is only one physics and one science of chemistry). But, worldwide, there are many ethical systems. Even western culture has many competing ethical systems. At the present time, the two principal ethical approaches are labeled *deontological* (or absolutist) and *consequentialist* (also called situation ethics or relativistic ethics). The deontological system assumes that duties are handed down to us by some unquestionable authority, duties that are independent of the consequences of actions. For this approach to abortion one may consult the writings of John T. Noonan, Jr. On the other hand, Joseph Fletcher is the most distinguished champion of the consequentialist approach. Discussion of the ethics of abortion is not strictly speaking part of a course in biology, but one should not let students escape with the illusion that there is only one system of ethics.

The next pedagogical point may come as a surprise to some biologists. It is this: *Abortion should not be treated under the heading of population control, but under the heading of development.* There are two good reasons for this decision, one theoretical and the other practical and political.

The theoretical issue is connected with the meaning we impute to the word "control." Laymen may use it loosely, but biologists are well-advised to restrict the word to its cybernetic meaning. Cybernetic control is achieved by negative feedback ("corrective feedback"). The room thermostat is a cybernetic control device; a valve on a gas pipe, if it is not connected with anything that can change its position, is not. The state of the room thermostat changes with the temperature; the state of the isolated valve does not.

Population control is achieved by "density-dependent" factors. The "crowd-diseases"—most notably enteric diseases like cholera and typhoid—are notably density-dependent. When the density of population rises tenfold, mortality from these diseases rises more than tenfold. Lightning bolts are not a population control device. On the reasonable assumption that lightning bolts strike completely at random as far as population size is concerned, they exert their mortality on a strictly proportional basis. Increase the density of the population tenfold, and mortality increases only tenfold. No method of birth control is, by itself, a method of population control. Birth control may be used in population control, but *it is the way in which birth control is used that constitutes population control*, as the following example shows.

From time immemorial abortion was a permitted method of family limitation in Japan. In the 1930s, when Japan set out upon a course of aggressive expansion in Asia, the Japanese rulers made abortion illegal. After losing the Second World War, realizing that further population increase was inimical to the national interest, the Japanese rescinded the abortion-prohibition law. The population *control* element in this case was not the technique of abortion but the changeableness of law, which proved to be sensitive to population density.

In brief, *"birth control" does not equal "population control."* Abortion is merely a method of birth control. It should not be presented as a form of population control. (Strictly speaking, abortion is the *only* method of *birth* control; all methods of contraception are *conception* control, as Joseph Fletcher has pointed out.)

The practical and political reason for insisting that abortion is not a method of population control lies in the danger of a serious misunderstanding. Those who oppose the prohibition of abortion want to ensure that no woman will be compelled to continue a pregnancy she does not want. They are opposed to mandatory motherhood, which they see as a latter-day form of mandatory servitude imposed upon only one sex. To them, mandatory motherhood is wrong for much the same reasons that slavery is wrong.

If a biologist presents abortion as a method of population control, he will soon find that some of the more emotional of his opponents will quite honestly think that he has come out for *mandatory* abortion. We should not risk this misunderstanding. To avoid it, all discussions of abortion should be preceded by this caveat: Only women's rights are being discussed, not the quite different issue of population control. With the caveat established, and sticking for the most part to strictly biological matters that are relevant to abortion, what can a biologist point out that should be of interest to those in his audience whose minds are still open?

First: Natural abortion—spontaneous abortion—is very common. A multitude of studies indicate that approximately 69% of all conceptuses are spontaneously aborted. If we equate normal with common (as we tend to do) it certainly cannot be said that abortion is abnormal. (On a purely statistical basis we would have to regard the completion of pregnancy as somewhat abnormal!) Not much should be made of this point beyond opening up the student's mind to new ideas.

It is, however, worth developing this point further to get across the idea that, to the biologically oriented mind, death is not abnormal. A bit of history is enlightening. In 1921 a Dr. Robinson was honored with an invitation to give the Struthers Lecture at the Royal College of Surgeons in Edinburgh. The terms of the lectureship required that the recipient *not* discuss problems in pathology. Robinson wanted to talk about the death of human embryos. Conventionally, in medical circles, death is viewed as pathological. Nevertheless, Robinson gave his lecture, justifying it on the grounds that embryonic death is so widespread in mammals that it should be accepted as a normal phenomenon. This was more than a "ploy"; it was an essential insight into biology.

One of the commonest questions asked of the biologist by the earnest inquirer into abortion is this: "When does life begin?" Human life is meant, of course. To this, the biologist must give an answer that is definitive and (unfortunately) initially quite unsatisfactory to the inquirer: *"Never!"* Life, evolutionists believe, began once some 3 billion years ago, but it has probably never started again on this earth. Life is merely passed on from one individual to another, from one cell to another. A living sperm unites with a living ovum producing a living zygote, which develops, step by step, through embryogeny to a baby and later to an adult. Life never begins—*not in human experience*. This may seem an oversubtle point to nonbiologists, but we must insist on it.

The question laymen are muddling toward is this: When does the life of the *individual* begin? When are we to call the thing that is alive a "human being"? In response to this question the most valuable thing a scientist can do is point out that what bothers people is not a question of fact but one of definition. *In matters of definition there is no right or wrong*; there are only definitions that are agreed upon and definitions that are not agreed upon. The question is: What definition can we agree upon? It is difficult to lay out all the considerations that enter into our deciding when to agree on a definition, but certainly among these considerations is the issue of the consequences of the definition.

In declaring that abortion is a permissible medical procedure the U.S. Supreme Court, in 1973, said: "The unborn have never been recognized in the law as persons in the whole sense." In other words, at the moment of birth the *biological* being becomes a *human* being in the eyes of the law. The transition is not a biological fact but a legal or cultural fact. Many societies have pushed the dividing line a few days farther along, making christening the rite of passage from mere biological existence to legal humanhood. Such is the primitive meaning of christening. (As a practical consequence this practice permitted the destruction of defective babies without committing the crime of murder.)

In our culture, killing before birth cannot be murder. Not long ago, in California, a pregnant woman was shot in the abdomen by her husband. The woman survived the shot, but the fetus did not. The man was charged with the murder of his child and the attempted murder of his wife. The court immediately dismissed the charge of murder, holding (consistently with all previous legal decisions) that the fetus was not a human being, and hence could not be murdered. The man was convicted only of the attempted murder of his wife.

Since the Supreme Court decision of 1973, the principal attempt of the abortion-prohibitionists has been to legally redefine humanhood as extending all the way back to the zygote. If this attempt succeeds, the prohibitionists will not only lay the grounds for forbidding all abortion as a form of murder, but they will also achieve other effects that will, I think, come as a surprise to them.

Remember: 69 percent of all multicellular human embryos that become implanted in the wall of the uterus end in spontaneous abortion. By the prohibitionists' definition of humanhood, these conceptuses would legally become human beings. All states have laws governing the burial or other disposition of dead human bodies. Once abortion-prohibition is established as law on this definitional basis it will then be logically necessary to bury (or otherwise legally dispose of) spontaneously aborted conceptuses. This means that we must first find these aborted "human beings."

Most spontaneous abortions occur in the first few weeks of pregnancy. Commonly the woman thinks she has merely had a delayed menstruation. Among those women who have regular menstrual cycles, and who are regularly indulging in intercourse, a "delayed menstruation" is more often than not due to impregnation followed by spontaneous abortion. Once the law defines the zygote (and all subsequent states) as a human being in every sense of the law, the law (to be consistent) must require every woman to save the flow from each delayed menstruation so that it can be given whatever burial is legally required by the state. With annual births in the United States standing at 3.5 million, there must be something like 7.8 million spontaneous abortions per year. If each of these menstrual flows has to be buried, at a modest cost of $500 per burial, the total cost would be approximately $4 billion per year— no small sum even in these days of inflation. (We can anticipate, of course, no objection from undertakers to the passage of this law.)

The economic cost of the law would by no means be the least. Those who really believed the new definition was morally right would psychologically suffer from all these additional "deaths" (as they do *not* now psychologically suffer from "late periods"). Those who held the law in contempt would bitterly resent its operation and seek to evade it.

So much for the costs of the proposed law. What are the benefits? Detecting the benefits might be an "exercise left to the class." But then again, perhaps this whole issue should be evaded. Esthetically, the consequences spelled out here are far from pleasing. I would have hesitated to mention them had not a courageous Jesuit, Father Tom Wassmer, first put the argument into print back in 1967. (Numerical aspects have been added to Father Wassmer's argument.) But perhaps biology teachers should usually keep the entire discussion in a secret armamentarium to be used only when circumstances seem appropriate.

The subject of abortion presents a splendid opportunity to get across to the student the significance of development, and the essential distinction between information and the *realization* of an informed code. The zygote of any animal contains all the information needed to produce the animal, but information should never be confused with reality. The egg of a salmon contains all the information needed to produce a delicious adult salmon, but noone, ordering a salmon in the fish market, would be satisfied with being handed a salmon egg. Putting the matter more in terms of the salmon's interest, if we saw a man destroying a million salmon eggs we would not accuse him of massively violating the fishing laws. (There might be laws against destroying salmon eggs, but they would not be as severe as those against destroying adult salmon.) The effect on the salmon population of destroying a million salmon eggs would be far less than the effect of destroying a million adult salmon.

A zygote is not an adult; it merely contains the information needed to produce an adult of a particular species. Its DNA constitutes, as it were, the blueprints of the species.

The destruction of the blueprints for a $100,000 house is not the same thing as the destruction of a $100,000 house. So long as the blueprints are replaceable, the loss occasioned by destroying them is equal only to the cost of the blueprints—not to the cost of the structure the blueprints encode. Compared with the final realization, blueprints are almost valueless; so also are zygotes and even fetuses.

The distinction between embryonic stages and born children has been made in language familiar to science, but it is interesting to note that some philosophers and theologians (e.g., E.-H. W. Kluge) have made an identical distinction in other words, noting that to call an embryo a person is to be guilty of committing a *moral prolapsis*. "Prolapsis" means confusing a future state with things that already exist—assigning a name to too early a stage in the developmental series. As regards matters of great moment in everyday human affairs, the findings of scientists are often anticipated by philosophers and theologians; but we have moved so far from the world in which these learned men were generally influential that the terminology they use is often unknown outside their professions. Subtle as the scientific concept of "information" is, this term now has a better chance of being widely understood than does "moral prolapsis."

The implications of information are far from being widely understood. Consider, for instance, the objection voiced by a political scientist to the suggestion that human fetuses already expelled from the uterus might be used for medical research: "If we really did not know that the fetus was a human offspring—if we really thought it could be a tadpole or a dog—we could hardly object to the selling of this kind of animal, among all others. But then again, if the fetuses were thought to be snail darters, the courts would rush in instantly to protect them." Ignoring the last sarcastic swipe at environmentalists it is obvious that the writer misses completely the distinction between information and realization. The clear implication of his argument is that there is no important distinction between house and blueprint. Biologists know better. So also does the ordinary citizen.

People trained in the law are very good at logical analysis, but that does not preclude their being entrapped by words. Consider the following remarks by a law professor commenting on a 1977 opinion of the Supreme Court. "The majority opinion [referred] to the unborn child as 'potential life.' As long as this term is employed, the issue of abortion is not squarely faced. If the unborn child is potential, he or she is not 'life'—a conclusion drawn by Judge Clement Haynsworth. . . . If the unborn child, as biologists and pediatricians and mothers claim, is alive, he or she is not merely potential. Judicial thinking would be clarified if potential and actual judges focused on the existence of unborn children."

Such entwined confusions surely merit the Shakespearean curse, "A plague on both your houses!" The judges on the bench make one biological error in labelling as "potential life" that which is actually alive, namely the living fetus. The law professor makes another in resolutely denying the biological phenomenon of development and the consequences that flow from it. The zygote produced by two adult members of the species *Homo sapiens* is a *Homo sapiens* zygote. But to insist that both zygote and adult must be referred to *only* by the single term "human being" is to lose *differentia* in a word. The lawyer unconsciously takes partial cognizance of this point when he refers to the fetus as "an unborn *child*." Why does he not refer to it as "an unborn voter" or "an unborn senior citizen"? Each of the nouns within quotation marks imputes to the fetal stage social properties that do not belong to it. The error would be immediately spotted if the lawyer spoke of "an unborn voter." By giving different names to different stages of development we manage to take the atomic, inflexible, time-blind elements of language and tailor them to the realities of fluid, progressive development, both biological and social.

That the most essential aspect of a zygote is its content of information has been implicitly recognized by biologists for about a hundred years and explicitly discussed for more than two decades. The implication of this insight for the abortion problem was first drawn in 1967. Yet still some lawyers and political scientists have not grasped the point. Information is a subtle concept. Biologists should not underestimate the difficulty of teaching the meaning of information, nor the social importance of succeeding in doing so.

One aspect of the resistance to the "blueprint analogy" deserves a serious response. *In the end, every analogy fails in some respect*; if it did not it would be more than an analogy. The proper response to this logical point is to examine each analogy carefully, asking this question: "When the analogy fails, is the failure significant for the issue at hand?" How, for example, does the blueprint analogy fail, and what bearing does this failure have on the abortion controversy?

Though the blueprints for a house can be exactly reproduced from the original drawings, the "blueprints" once existent in the DNA of a zygote that has been destroyed can never be reproduced exactly. . . . What, never? Well, hardly ever. It is so improbable that another spermatozoon and another ovum will bring to another zygote exactly the same coded instructions that we can (for practical purposes) assume that the probability is zero. Thus, does the analogy fail. But has the failure any significance for the case in hand? Long before the blueprint analogy was developed, abortion-prohibitionists were fond of asking this question: "What if Beethoven's mother had had an abortion?"

What indeed? With equal justice one can ask, "What if Hitler's mother had had an abortion?" The point is, almost all mothers have one or more spontaneous abortions during their childbearing years (not to mention their induced abortions). That which is lost by an abortion—and it does not matter whether it is spontaneous or induced—is, on the average, an average zygote. It may be a Hitler or a Beethoven. More likely it is just an average human being. In any case, it never becomes an existent adult, so we never know what we have lost.

*Of the never-existent, nothing useful can be said.* This is an extremely valuable insight that science can give nonscientists. On analysis it turns out that the way in which the blueprint analogy fails is of no practical human importance. Therefore the blueprint analogy is sound. It emphasizes the fact that whatever is lost in abortion—spontaneous or induced—is (on the average) of very little value, as value is reckoned by men and women of common sense.

Since human beings have had some understanding of the facts of embryological development for thousands of years it is surprising to note that some scholars actually deny the whole concept of development. For example, the theologian Karl Barth wrote: "He who destroys germinating life kills a man." And we find the writer of a letter-to-the-editor asking this rhetorical question: "Surely the advocates should not consider killing at one stage of human life as fundamentally different than killing at another?" But, in fact, that is exactly what biologists must insist upon. An acorn contains all the information needed to produce a magnificent oak tree—but who would regard smashing 10,000 acorns as an act of deforestation?

On an objective basis it matters a great deal what the stage of life is, whether one is talking about oak trees or human beings. The nearly 8 million embryonic deaths that result from spontaneous abortion in the United States each year have nothing like the effect on society that the same number of deaths of adult Americans would have. Nor should they have. Development makes a difference. Development is a fundamental concept, and it has consequences of great importance.

Involved here is the important issue of "numeracy" in thinking. All too many people think only in terms of words divorced from numbers and quantities. Particularly at fault are the people who are very clever with words, the literary·people. Numeracy should be contrasted with literacy (understood in this special sense). The merely literate people have all too much influence on public policy. Their repugnance at numbers leads at times to some astonishing statements. Consider the following examples. Father Austin O'Malley: "An innocent fetus an hour old may not be directly killed to save the lives of all the mothers in the world." Father Edwin F. Healy: "It is preferable by far that a million mothers and fetuses perish than that a physician stain his soul with murder"—as he would if he killed a fetus to save the life of a mother. These are statements that surely 99 percent of the populace rejects out of hand. The extremism of these statements is a consequence of an intoxication with words ("innocence" and "murder") that afflicts people who are merely literate and determinedly antinumerate.

Why this intoxication with literacy, this deliberate blindness to numbers and quantification? I think we can understand it. Mother Teresa, famed for her compassionate work in Calcutta, said: "If a mother can murder her own child, in her own womb, what then is left for you and me but to kill each other?" What Mother Teresa is expressing is what has been called "the fear of the slippery slope." If we allow ourselves to draw an arbitrary line, on one side of which killing is to be called murder, then have we not entered upon a moral "slippery slope" down which we will steadily slide? Will we not (it is argued) descend from what was originally intended to be a compassionate decision into the moral degradation of Nazi Germany?

There is a certain plausibility to the slippery slope argument, but against it we must urge that in real life we have to draw many lines that are purely arbitrary and absolutely essential. When automobiles are driven at unsafe speeds there is the danger of an accident that will kill some human being. At what level does the "unsafe" speed begin? There is no objective, scientific, absolute answer to this question, and there cannot be. At 55 miles an hour, 65 miles an hour, or 75 mph? These are purely arbitrary lines. No matter where the line is drawn, some deaths will result. If cars were restricted to 5 miles an hour, there would still be some deaths—not many, but some. The only safe speed is zero. Permitting the slightest speed greater than zero puts us on the slippery slope. We run this risk, knowingly and willingly. No particular figure is defensible, but we need to agree on *some* figure. In a very rough way we balance the advantages and disadvantages of going (say) 55 mph against the advantages and disadvantages of moving at slower or faster speeds. In some approximate way we decide where the best balance is. We pass laws, and set up the machinery to enforce the laws. The machinery is never perfect. There is always some cheating at the line. But it is better to have some line than none at all.

One of the important lessons that comes out of this analysis is that the word "arbitrary" as used by scientists is not a pejorative word, as it generally is in the legal context. (Every statistical test of significance in science requires, for its interpretation, an arbitrary decision.) To get the world's work done there must be arbitrary decisions.

In connection with the abortion problem, it turns out that drawing a reasonable, arbitrary line runs no danger of putting us on a slippery slope. Abortion is quite different from speeding in automobiles. No matter what speed limit we establish by law, people will push against it; they will drive just a little bit faster to see what they can get away with. With abortion there is no such danger. Women do not want late abortions. They want early abortions—the earlier the better. So if we establish an arbitrary line at, say, 24 weeks, we will not find cases crowding up against the 24-week line. On the contrary, most elective abortions will occur before the eighth week—as they do now, except when officious administrators interpose difficulties. Only rarely will the request for an abortion come late in pregnancy—as it may when prenatal tests reveal a congenital defect. Such special cases create no slippery slope. They are special, and they do not escalate in number when we deal with them compassionately on an individual basis.

Such are the major biological and scientific considerations. Before closing, let us examine some areas where the discipline of biology intersects with the academic discipline of ethics. The intersections require semantic analysis, that is, taking a hard look at words and the way we use them.

Most abortion-prohibitionists put their case in terms of religion, specifically the Christian religion. They cite the Sixth Commandment as it is stated in the King James version of the Bible: "Thou shalt not kill." They seem unaware of the fact that recent, and more exact, translations of the Bible (e.g., the "Goodspeed Bible") give the Commandment thus: "You must not commit murder." What is the difference in meaning between the two wordings?

The difference brings us back to the idea of arbitrary discriminations. Like us, the ancient Hebrews made a distinction between killing and murder. Murder was an unapproved killing. Mere killing was (by definition) an act that was approved, or at any rate not forbidden. The grounds for forbidding killing vary in different cultures. Most societies recognize the right of an individual to kill in self-defense. Most societies recognize the right—often the obligation—of its members to kill the members of another society in time of war. We can argue about where the line between killing and murder should be drawn, but we must recognize that, with very rare exceptions, societies do draw a line somewhere. And—*by definition*—only murder is forbidden.

The issue is more than semantic. The first three verses of the third chapter of *Ecclesiastes* will bear close scrutiny:

> To every thing there is a season,
> and a time to every purpose under the heaven;
> A time to be born, and a time to die;
> a time to plant, and a time to pluck
> up that which is planted;
> A time to kill, and a time to heal. . .

What are we to make of this? Is the second part of the second verse no more than self-evident agricultural advice? Or does it have reference to human affairs?

I support the latter view on the grounds that the orientation of the Old Testament is overwhelmingly humanistic. More: I submit, *as a hypothesis*, that what Koheleth, the Preacher, is recommending is induced abortion. This is a radical hypothesis. It cannot be proved (or disproved, for that matter); but I present an argument for its plausibility.

First of all, the accurate translation of the Goodspeed Bible shows us that the ancient Hebrews did not have the horror of killing that many people in our time express. Secondly, the approach of the Preacher is that of a situation ethicist: "There is a season" to everything—even killing. Maybe not a long season, but a season nonetheless. What is taught by *Ecclesiastes* is at the other pole from absolutist ethics.

The statement that there is "a time to pluck up that which is planted" takes on added significance when we note that the Japanese, who have approved of abortion for many centuries, refer to the practice as *mabiki*, "thinning seedlings." The parallelism of language is striking.

Both the ancient Hebrews and the Japanese were closer to the soil than academic scholars are now: it was natural for them to discuss human affairs in agricultural terms. This mode of speech had the advantage that it emphasized the quantitative, situational similarities between plant populations and human populations. Sound bioeconomics leads the good husbandman to pluck up and thereby to kill some of the corn seedlings that have been planted too close together in the row. Moving to the human realm, bioeconomics becomes bioethics as the good wife aborts and thereby kills some of the fetuses that come too close together in time to permit good mothering, were all the fetuses permitted to develop to term.

If this hypothesis is justified, we interpret the use of the metaphor "to pluck up" as springing not only from the agrarian experience of the Hebrews but also, in its indirection, from a certain delicacy in dealing with ambivalent situations in which moral considerations play a central role.

If this hypothesis is true, our past failure to recognize the core significance of *Ecclesiastes* 3:2 is one more example of the loss of common sense which has followed the alienation of modern man from realities of life that people close to the soil naturally and easily comprehend.

# 15

## *Ecology and the Death of Providence*

Why are ecologists and environmentalists so feared and hated? This is because in part what they have to say is new to the general public, and the new is always alarming. Moreover, the practical recommendations deduced from ecological principles threaten the vested interests of commerce; it is hardly surprising that the financial and political power created by these investments should be used sometimes to suppress environmental impact studies. However, I think the major opposition to ecology has deeper roots than mere economics; ecology threatens widely held values so fundamental that they must be called religious. An attack on values is inevitably seen as an act of subversion.

The ecologist Paul Sears was apparently the first to call ecology subversive; he was followed by Paul Shepard and Daniel McKinley who made *The Subversive Science* the title of a collection of essays. The charge generally has been regarded as sound by both the ecologists and their opponents. It is significant that Sears chose the adjective "subversive" rather than "revolutionary." The latter (and more fashionable) term comes from the Latin verb *revolvere* and is apt to connote an alteration that is as impermanent as the changing of the palace guard in a military dictatorship; no doubt this is what some of the opponents of "the ecological revolution" hope it will be. The word "subversive" is, to my mind, better fitted to describe the sort of change ecological insight brings about. *Sub* means under or below, and *vertere* means to turn. To subvert a world view is to change it from below (which is where the foundations of any subject are to be found). Subversion is more profound than revolution.

In what way does the ecological view subvert the political and economic faiths we live by? We must ask first who is "we"? I suggest that our inquiry be limited to people living at the present time in the North Atlantic version of civilization, particularly the American variety. The extent to which what I have to say is true of other civilizations is a topic for other times, other places. As for our own culture, I wish to express a sympathy with those who draw back from a rational, ecological analysis of our way of life. I think it is inappropriate to dismiss their views as simply irrational. We need to plunge beneath the surface of their rhetoric. Ralph Waldo Emerson truly remarked that "we are wiser than we know," an idea that the scientist-philosopher Michael Polanyi elaborated on in his exposition of what he called "tacit knowledge." If the creative mind is indeed a sort of computer, it is one that is characterized in this remarkable way: Most of the time its "programs" run to completion without producing any explicit readouts. Our more mundane behavior we attribute to habit; less repetitive and more surprising behavior we ascribe to intuition. "Readout" seems too definite a term to apply to the products of that veiled computer we call "mind."

Hidden deeply behind the veil are repressive mental processes that generate taboo, which takes the form of silence or nonaction. In its most effective form taboo prevents any readout at all, since a taboo is a sort of Chinese egg. Inside is the primary taboo, surrounding a thing that must not be discussed; around this is the secondary taboo, a taboo against even acknowledging the existence of the primary taboo. The double nature of taboo has not been generally recognized, but a little thought shows that this bivalence is necessary for the stability of a taboo. If only the primary taboo existed, its power, like Rumpelstiltskin's, could be shattered by a single word. A univalent taboo would not long be operational.

Case studies of the creative process show that the generation of intellectual novelty takes place first in the unconscious. If the unconscious mind senses a painful incompatibility between the unfolding intellectual novelty and the traditional values it is committed to, the mind is all too likely to put an end to inquiry by imposing a taboo on further thought. Since the imposition cannot be explicitly acknowledged, the maneuver is covered over with clever rhetoric. Once we understand the origin of such rhetoric we become somewhat tolerant of it. To protect rather than examine inherited values is all too human an impulse. Simple decency dictates that we deal compassionately with individuals who disguise taboo with rhetoric; but concern for the long-term well-being of society demands that we be intolerant of anything that protects inconsistencies in action. Those of a scientific bent assume that the dissolution of inconsistencies is, in the long run, the least painful policy.

How do ecological insights conflict with contemporary workaday values? Without claiming exhaustiveness I suggest five major areas of conflict, clustering around the codewords "limits," "scale effect," "interrelatedness," "development," and "irreversibility." Let us explore these one by one.

*Limits.* The progress of pure science can be measured by its discovery of conservation laws, which presuppose limits. When the laws are worded with practical aims in mind we have what Edmund Whittaker called "impotence principles." By contrast, the world outside science for the past two centuries has been inspired largely by the anticonservation orientation we call the "idea of progress."

In the popular view this idea justifies us in presuming that there are no limits worth mentioning: In planning for the future we simply assume that the world is a cornucopia. The perils of this assumption are obscured effectively by the bias of the record: Those who lose by making it are wiped out, whereas those who prosper survive to bear witness to the wisdom of the cornucopians' position. The crunch comes whenever the *last* prediction of the cornucopians is thwarted. Unfortunately, the next-to-last prediction seems innocent enough.

*Scale Effect.* If conflicting values are related to population size by variables that have different exponents, the action that is judged best necessarily changes with change in population size. The politico-economic system of the commons can work well with less than 150 people in the community but breaks down and must be replaced by one of two other possible systems when the number goes higher. Rhetoric applicable only to small communities is called upon all too frequently to prevent the modifications required by growth to a larger size.

*Interrelatedness.* The sanctions of traditional ethical systems paradoxically presume an almost systemless ambience in which to operate. Ecologists know that nothing can escape the web of life, and precisely where an entity stands in the web is important in determining the best action. The behavior of each entity influences the state of many other entities: "We can never do merely one thing."

I think ecologists can take credit for getting people at last to take the web of life seriously, but now our success has created the dialectical danger of "too much of a good thing." Consider, as an illustration of going too far, this advice given by a scholar of literature who became converted to ecology: "If a decision taken in Moscow or Washington can effect a catastrophic change in the chemical composition of the entire biosphere, then the idea of a San Francisco, or Bay Area, or California, or even North American ecosystem loses much of its clarity and force. Similar difficulties arise when we contemplate the global rate of human population growth. All this is only to say that, on ecological grounds, the case for world government is beyond argument."

This is asking for trouble. We can grant of course that if a decision made in one city can indeed cause a catastrophic change that is global, then global decisions will be necessary. The greenhouse effect, if it proves as bad as we fear, will require global cooperation to control the emissions of carbon dioxide, nitrous oxides, and other atmospheric pollutants. But let us not forget that global cooperation is always more difficult to obtain than local. It is a mistake to adopt a policy of preferring the global approach to a local one. If Lake Cayuga is polluted it is pretty silly to try to get Moscow, Paris, and Rome to share the responsibility for cleaning it up. I sometimes suspect that those who systematically prefer global solutions are driven by a death wish.

What then are we to make of the cliche "global population growth"? Population does not grow globally: It grows very locally, at each spot occupied by a fertile woman. When we are dealing with the problems created by a too large population of deer we do not dream of seeking a global solution. The "population problem" is shorthand for a "population-to-resources ratio." In animal and plant demography population problems always presuppose a local habitat. When there are too many reindeer on Saint Matthew Island noone is so foolish as to speak of a "global reindeer population problem." To any such problem there are only two possible rational solutions: Reduce the size of the local population or increase the local carrying capacity. For animals other than man, the second approach is usually out of the question. That leaves only the first.

What about man? For two centuries we have had marvelous success in increasing the carrying capacity of the environment. Each major technological revolution has been reflected in a demographic saltation, as Edward S. Deevey, Jr., has pointed out. Those who take limits seriously, however, cannot believe that the demographic effects of the present revolution—the scientific-industrial revolution—can keep pace forever with the present rate of population growth, which is exponential. Someday, if we unwisely insist on viewing population as a global problem, we shall have either to find ways of globally reducing population or to give up all attempts to solve the problem; this would mean turning it over to forces of the purest Malthusian sort. The population problem is, more than most problems, a semantic one. We are the inheritors and the victims of a sharing rhetoric that was developed in a tribal setting. Sometime during the 1950s we unconsciously started applying tribal rhetoric to nontribal situations, generating the new terms "global hunger" and "world hunger." To speak of global hunger is to imply that hunger is not spatially limited; this implies that the ownership of resources is not spatially limited; in turn this implies that the world must be treated as a commons. Since it is beyond doubt that there is no positive responsibility in a commons once the size of the population exceeds a hundred people or so, the predictable and certain result of thoughtlessly succumbing to the rhetoric of global hunger is tragedy. Though hunger is not global, the tragedy generated by presuming so will be global; when it comes, it will be an unprecedented event in the history of mankind.

*Development.* Does time matter? Heraclitus in the fifth century B.C.

said it mattered greatly: "You cannot step twice into the same river." This Greek insight was largely lost in the first growth of science after the Renaissance, dominated as it was by physics. Time came back into the picture in the nineteenth century with the creation of the concept of entropy—"time's arrow," as A. S. Eddington later called it. Geology also made much of time but on a scale too great for easy human comprehension. Ecology, with its study of succession and synergy, brought the human scale back in. Ecologists pointed out that a biocide that reduces the population of an insect pest in year 1 may increase it greatly by year 5, much to the surprise of the timeless minds of engineers and so-called developers. Every well-meant intervention in the web of life is challenged by ecologists with the Heraclitian question, "And then what?" Since the intentions of would-be interveners are noble, this chilling question evokes vituperation, as Rachel Carson discovered. But Carson was right, and so was Heraclitus. "Developers" and "promoters" have yet to acknowledge this fact fully; perhaps by their nature they cannot.

*Irreversibility.* The final major concept substantially lacking from the conventional wisdom of promoters is the idea of irreversibility. It is not in their interest of course to admit that the damage they do may be irreversible, or practically so. "Develop now—worry later" is their motto. Childishly they assume that science will provide an answer—in time. Strip miners manage to get legislation passed that permits them to continue their destructive business by posting a bond of a mere $500 per acre, though there are sites where it is doubtful if $10,000 could create an acceptable substitute for the beauty destroyed. We continue to load the atmosphere with gaseous pollutants, and the earth and water with long-lived radionuclides, trustfully assuming that we are causing no irreversible harm.

I will spend no more time on a substantive analysis of the major areas of conflict between ecologists and promoters because I think we need to plunge into a deeper level to gain a sympathetic understanding of the anguish of the promoters, an anguish, I believe, that can be called truly religious. The word "religion" is ambiguous and overused, so its introduction here needs justifying. The etymology of the word is uncertain, but according to the *Oxford English Dictionary* a highly probable root is *religare*, to bind. We may define religion as that which binds our views of the world; it also binds the men and women holding a particular set of views. It is not surprising that our most conservative impulses show themselves in the defense of religious beliefs.

Whenever a social arrangement or intellectual orientation has a name, our desire to conserve that which has long existed is satisfied often by conserving the name even though the fact behind the name changes. Thus it has come about that England has a "monarch" who does not rule, and America an electoral college that does not elect. "Institutions may with impunity be altered or destroyed," said Will Durant, "if their names are left unchanged."

Not so well recognized is the fact that conservation sometimes takes the opposite path, the name being abandoned in the face of critical attack while the concept is preserved under a new name. That our civilization has been powered by the idea of progress during the past two centuries is widely recognized. For most people progress has been largely held to mean technological progress. Many observers, Norbert Wiener among them, have noted that the fervor with which we cling to progress implies that it is a religious concept. The vulgar motto "You can't stop progress!" is no longer fashionable, but a very able physicist, Freeman J. Dyson, recently gave the thought new life in his essay, "The Hidden Costs of Saying NO!" Dyson begins by quoting, with obvious approval, a poet who was hardly an apostle of technological progress, William Blake: "You never know what is enough unless you know what is more than enough." In other words, confronted with the potential dangers of mass supersonic travel, large-scale chemical pest control, worldwide nuclear energy, global climatic alterations, preservation of food by x-radiation, and uncontrolled genetic engineering, our motto always should be "Experiment now—pay later!" For such as Dyson technological progress is seen as an ethical imperative.

The guidebook to the exhibits of the 1933 "Century of Progress" World's Fair in Chicago boldly stated: "Science discovers—Industry applies—Man conforms." Resistance to this imperative is regarded as irrational. As one editor (of *Look*) put it, "a strong case can be made for positing the onset of the Age of Unreason in America at the instant when Rachel Carson's *Silent Spring* was unleashed on a moderately happy and justifiably tranquil populace." This statement occurs in a chapter entitled "The Worst of Madmen" in a book called *The Disaster Lobby*, which bears the subtitle, *Prophets of Ecological Doom and Other Absurdities*. The editor of the journal *Nature* concurs in spirit by entitling his book, *The Doomsday Syndrome*, which the dust jacket identifies as "an attack on pessimism." Antiecologists at Sussex University entitled their attack *Models of Doom*. A very capable promoter of unlimited hydroelectric power in the Northwest categorized his opponents in the following terms: "The environmental movement has fallen into the hands of a *small, arrogant faction which is dedicated to bringing our society to a halt*. . . . The environmental extremist . . . is . . . *a spoiler*."

What is it about the ecological orientation that upsets these critics? Just this: that the ecologist insists that we ask the time-binding question "And then what?" before we go off half-cocked. During all of man's history on earth, except for the last 200 years, asking this question was viewed as the mark of a mature, thoughtful person. It is one of the wonders of the world that the great question "And then what?" is now regarded as the demand of a crackpot. Crackpots, ecofreaks, neo-Luddites, pessimists, bird-watchers, pansy-pluckers, merchants of doom, spoilers—the semantic defenses against a return to the wisdom of the ages are legion. Antiecologists would, if they could, repress the great question completely. At times, their religious fervor has a querulous cast. A recent set of "institutional" defenses of technological progress put out by an electric company had as its leitmotif these two sentences, in boldface: "Science and technology can solve many problems. If they don't, what else will?" The latter was intended undoubtedly to be merely a rhetorical question. One of the pamphlets plaintively pleaded, "Let's put the magic back in the marketplace."

Magic. Religion. How did progress come to be linked up with these ideas, these feelings? I think a good case can be made for the term "progress" being the most recent verbal form of an idea that earlier went under the label "providence," which in turn was a still earlier rewording of "god." The word "god" of course stands for a vast array of predications. The only one we are concerned with here is that preserved in the word "providence." The meaning of philosophical terms such as this cannot be discovered as easily as the meaning of terms such as "chemical valence," "genetic dominance," or "ecological succession," so I shall lean heavily on the works of recognized theological authorities, namely, W. T. Davison and Theodorus P. van Baaren.

The word "providence" comes from the Latin *providentia*, meaning foresight. Providence is an act of providing or provisioning for the future. Long before Christ this act came to be viewed as characteristic of the deity. The transition from property to person was made easily. After Caesar Augustus, Providence was a synonym for God, and "Providence," says van Baaren, "is the quality in divinity on which man bases his belief in a benevolent intervention in human affairs and the affairs of the world he inhabits." In a strict and narrow etymological sense, a climatologist with a prevision of a global catastrophe brought about by a temperature change of a few degrees may be said to be taking a providential view, but such is not the usage. As van Baaren says, "benevolence is the primary requirement" of what we call Providence.

## God = Providence

For centuries this equation merely created a harmless redundancy in the language. In the eighteenth century, however, the equivalence became the means whereby the concept of God escaped the suppression of the word "God." The Age of Reason as this period was called, brought with it a widespread, overt acknowledgement of personal atheism. In earlier days many an atheist hesitated to admit his disbelief; in the eighteenth century, in certain circles, the contrary was the case. "Atheism is the vice of a few intelligent people," said Voltaire, and Robespierre remarked that "atheism is aristocratic." No doubt many people who believed in God hesitated to pronounce the name. The word "providence" saved them the embarrassment. By whomever used, the newly fashionable word implied benevolence.

So did the word "progress." As appeals to and praises of technological progress became ever more common in the nineteenth century, it was obvious that progress was nothing if not benevolent. The equation had grown:

$$God = Providence = Progress .$$

The idea of benevolence was one more stage removed from the idea of

God, making its nearly universal acceptance in a largely godless society much easier.

There is another aspect of the idea of deity that needs clarifying. Theologians, wrestling with many different conceptions bearing the singular name of God, distinguish between transcendent gods and immanent gods. A transcendent god stands outside the world (as a puppeteer stands outside his miniature puppet theater), manipulating the actors to produce the results he wants. Transcendent gods have been given a hard time by the increasingly rigorous skepticism of science.

Matters have not been so bad for immanent gods. Immanent literally means "indwelling"; an immanent god dwells inside all objects and forces. An immanent god does not meddle in everyday affairs, does not arbitrarily intervene in the workings of nature. Those who believe in this God believe in his immanence; those for whom God has dropped out of the picture, for whom Providence has been replaced by progress, perceive a depersonalized, benevolent immanence in things. The publisher of *Scientific American*, for instance, said: "If ever an invention arrived on earth in the nick of time, it was the discovery and release of the energy of the nucleus of the atom." This is a most remarkable assertion. If it implies anything, it is that if we had not learned how to extract energy from the atom in 1942 the early death of civilization (if not of mankind) now would be certain. Mankind has lived for hundreds of thousands of years with an energy supply that was increasing yearly at a rate so low as to be perceptibly near zero; yet from now on, it is asserted, we cannot survive without an energy supply that is doubling every fourteen years or less into perpetuity. *Homo sapiens*, tamer of fire, domesticator of animals and plants, inventor of writing, designer of computers, fabricator of satellites, and traveler to the moon, suddenly is grown too stupid to do what all other animals and plants can do, that is, live within a fixed energy budget. I do not believe it.

Since the word "ecology" entered popular speech many observers have commented on the truly religious fervor of the nonprofessionals converted to ecology's banner. The struggle between ecologists (in this new and extended sense) and antiecologists can properly be viewed as a religious battle. The earlier wars of religion were notably bloody. Must this one be, too?

Perhaps bloodshed can be averted if we uncover the unspoken dogmas of both the combatants. The religion called progress is built on two dogmas: (1) The Dogma of Aladdin's Lamp: If we can dream of it, we can invent it. (2) The Dogma of the Technological Imperative: When we invent it, we are required to use it.

The religion called ecology—and let us admit it is a religion, a set of beliefs that bind us—also is built on two dogmas, the contradiction of the ones just given: (1) The Dogma of Limits: Not all things are possible (though death is!). (2) The Dogma of Temperance: Every "shortage" of supply is equally a "longage" of demand; and, since the world is limited, the only way to sanity ultimately lies in restraining demand.

At the root of our troubles is the very human desire to be taken care of, as a little child is taken care of—by a parent, by God (a "father figure"), by Providence, or by progress. As we wrestle with our problems we want to be helped by a transcendental—or immanent—and benevolent force. We choose to forget what Benjamin Franklin said: "God helps those who help themselves."

The eventual demise of the idea of progress was foreseen by J. B. Bury in his classic history, *The Idea of Progress*. In a moving epilogue he wrote:

> Will not that process of change, for which Progress is the optimistic name, compel "Progress" too to fall from the commanding position in which it is now, with apparent security, enthroned? . . . A day will come, in the revolution of centuries, when a new idea will usurp its place as the directing idea of humanity. Another star, unnoticed now or invisible, will climb up the intellectual heaven, and human emotions will react to its influence, human plans respond to its guidance. It will be the criterion by which Progress and all other ideas will be judged. And it too will have its successor.

Every successor to "progress" is in danger of being tarred by the brush of benevolence. What we are loath to admit is that in a limited world the pleasure of benevolence must be sought in reducing longages of desire, not in vainly expecting shortages of supply to disappear.

Benevolent progress is a religious idea. When we see the conflict of our time as fundamentally a religious one we may be able to solve it. One can hardly argue against progress, *properly understood*, but our problem is to give meaning to these italicized words. At the moment perhaps only two aspects of the progress of tomorrow are clear: Progress will no longer be equated with technological progress alone, and the concept of progress must be divested of the illusion of Providence. "Man makes himself," Jean-Paul Sartre said, and it is high time that we try to reshape human beings into mature creatures who no longer depend on the support of a benevolent Providence (under any name).

# 16

## *Why Plant a Redwood Tree?*

*Scientists, committed to rationality, are loath to fall back on religious or transcendental justifications for any human action. Most of the time their attitude pays off. But there are some areas in which rationality fails to give the answer we know "intuitively" to be right. Does this mean that intuition is in error? Or is it rationality that is at fault? Can rationality grow to take care of all cases? Or, if we must sometimes abandon rationality, how are we to keep the destructive forces of unreason at bay? We still remember that Hitler (successfully) urged his people "to think with their blood."*

*At the present moment in history perhaps no intellectual problem is as pressing as working out an acceptable method of planning for the future in a resource-poor, overpopulated world. The paragraphs below were written in 1974. I was puzzled and uncertain then; I am still puzzled.*

*Fortunately the tree I planted is bothered by no such doubts: it grows steadily, day by day.*

"Would you plant a redwood tree in your back yard?" the ecologist asks the economist. "I mean, assuming that you had a large back yard, and suitable soil and climate?"

The economist smiles wanly and shakes his head.

"Well, I would," says the ecologist. "In fact, I did."

"Then you're an economic fool," retorts his antagonist.

The economist is right, of course. The supporting economic analysis is easily carried out. A tree can hardly be planted for less than a dollar. To mature to the stage the ecologist has in mind takes some two thousand years, by which time the tree will be about three hundred feet high. How much is the tree worth then? An economist will insist, of course, on evaluating the forest giant as lumber. Measured at a man's height above the ground, the diameter of the tree will be about ten feet, and the shape of the shaft from there upward is approximately conical. The volume of this cone is 94,248 board feet. At a "stumpage" price of 15 cents a board foot—the approximate price a lumberer must pay for a tree unfelled, unmilled, untransported—the tree would be worth some $14,000.

That may sound like a large return on an investment of only one dollar, but we must not forget how long the investment took to mature: 2,000 years. Using the exponential formula to calculate the rate of compound interest we find that the capital earned slightly less than one-half of 1 percent per year. Yes, a man would be an economic fool to put his money into a redwood seedling when so many more profitable opportunities lie at hand.

Is that all there is to say about the matter? If it is, then sooner or later mankind will have no great groves of redwood trees for his delight. It is the groves of trees that we are interested in. A single redwood tree, remarkable though it may be for its size, is not that which evokes those religious feelings that seize sensitive people who find themselves enveloped in the hush of a forest of towering trees. But how can we assign a value to religious feelings? Encapsulated in the prejudices of the market place the economist must advise us not to plant a forest of redwoods.

(A "tree farm" is something else. Depending on the price of land and lumber, and on our theory for discounting an uncertain future, economic analysis may justify planting an esthetically sterile, disciplined array of trees that will be harvested in less than a century for the lumber. But that is not our problem.)

Among contemporaries, rationality demands that there be a *quid pro quo* in every exchange. But what if the exchange is between generations? This logical sticking point was brutally laid bare two centuries ago by the American poet John Trumbull, who wrote scornfully of those who would have us act—

> As though there were a tie
> And obligation to posterity:
> We get them, bear them, breed, and nurse:
> What has posterity done for us?

By asking that question do we prove that all redwood forests must go? Is this the best that rationality has to offer? Or is it true (as Pascal said) that "the heart has reasons that Reason knows not of"? Can we delve deep into the abysses of the heart, and expose the reasons that Reason sometimes denies?

I think we can. A clue is given us by the great English voice of conservatism, Edmund Burke: "People will not look forward to posterity who never look backward to their ancestors." His aphorism asserts a sort of symmetry to the psyche. If a man is so brought up that he feels a tie to the past, by symmetry he can perceive and acknowledge a similar tie to the future. By contrast, a hard-headed rationalist lives only in the present. To him, the remembrance of things past as well as concern for the distant future bespeaks a sort of mental corruption. It is not easy to refute this view which, tragically, is shared by some of the most radical as well as some of the most reactionary people in our time.

*Must* we be concerned with posterity? It is always tempting to try to get others to do our will by bringing in the word *must*. Rationally it is more useful to point out the ecological implications of Burke's insight. If we want a community to care for the future, we must raise its members with a strong sense of place, of ancestry—with a pervasive feeling of connectedness with their origins. The managers of great enterprises, seeking the maximum economic "efficiency," are quite willing to treat people as objects, moving them around like so many men on a chess board. The resulting mobility erodes the sense of place and past-connectedness. When the past disappears the future soon follows.

Make a society fully mobile and you can kiss the redwood trees—and all that they stand for—goodbye.

Some journalist, a few years ago, coined the phrase "the now generation." He intended it to be laudatory. Edmund Burke would surely view it in another light. So also must his spiritual descendants, people now called conservationists, environmentalists, and ecologists. Pure "nowness" to them indicates a poverty of the spirit that should be strongly deprecated. To them, the world is richer if the psyche has an enduring awareness of both the unalterable past and of a future that can, with effort and intelligence, be molded "nearer to the Heart's desire."

# 17

## Setting Limits to the Global Approach

Infection of the public mind by ecological thinking has been brought about by a succession of Anderson's children crying out the Emperor's nakedness. First there was Rachel Carson's *Silent Spring* in 1962; then the so-called Report to the Club of Rome, *The Limits to Growth*, in 1972; then, not quite ten years later, *The Global 2000 Report* by the President's Council on Environmental Quality in 1980. The outcry from the indignant crowd was deafening in each instance, but by this time it is clear that the authors of the first two works were substantially correct, and no doubt the authors of the last will prove to be so, too.

The informal group known as the "Club of Rome" tried to capitalize on their initial success by publishing follow-up studies. In terms of public relations, the attempt failed. It was hardly their fault: they were "bucking the system" that decrees that each dog gets one bite. The first Kinsey report on human sexuality was a runaway best-seller; the second report had to be "remaindered" to the tune of tens of thousands of copies. The response of the public to a new point of view is like the stock market's response to fresh financial news: the new report or new idea is "discounted" (responded to) only once.

This is a pity because the second report to the Club of Rome, *Mankind at the Turning Point*, by Mihajlo Mesarovic and Eduard Pestel (1974), deserves thoughtful attention. The authors raise difficult issues about the relations between nations. The second report is based on a finer analysis than the first, and the results are significantly closer to reality. The first "aggregated" the variables—that is, it treated population, minerals, energy, etc., on a worldwide basis. This procedure would be justified if there were no inequalities in the distribution of these variables, or if there were no barriers to the free flow of people and materials from one region to another. But such inequalities and barriers exist. Barriers have always existed, and at the moment there is no reason to think they will disappear (though they may change). In fact, it has yet to be shown that the world would be better off without barriers (though this is a question that can be put aside for the present). A barrierless world is a pure hypothesis.

Mesarovic and Pestel accept a compartmentalized world and repeat much of the computer analysis of the preceding study in the framework of a world divided into ten regions: North America, Western Europe, Japan (the only region including but a single nation), Eastern Europe, Latin America, North Africa and the Middle East, Main Africa, South and Southeast Asia, and Centrally Planned Asia (including China). In terms of geography, history, and current political realities, the groupings seem well chosen (though Cambodia and South Vietnam may by this time have moved from the next-to-last into the last category). Current trends clearly indicate different futures for the ten regions. To assume an aggregate common future, which some have inferred from the Meadows' study, is surely not realistic. We do not live in One World.

Mesarovic and Pestel do not, however, hold out any hope for the world if the ten regions, or individual countries, insist on pursuing their own courses in opposition to, or in whole-hearted competition with, each other. On the contrary, they say that the peoples of the world must "embark on a path of organic growth," producing a world that is "a system of interdependent and harmonious parts." On page 147 of

*Mankind at the Turning Point* they give four *musts*, the first of which is
this:

> A *world consciousness* must be developed through which every indi-
> vidual realizes his role as a member of the world community. Fam-
> ine in Tropical Africa should be considered as relevant and as dis-
> turbing to a citizen of Germany as famine in Bavaria.

Such a call for global unity is strangely at variance with the meth-
odological analysis on page 37:

> In the "one-world" or homogeneous view of the world develop-
> ment in which differences between various parts of the world are
> suppressed and one talks only about global indicators and vari-
> ables, *the entire system reaches its limits at one time and either collapses
> or not.* In the world view based on diversity . . . collapse, if it oc-
> curs, would be regional rather than global, even though the entire
> global system would be affected. [Italics added.]

It seems to me that the latter view is far closer to the truth, and a far
better guide to realistic action at the present time, than is the inspiring
*must* of the first quotation. No matter how strong our humanitarian sentiments may be, the blunt fact is that 1 million people dying in Bavaria
is more relevant and disturbing to the citizens of Germany than the
same number dying in the Sahel. Would the world be a better place to
live in if distance—in space, in time, and in culture—made absolutely
no difference at all to men and women?

The authors' example is a variant of the old complaint that the splinter in the finger of the little girl next door matters more than the death
of a man in China. When we first hear this complaint, we may think we
ought to change our ways. But suppose we did? We *could* say to the
little girl, "I'm sorry, my dear, but please don't bother me about your
little splinter; I must sit here and agonize over a man dying 10,000 miles
away." If that were our attitude, would the world be a better place to
live in? Would the problems of the world be sooner solved?

We sense, of course, a conflict between the instinctive—the adjective
is used advisedly—the instinctive preference for those near and dear to
us and our intellectual recognition of the many ways in which events

distant in space, time, and empathy can, in fact, ultimately affect our well-being. As the world fills up, the relative importance of distant interrelationships increases. That being so, there is ever more need for some sort of resolution between opposing impulses, a resolution that will make survival possible.

Survival of what? Of life, at least—the life of *some*, at least; of many or all, if possible. And the survival of civilization. Defining "civilization" is difficult, but for the purposes at hand we should be able to agree on a rough and ready definition so that we can get ahead with the work of trying to save for our descendants something of greater value than mere physical existence. Culture? Dignity? Decency? Benevolence? It is hard to know what word or words to put to this "something else," but mere physical survival is not enough. (In the language of mathematics, physical survival of some—but not necessarily all—human beings is a *necessary but not sufficient* condition for achieving our goal.)

If a crowded world is not to be torn apart by conflicting forces, some sort of organic organization of these forces is a necessity. But what does "organic" mean? Mesarovic and Pestel do not tell us, so we must think further about this matter. The adjective "organic" is related to the noun "organism." In the embryological development of an organism we observe one tissue after another, one organ after another, dominating the growth process—*but each only for a time*. If the liver is growing most rapidly today, tomorrow it will be the lungs; today the nervous system, tomorrow the long bones. Everyone who knows anything at all about population growth knows that continued exponential growth of a population of organisms is intolerable in the long run (and not such a very long run at that). The indefinite exponential growth of a population of cells is equally intolerable. Each little organ has its exponential day. But the exponent of its growth has a negative exponent of its own: ultimately, for each tissue, a state of ZPG (zero population growth) is reached. Sometimes the negative exponent carries growth below the ZPG point, and the tissue disappears. The thymus gland, so large in early childhood, usually disappears before adulthood. A tissue may even have more than one "grand period" of growth—for example, the reproductive tissues which grow exponentially once during embryonic life and again during adolescence.

The organization of scores of separate growth processes in space and time is immensely complex, far beyond our certain knowledge. Were they in charge, today's scientists would not know how to orchestrate the multitude of cellular voices; but the organism "knows." The more we study the orchestration, the more we are impressed with "the wisdom of the body," to use Walter B. Cannon's pregnant phrase. Can we human beings, the inventors and elaborators of politics and political economy, discover or create a comparable wisdom of the body politic? Can we orchestrate the multitude of countervailing forces that wrack this poor body, compelling or persuading each force to mitigate its power after a time, for the sake of the whole? This is the hard question that underlies the facile appeal for the establishment of an "organic" arrangement of competitive powers in the body politic.

Perhaps a look at the problems of biological bodies may throw light on the issue. The orchestration of contrary forces is awe-inspiring when it is successful, but let us not forget how often it fails. In mammals, from a quarter to a half of the embryos started normally are aborted. About half of these are visibly abnormal; no doubt many of the remainder are biochemically, though not visibly, abnormal. The embryos that are aborted are ones in which the orchestration of forces went astray to such a degree that survival became impossible even in the highly protective and nurturent uterine environment. To use a musical analogy, the fertilized egg starts off life with a beautiful "score," but one not quite like that of any composition before it. Harmony and chaos are only a half tone apart. If the new orchestration given the fertilized egg is reasonably harmonious, the embryo survives; if it is not, the embryo soon perishes. No external intelligence writes the score; the score is inherited, with variations, from the survivors of earlier tests of existence. Harmonic variations produced by the new combination may be too extreme to permit survival. But life—mere life—is so cheap that the species is not in the least threatened by a mortality rate of 25 or 50 percent in the embryonic phase.

Is there any analogue of this situation in the survival of variants of the body politic? It is not obvious if there is. Perhaps in an earlier day there was. When the human species was divided into thousands of more or less equal tribes, a tribe that prospered in war because it had devised more effective communication among its members displaced less gifted tribes. In this way the average level of language skill in the tribe rose. The improved language could be used not only for integrating war activities but also for writing poetry, inventing mathematics and science—and debating about the future of the species.

But, in our time, the existence of powerful *exosomatic* adaptations such as nuclear bombs gives us good reason to doubt that a battle to the death would necessarily result in survival of the best, by any defensible definition other than a purely tautological one. How are we to harness the divergent and conflicting forces of the body politic into an organism that can survive? How can we program self-limitation into the economic and social forces needed for doing the work of the world? It is not obvious that answers to these questions exist.

Certainly the authors of the Second Report to the Club of Rome do not give us the answers. I am not even sure that they appreciate the full complexity of the problem. William James divided the thinkers of the world into hard-headed and soft-headed. The authors of this work begin bravely as hard-headed thinkers, but toward the end they lose their nerve and fall into the camp of the soft-headed, calling for more concern for our fellow men and for Nature, trying to create the One World they regard as necessary by the fiat of the word "must."

In a commentary at the end, Alexander King and Aurelio Peccei (the godfather of the Club of Rome) give two warnings from the club that merit meditation:

> No fundamental redressment of the world conditions and human prospects is possible except by worldwide cooperation in a global context and with long views.
>
> The costs, not only in economic and political terms, but in human suffering as well, which will result from delay in taking early decisions, are simply monstrous.

These two statements look suspiciously like an ultimatum. The authors seem to be saying that they won't play ball unless reforms are accomplished instantly, and in the framework of One World. I hope this is not a valid inference from their statements, for if so, they define a no-win game.

Near the end of their book Mesarovic and Pestel argue that the initiation of a suitable population policy in South Asia in 1975 would reduce the number of child deaths from starvation in the period from 1975 to 2025 by half a billion, as compared with delaying the beginning of such a policy until 1990. This may be so, but is there the slightest chance that the publication of their computer curves will generate the political and social changes needed to save half a billion children? Computer-simulation competes with Freudian denial. Is there the slightest doubt what the outcome will be? In another connection, the authors quote Winston Churchill as saying, "A problem postponed is a problem half solved." This surely is the conventional wisdom of most politicians, particularly of those who owe their posts to election.

It's no good saying that mankind *must* reform immediately. We'll do the best we can, and that undoubtedly means learning from horrible, though not overwhelming, catastrophes. *We dare not make practical solutions contingent upon worldwide cooperation.* It is the better part of wisdom to use the little cooperation we can muster at the moment, protecting the cooperators from the noncooperators by suitable barriers, while we cautiously seek to enlarge the circle of cooperation. Better that some civilization be saved here and there in an imperfect world than that we stake our all on a perfect world and lose all when ideals collide with reality.

Scientists trained in the simplicity of classical engineering and economics constantly look for maximum points. The political scientist William Ophuls, surveying the almost infinitely more complex world of human politics, has remarked that "Nature abhors a maximum." We may call this *Ophuls' Axiom*; it is a more general statement of the ancient wisdom that "The best is the enemy of the good." Pursuit of the unattainable "best" prevents achieving the attainable but lesser "good." The thinkers of the Club of Rome have done a real service in persuading large numbers of people that death is possible. But occasionally (as in the passages quoted above) spokesmen for the club lapse into the millennial thinking that threatens to undo the good they've wrought. Survival will be difficult enough; let us not complicate our task by making survival contingent upon the creation of One World, or insisting that the loss of life be kept at a minimum (i.e., that survival be kept at a maximum). Ophuls' axiom is more powerful than good intentions.

# 18

## *Ecological Conservatism*

*India*: The name conjures up a scene of a village road down which a half dozen cattle are being driven by a man and several children. At the rear of the procession, carrying a basket, is an old woman—at least she looks old, though it is doubtful if she is yet forty. From time to time one of the cows defecates in the road, and the woman scoops up the warm feces with her bare hand, slapping it into her basket. Her motions have the happy briskness of a miser fondling his gold.

Later she plasters the wet dung on a convenient wall, the finger-ridged patties forming an attractive mosaic. The wall is not her property—she is too poor for that—but it is her territory and will be respected by others. When the patties are dry she will use a few of them as fuel to cook her rice; the rest she must sell to buy the rice.

To a generation of westerners now rediscovering the morality of environmental housekeeping the practice may be superficially attractive. Certainly Indian roads are kept free of dung. Ecologically, however, the neatness is pathological. In the long run the community would be better off if the dung were put back into the soil. But who can wait for the long run? It is today's rice that needs cooking.

The making of dung patties is a sign that a cultural sink has been reached. Too large a population exhausts the soil and destroys the forests, thus producing a fuel shortage; then dung is burned and the soil impoverished, thus diminishing future crops and increasing poverty. Unrestrained human reproduction, another positive feedback, locks the culture into its poverty.

An extreme case illuminates the general. Ecologists warn that it is *possible* that population growth and polluting technology will bring irredeemable harm to the global environment, ultimately causing a "population crash." The doomsayers are called "econuts." They may be wrong, of course; the future is unclear.

Given uncertainty, what constitutes true conservatism? Refusing to change existing social arrangements is one form of conservatism. But it can be argued that changing the social and economic structure drastically is another form of conservatism, if the survival of civilization is at stake. It is objectively easier to finance change out of prosperity. A rich country can pay for ecological reform. A poor country cannot; it is locked into an ecological downward spiral.

Econuts ask that we mend our ways before we reach the brim on the cultural sink. If conservative action results in putting on the brakes too soon, no permanent harm is done. Putting them on too late is fatal. Unfortunately, it is difficult to believe in bad news until ruin is fully upon us.

Whether the poor countries—the majority of the world's population—can be helped significantly by the rich minority is doubtful. But the rich can benefit from the object lesson of the poor, if they will only pay attention.

# 19

## *Property Rights:*
## *The Creative Reworking of a Fiction*

From our ancestors we inherit three sorts of things: material objects, genes, and ideas. Of these three the first is least important, for "a fool and his money are soon parted." The other two inheritances leave more lasting traces. Genes and ideas are both stable as a rule, but the rule is normally broken at a low frequency. Genes and ideas are both mutable. The diversity created by change constitutes the field in which the forces of selection operate. On the biological plane selection is called "natural," and the result is judged "adaptation." Selection at the level of ideas goes by various names, "criticism" and "rational evaluation" among them; the results are generally referred to as "progress" (which they may indeed sometimes be).

The mutation of ideas differs strikingly from the mutation of genes in this way: change in an idea by which we have previously been unconsciously ruled becomes much more probable once the idea has been explicitly brought out into the open. Such a change in changeability does not hold for genes. The gene for the normal alternative to the disease hemophilia mutates to the hemophilic form about once in every 50,000 opportunities, with Olympian indifference to our awareness of it.

In the mental realm, to express an idea clearly is to invite its denial. Our lives are no doubt ruled tyrannically by a wealth of ideas we have no idea of—until, without warning, we become aware of them one by one. As each ruling idea surfaces it becomes subject to a mutation process that is faster by many orders of magnitude than is the natural mutation of genes.

The foregoing assertions may sound suspiciously like the elements of a "waterproof hypothesis," since they assert the existence of unconscious forces that lose their force once they cease to be unconscious. Such a postulation would seem to be beyond proof or disproof; if so, we should refuse it admission to the realm of rational discourse. But I think the postulation is better than that. *Looking backward* we can see that we—and by "we" I mean both ourselves and the ancestors with whom we psychologically affiliate ourselves—were formerly ruled by ideas that "we" were unconscious of at the time when the rule was effective. For example, the "divine right of kings" was calmly accepted before the phrase was invented. The invention of a legitimating phrase is often the first step to doubt and the opening of a door to the exploration of alternatives. He who explicitly asserts that kings have a divine right to rule cannot keep others from asking, "But how do you know that? And what if they don't? What would the world be like then?" In fact, the speaker cannot shield even himself against subterranean doubts once he has been so imprudent as to make a ruling assumption explicit.

Aware of tyrannical ideas we escaped in the past we cannot but wonder what unconscious ideas rule us still. How can we discover them, and so take one more step in the endless journey of escape from intellectual tyranny? There is no royal road to the discovery of the unconscious, but the economist John Maynard Keynes blazed a useful trail when he said that "a study of the history of opinion is a necessary preliminary to the emancipation of the mind." Becoming aware of the indefensible in the mental baggage of our ancestors we become sensitized to that which is dubious in our own minds.

The American naturalist Aldo Leopold opened the way to escape from one of the ideological tyrannies of our time when he made us acutely aware of the hidden implications of the terms "rights" and "property," by recounting the history recorded in the myths of Homer:

> When god-like Odysseus returned from the wars in Troy, he hanged all on one rope a dozen slave-girls of his household whom he suspected of misbehavior during his absence.
> This hanging involved no question of propriety. The girls were property. The disposal of property was then, as now, a matter of expediency, not of right and wrong.
> Concepts of right and wrong were not lacking from Odysseus' Greece: witness the fidelity of his wife through the long years before at last his black-prowed galleys clove the wine-dark seas for home. The ethical structure of that day covered wives, but had not yet been extended to human chattels. During the three thousand years which have since elapsed, ethical criteria have been extended to many fields of conduct, with corresponding shrinkages in those judged by expediency only.
> This extension of ethics, so far studied only by philosophers, is actually a process in ecological evolution. Its sequences may be described in ecological as well as in philosophical terms. An ethic, ecologically, is a limitation on freedom of action in the struggle for existence. An ethic, philosophically, is a differentiation of social from anti-social conduct. These are two definitions of one thing. The thing has its origin in the tendency of interdependent individuals or groups to evolve modes of co-operation. The ecologist calls these symbioses. Politics and economics are advanced symbioses in which the original free-for-all competition has been replaced, in part, by co-operative mechanisms with an ethical content.

This passage, from the essay "The Land Ethic," first published posthumously in 1949, has been often reprinted. The essay has had a great effect, first on biologists and ecologists, and latterly on the general public. Leopold went on to say:

> There is as yet no ethic dealing with man's relation to land and to the animals and plants which grow upon it. Land, like Odysseus'

slave-girls, is still property. The land-relation is still strictly economic, entailing privileges but not obligations.

The extension of ethics to this third element in the human environment is, if I read the evidence correctly, an evolutionary possibility and an ecological necessity. . . . Individual thinkers since the days of Ezekiel and Isaiah have asserted that the despoliation of land is not only inexpedient but wrong. Society, however, has not yet affirmed their belief. I regard the present conservation movement as the embryo of such an affirmation.

An ethic may be regarded as a mode of guidance for meeting ecological situations so new or intricate, or involving such deferred reactions, that the path of social expediency is not discernible to the average individual. Animal instincts are modes of guidance for the individual in meeting such situations. Ethics are possibly a kind of community instinct-in-the-making.

The animal instincts Leopold refers to include the territorial behavior of higher animals. Animal territoriality is no doubt the progenitor of the human concept of "property," a concept which has, like all things human, undergone a wealth of variations. Asserting that property is natural in its origin does not justify any and all of these variations. Equally natural is the concern for the welfare of other human beings that periodically brings the rights of property into question.

The most rigid defenders of the momentary legal definition of "property" apparently think "property" refers to something as substantive as atom and mass. But every good lawyer and every good economist knows that "property" is not a *thing* but merely a verbal announcement that certain traditional powers and privileges of some members of society will be vigorously defended against attack by others. Operationally, the word "property" symbolizes a threat of action; it is a verb-like entity, but (being a noun) the word biases our thoughts toward the substantives we call *things*. But the permanence enjoyed by property is not the permanence of an atom, but that of a promise (a most unsubstantial *thing*). Even after we become aware of the misdirection of attention enforced by the noun "property," we may still passively acquiesce to the inaccuracy of its continued use because a degree of social stability is needed to get the day-to-day work accomplished. But when it becomes painfully clear that the continued unthinking use of the word "property" is leading to consequences that are obviously unjust and socially counterproductive, then must we stop short and ask ourselves how we want to redefine the rights of property.

Law, to be stable, must be based on ethics. In evoking a new ethic to protect land and other natural amenities, Leopold implicitly called for concomitant changes in the philosophy of the law. Now, less than a generation after the publication of Leopold's classic essay, Professor Christopher D. Stone has laid the foundation for just such a philosophy in a graceful essay that itself bids fair to become a classic. The occasion of its writing was the preparation of a special issue of the *Southern California Law Review* devoted to "Law and Technology," which was published as Volume 45, Number 2 in the spring of 1972. Professor Stone later explained the background to me in detail:

> For some time I have been thinking about the interplay between law and the development of social awareness, emphasizing to my students that societies, like human beings, progress through different stages of sensitiveness, and that in our progress, through these stages the law—like art—has a role to play, dramatizing and summoning into the open the changes that are taking place within us. While exemplifying this in class and trying to imagine what a future consciousness might look like, I began to discuss the idea of nature or natural objects being regarded as the subject of legal rights.
>
> The students were—to say the least—skeptical. After all, it is easy to say, "Nature should have legal rights," but if the notion were ever to be more than a vague sentiment, I had to find some pending case in which nature's having legal rights would make a real operational difference.
>
> It was in this context that I turned to the Mineral King case, then recently decided by the Ninth Circuit Court of Appeals. The U.S. Forest Service had granted a permit to Walt Disney Enterprises, Inc. to "develop" Mineral King Valley, a wilderness area in California's Sierra Nevada Mountains, by construction of a $35 million complex of motels, restaurants, and recreational facilities. The Sierra Club, maintaining that the project would adversely affect the

area's esthetic and ecological balance, brought suit for an injunction. The District Court had granted a preliminary injunction. But the Ninth Circuit reversed. The key to the Ninth Circuit's opinion was this: not that the Forest Service had been right in granting the permit, but that the Sierra Club had no "standing" to bring the question to the courts. After all, the Ninth Circuit reasoned, the Sierra Club itself does not allege that it is "aggrieved" or that it is "adversely affected" within the meaning of the rules of standing. Nor does the fact that no one else appears on the scene who is in fact aggrieved and is willing or desirous of taking up the cudgels create a right in appellee. The right to sue does not inure to one who does not possess it, simply because there is no one else willing and able to assert it.

This, I saw at once, was the needed case, a ready-made vehicle to bring to the Court's attention the theory I was developing. Perhaps the injury to the Sierra Club was tenuous, but the injury to Mineral King—the park itself—wasn't. If I could get the courts thinking about the park itself as a jural person—the way corporations are "persons"—the notion of nature having rights would here make a significant operational difference—the difference between the case being heard and (the way things were then heading) thrown out of court.

It was October 1971. The Sierra Club's appeal had already been docketed for review by the United States Supreme Court. The case, we calculated, would be up for argument in November or December at the latest. Was it possible that we could get an article out in time to influence, perhaps, the course of the law? I sat down with Dave Boutte, then the editor of the *Southern California Law Review*, and we made some quick estimates. The next issue of the *Review* to go to press would be a special Symposium on Law and Technology, which was scheduled for publication in late March or early April. There was no hope, then, of getting an article out in time for the lawyers to work the idea into their briefs or oral arguments. Could it be published in time for the Justices to see it before they had finished deliberating and writing their opinions? The chances that the case would still be undecided in April were only slim. But there was one hope. Justice Douglas (who, if anyone on the Court, might be receptive to the notion of legal rights for natural objects) was scheduled to write the Preface to the Symposium on Law and Technology. For this reason he would be supplied with a draft of all the manuscripts in December. Thus he would at least have this idea in his hands. If the case were long enough in the deciding, and if he found the theory convincing, he might even have the article available as a source of support.

We decided to try it. Dave made some last-minute room for my article in the Symposium and I pulled it together at a pace that, as such academic writings go, was almost break-neck. The manuscripts for the Symposium issue went to the printer in late December, and then began a long wait; the two of us hoping that—at least in this case—the wheels of justice would turn slowly. Our excitement at what happened next I leave to you to imagine.

What happened next was that the Mineral King decision was held up until 19 April 1972. On that date the U.S. Supreme Court (the new appointees Powell and Rehnquist not participating) upheld the Ninth Circuit. The Sierra Club itself had no sufficient "personal stake in the outcome of the controversy" to get into Court. Stone's theory (or some alternate) not having been raised, Justice Stewart, writing for the majority, did not feel called upon to pass upon its validity. But in a footnote, he dropped a broad hint: "Our decision does not, of course, bar the Sierra Club from seeking in the District Court to amend its complaint by a motion" invoking some other theory of jurisdiction.

Then came Justice Douglas's dissent. Although the theory of nature itself being the rights-holder had not been pleaded, he decided to deal with it then and there. In his very opening paragraph—which was to resound in newspapers and editorials across the country—he proclaimed:

> The critical question of "standing" would be simplified and also put neatly in focus if we fashioned a federal rule that allowed environmental issues to be litigated before federal agencies or federal courts in the name of the inanimate object about to be despoiled, defaced, or invaded by roads and bulldozers and where injury is the subject of public outrage. Contemporary public concern for pro-

tecting nature's ecological equilibrium should lead to the conferral of standing upon environmental objects to sue for their own preservation. This suit would therefore be more properly labeled as *Mineral King v. Morton.*

Douglas was not alone. Theretofore Justice Blackmun (a Nixon appointee) had been in agreement with Justice Douglas on a major issue perhaps only once, but the two were brought together on this. Blackmun endorsed the idea in the following terms:

> . . . Mr. Justice Douglas, in his eloquent opinion, has imaginatively suggested another means [to establish standing] and one, in its own way, with obvious, appropriate and self-imposed limitations. . . . As I read what he has written, he makes only one addition to the customary criteria (the existence of a genuine dispute; the assurance of adversariness; and a conviction that the party whose standing is challenged will adequately represent the interests he asserts), that is, that the litigant be one who speaks knowingly for the environmental values he asserts.

Justice Brennan agreed.

Thus, when the dust settled, three justices had endorsed the notion and would have "interpreted" the Sierra Club's complaint as though it had been intended to raise Stone's thesis (conceiving Mineral King as the party in interest and the Sierra Club as its guardian). Two judges not on the Court at the time of the argument had abstained, and the other four (a bare majority) had chosen not to reach the theory because it had not, technically speaking, been raised.

In a way, the trees lost, albeit narrowly—and perhaps temporarily. Had they won, the Mineral King decision would no doubt have been called a "watershed decision." A watershed—the topographical image must be kept in mind—is ordinarily recognized only after one has passed over the ridge and is ambling down the other side. (If we haven't passed the ridge, how do we know there is one?) In the present instance, however, I submit that it is a good bet that we are near the ridge of a watershed. It is not merely the closeness of the decision (4 to 3) that leads to the suspicion; it is also the tone of the majority opinion—which is not unfriendly to the trees—as well as other evidences of a changing climate of opinion in this country. Within a month of the Court's decision Senator Philip A. Hart of Michigan praised Stone's article on the floor of the Senate and received permission to have it reprinted in the Congressional Record. The rapidity with which Stone's work has been favorably commented on by jurists, journalists, and legislators gives grounds for optimism as to the early incorporation into law of Stone's thesis that natural objects should have standing in court.

Justice Blackmun, at the conclusion of his opinion, calls attention to the deep reason why change is called for when he quotes the famous lines from John Donne:

No man is an island, entire of itself; every man is a piece of the continent, a part of the main. If a clod be washed away by the sea, Europe is the less, as well as if a promontory were, as well as if a manor of thy friends or of thine own were.

The poet's rhetoric does not automatically give us answers to the thousand and one practical questions with which we are daily confronted, but it does furnish a framework within which acceptable solutions may be found, namely the ecological framework. The world is a seamless web of interrelationships within which no part can, without danger, claim absolute sovereignty in rights over all other parts. Even those who agree (as not all do) with Alexander Pope that "Man is the measure of all things" must admit that man's interests are sometimes served best by taking seriously Christ's advice: "Consider the lilies of the field. . . . They toil not, neither do they spin: and yet I say unto you that even Solomon in all his glory was not arrayed like one of these." Even the narrowest view of the interests of mankind, if pursued to its farthest bound, leads us to conclude that our greatest happiness, especially if we are mindful of the survival in dignity of our posterity, demands that we give some sort of standing in court to the lilies, the trees, and all the other glories of nature.

"Poets," said Percy Shelley, "are the unacknowledged legislators of the world." During the last two centuries the words of William Blake, William Wordsworth, Henry David Thoreau, John Muir, John Burroughs, Rachel Carson, Aldo Leopold, and a host of others have been giving form to the statute books of our unconscious minds. But that which is unconscious is seldom precise, and in any case is not suited for action in a world of differing opinions. The statute law of the moment that is precise enough for action does not adequately take into account what many of us see as our responsibilities as trustees of the earth. Surely it is time now to make explicit the implications of the poets' insights and rebuild the written law "nearer to the heart's desire."

# 20

# *Cash Crops and Redistribution*

Viewing the poverty of the so-called Third World countries, the "Man from Mars" would have no difficulty in assigning the greater part of the blame to overpopulation. Earthlings, addicted to a more personalistic way of looking at things, look for devils to blame. The two most common of these are cash crops and maldistribution.

The earthlings' point of view is adopted by William H. Durham in his *Scarcity and Survival in Central America: Ecological Origins of the Soccer War*. Before Durham, a more Martian conclusion prevailed as regards the cause of the four-day "Soccer War" of 1969, which was commonly presented as a simple consequence of overpopulation, with El Salvador overflowing into the less heavily populated Honduras. The hostilities were touched off by a riot at a soccer game in El Salvador. Durham presents data that cast doubt on the population hypothesis. The population density of El Salvador is about seven times that of Honduras when all land is counted in, but only twice as great when only agricultural land is considered. The lesser fertility of Honduran soils decreases the effective difference even more.

The poverty of Salvadorans is attributed to three sources: a high ratio of population to arable land, inequitable distribution of farmlands, and the growing of exportable cash crops like coffee and cotton in preference to food crops. Outside the haciendas of the wealthy, farms have greatly diminished in size, from an average of 7.41 hectares in 1892 to 1.94 in 1971. Some 266,805 farms now make up 51 percent of the farmland, which means an average of 2.76 hectares per farm in this group. The other 49 percent of the farmland is in the hands of 4,063 owners holding an average of 176 hectares each. Since 1950 there has been a relative increase in the amount of land devoted to export crops over that planted to basic food crops.

Such a shift from local food crops to export crops does not necessarily create hunger. An all-powerful and benevolent dictator would, in many instances, mandate the shift. I am informed by an experienced tropical agronomist that land that yields $300 per hectare when planted to coffee will typically yield only $60 per hectare if converted to corn. Moreover, on sloping land, soil erosion will be more serious in the latter case. A benevolent dictator would, then, prefer the cash crop to the subsistence crop—and then use the cash to buy his people more corn than could be grown on the same land planted to corn.

"Cash crop" is the wrong whipping boy. The real issue is the distribution of income. Outsiders who castigate the growing of cash crops when they have no power to institute a better distribution of income in another sovereignty are simply wasting their time. If the *hacendados* of El Salvador were compelled to grow subsistence crops instead of cash crops, would the situation of the *peones* be improved? It is difficult to believe so.

Thus are we brought back to the distribution problem. Since Reutlinger and Selowsky's *Maldistribution and Poverty* it has been the conventional wisdom of those who would reform other nations that (in Durham's words) "in most countries around the world the problem of malnutrition is a problem of distribution." As a first approximation there is much to be said in favor of this view. If the rich were prevented from buying Mercedes and forced to buy—and distribute—food, their subjects would certainly be better fed. But for how long? When we deal with processes, every reform measure proposed must be confronted with the question, *And then what?*

From data presented on page 38 of Durham's *Survival and Scarcity in Central America*, it can be calculated that a totally equitable distribution of Salvadoran farmland would increase the size of 51 percent of the farms from an average of 2.76 hectares to 5.36 hectares, an increase of 94 percent. The effects of this would surely depend on the way in which redistribution took place. If the change was sudden and peaceable there would be a general improvement in nutrition; this, as Rose E. Frisch has shown, would increase fertility, and population increase would soon negate the improvement. Even without increased fertility, the present rate of increase (3.2 percent per year) would absorb all the benefits of redistribution in twenty-one years.

More realistically, we should expect redistribution to be either violent (accompanied by some erosion of productive capacity) or so slow that its beneficial effects would be indiscernible under the juggernaut of population increase.

There are many aspects to the "cycle of poverty," but perhaps the most tragic one is the attitude toward the future that poverty creates among those who habitually suffer from it. What is the perceived value of a present good relative to a future good? It is an observed fact that this ratio is greater for a poor man than for a rich. In economic terms, it is as though the poor man discounts the future at a higher rate than does a rich man. As confirmation of this prediction we note that the interest rates in poor countries are much higher than those in rich. But, in the long view, the real value of the future is not determined by interest rates. It follows that those who are wealthy can forego present gain for the sake of the future, and the poor cannot. Thus it comes about that poverty creates maldistribution. This is not to deny the reverse causation; what we are dealing with is circular causation. There is no simple recipe for breaking the circle.

The Man from Mars would say, "Decrease population!" The Man from Earth, more aware—perhaps too aware—of the multiple practical difficulties of such a program, would say, "You might as well demand that we bell the cat!" Perhaps that is why books like Durham's ignore the possibility of population control.

Unfortunately, a population-blind "solution" to population-created problems has no more reality than the Emperor's new clothes.

# 21

## Exploited Seas—An Opportunity for Peace

By now everyone recognizes that the discouraging prognosis for oceanic fisheries derives precisely from the status of the oceans as an unmanaged commons. Few scenarios of the future offer any hope: I see only three.

First, chronic military action might render the oceans unsafe for fishing. This happened to the Mediterranean during the First World War. Four years of interrupted fishing permitted the fish stocks to recover remarkably. For the global seas this seems an unlikely scenario, though perhaps a sufficient rise in the price of fuel for motors may bring it about.

Second, a monstrous new plague, whether natural in origin, or created by experimental inadvertence in genetic laboratories, might wipe out 90 percent of the human population. The probability of this event is, in the strictest sense of the word, incalculable.

Third, humanity might "do the impossible" and create a global government that could manage the global commons. I doubt if there is any profit in trying to calculate the probability of such a lifting of ourselves by our bootstraps, but there may be some benefit in trying to dream up ways of making such an advance. What follows is my modest proposal. It is no doubt naive, but perhaps some naivete is called for. The creation of the American nation out of a loose federation of bickering states was also an impossibility, but somehow it was accomplished. We need to examine more closely the impossibility that faces us.

Niels Bohr once said, "There is not much hope if we have only one difficulty, but when we have two, we can match them off against each other." It seems to me that the oceans present us with a "Bohr pair" in the political realm.

The future of oceanic fishing looks hopeless. Since no one owns the seas, each nation tries to get all the whales and fish it can "before the pigs get there." It would be futile for one public-spirited nation to fish less: its share would simply go to the others, and fishing would ultimately be ruined anyway. Competition favors national greed in the short run and the ruin of all fishing in the long. Conclusion: It is impossible to save the seas.

International peace looks equally hopeless. The fissionable-fusible atom hangs over our heads. Weaponry increases without limit because each major nation wants to be "second to none." Competition favors national paranoia in the short run and universal destruction in the long. Conclusion: International peace looks impossible, too.

Here we have the raw material for a "complementary" solution in the style of Bohr: two difficulties—or rather, two impossibilities—to be fused into a single solution. "Impossible" is always relevant to a particular frame of reference. In both problems national sovereignty is part of the frame. In our most searching investigations sovereignty is left unexamined; it is the Emperor's new clothes. Let's see if there is not something we might do about sovereignty.

The League of Nations failed, and now many say that the United Nations is failing, too. This should surprise no one: both institutions were designed as failures by the founding nations, which did not look at sovereignty in a creative way. They failed to consider the possibility that sovereignty could be subdivided.

The sovereignty of the oceanic fisheries could be separated from the sovereignty needed to ensure national survival. Fishery sovereignty could be assigned to a suitably limited supranational agency without peril to the nations agreeing to this partial relinquishment of sovereignty. The minimal armament needed for an effective international fish patrol would be no threat to national navies.

The size of the annual catch of each species should be determined by a scientific council; but the division of the catch should be determined by a political body. The system would have to be asymmetrical: rich nations would finance and run it, but only poor nations would be allowed to benefit from it. Fortunately, rich nations can afford to be generous about the ocean fisheries because they are only a minor source of proteins for most of them. (Patient diplomacy would be required to deal with Japan, a special case.) Any controlling agency is properly suspected of being self-serving. The *bona fides* of this one would be the abandonment of the possibility of direct gain to the controllers.

To some, this proposal will seem shamelessly paternalistic. Perhaps it is: but what is the alternative? It is inconceivable that poor countries, envious of one another as they are, could agree to manage such a system themselves. It takes only a single noncooperator to make a cooperative system of equals fail. So which is it to be: paternalism, or more hunger?

Looking at the other side of the coin, what's in this proposal for the rich countries? Such an operation would save something for posterity, and the intelligent rich should be more concerned with posterity. But the proposal also offers a more immediate *quid pro quo* to the rich and powerful. It holds out the potential of an evolution of a truly supranational authority that all nations, the rich especially, need if thermonuclear destruction is to be avoided.

In the strictly limited area of the seas the generation of supranational power is credible. Not easy, but credible. Once this was accomplished other extensions of supranationality might be brought into being. For instance, the large reserves of coal in the Antarctic might be managed in a similar way. Whatever the details (and they are unforeseeable), the evolution of supranational power must be slow, so as to allow for the correction of sublethal mistakes, and to allow people's minds to adjust. There must be a building from strength to strength as trust grows. Trust is the key.

The prospect of laying a stable base for international peace should be an adequate *quid pro quo* for rich nations, quite a sufficient recompense for relinquishing to the poor all the benefits from the ocean fisheries, which need to be managed by strong hands if the seas are not to be exhausted in our lifetime.

# 22

## *Conservation's Secret Question*

Only once have I seen a California condor. I saw it just south of Big Sur, where the steep canyons dip abruptly into the Pacific. I don't know how I happened to look up. Certainly there was no sound, and human vision upward is so cut off by our brow-bones that movement in the vertical sector of the periphery seldom activates the tracking reflexes of our eyes.

But for some reason I did look up; there, no more than a hundred yards directly overhead, was the magnificent sail of wings, feather-splayed at the tips, motionlessly riding the upcurrents. The condor's naked head turned alertly from side to side. "What luck!" I thought.

That was forty years ago.

I wish all human beings could be as lucky, not only in my time but for generations to come. But luck is running out all over the world.

I have had the good fortune to see the great panorama of the Serengeti: gazelles, wildebeests, zebras, giraffes, hyenas, and jackals, several hundred thousand animals at one time. I can still feel the wonder of sitting in an automobile on the plain, motor turned off, my wife and I gazing at the sea of large, living beings that extended clear to the horizon in all directions. The animals left only a rather small avoidance area around our car as the herds moved slowly along their migration. The shimmering air was paradoxically quiet and yet buzzing with life. The principal sound came from the wildebeests—the deprecatory coughs of thousands of shy creatures seemingly saying "Oh, pardon me!" A suitable sentiment for a species that hangs on to existence by human sufferance.

Again I wished that all men and women, all girls and boys, now and into the indefinite future, could know such luck. I know this cannot be. The myriad African mammals are on the same steep down curve as that one condor, a curve ending in zero or, almost as bad, with a few creatures in zoos, deprived of their multitudes, their essential beauty. It makes one weep, not only for the animals but for us.

"Surely if we human beings can fly to the moon we can also. . . ." How often we have heard this remark in its many variants! The implication is wrong, however. Going to the moon was easy. The needed theory had been known since Newton, though the admirable technology was only recently perfected. True, it cost a bit of money, but the cost was commonized over 200 million people and spread over a decade. Every taxpayer contributed a little bit. A handful of suppliers made a great bit. That is the combination of profit and loss that gets things done.

Unfortunately saving wildlife threatens people's pocketbooks, and it is not easy to make a profit from doing good. This does not mean it is impossible, but it does mean that saving wildlife is difficult. Our greatest chance of success lies in openly exposing the difficulties, to see what we can do about them. Let us see what the problems are.

It is evening and the television set is on. The camera zooms to a hunter facing an elephant. The man raises his gun and fires. The elephant falls down dead.

The commentator would have you believe that you are witnessing the extinction of a species. Perhaps not. If this elephant is being killed in Tsavo, which is vastly overpopulated by elephants, the killing of one elephant, or even a hundred, is actually good for the population of elephants living there. The concept of "carrying capacity" is the great organizer of game-management theory. When the carrying capacity of the environment is transgressed, the too-numerous population destroys its own environment, reducing carrying capacity in future years.

In the picture, the hunter shooting an elephant is doing the population of elephants (and the species) a favor—*if* the carrying capacity has been transgressed. On the other hand, if the dying elephant is the last of its herd, great harm is done. Is the hunter a benefactor or a scoundrel? You cannot tell from a photograph. You cannot photograph morality.

We do not have to go to Africa to confront the moral problems of game management. Wild burros have multiplied in the Grand Canyon until they are their own worst enemy, as have wild horses in several western states. Under natural conditions (meaning, no human intervention at all) predators are the force that prevents overpopulation among prey animals. But when men intervene and cut down the mountain lions, wolves, and coyotes, prey animals become victims of their own reproductive powers.

Some of the people who killed predators thought themselves defenders of a particular form of wildlife. A limited view, but let it pass for the moment. Accepting at face value their excuse, we still must point out that the first intervention in the natural order must be followed by a second, namely preventing the nearly predator-free prey species from breeding beyond the carrying capacity of its habitat. It is impracticable to force birth control on wild animals, so the second intervention has to be in the form of death control—the deliberate killing of excess animals.

At this point a new problem arises. In every case of this sort, there are human beings who stand to profit from killing—even to the point of extinction—wild animals. Herdsmen and ranchers wanting to graze the maximum number of sheep, cows, and domestic horses on the western range will be only too happy to kill burros and wild horses, down to the last animal. When someone says we must kill some burros and wild horses for the good of the wild herds, how do we know his concern is for the wild animals rather than for his own pocketbook? Game management is easily perverted into one more excuse for sacrificing nature to serve mammon. There is no escaping this difficulty; we must learn to examine proposals critically, to evaluate the experts, and then to ride herd continuously on every game-management program.

Killing an animal is not the same as killing a species. Yet such is the tyranny of the camera that too many people mistake one for the other. Producers of television shows take advantage of the confusion because it makes their job easy. But it makes more difficult the job of saving wildlife.

Many of the human actions that extinguish species almost defy photography. The actions that "kill" a species generally do not directly involve members of the species affected. For instance, the forceable settling of the Masai people on the flanks of the Ngorongoro crater constricts the migration route of animals into and out of the caldera. Ultimately, this settling of herdsmen-turned-agriculturalists will completely cut off an important habitat for more than a dozen species.

Unless we do something to stop it, habitat piracy will take place in one area after another. Yet piracy looks so peaceful. No gore as animals fall before a gun, just peaceful farmers tilling their crops. Animals starve as herds are confined to smaller areas that are exploited past their carrying capacity. Photographs of the emaciated beasts may lead shallow thinkers to demand that we fly food to the starving herds. At best, such charity merely prolongs the agony of extinction.

Citizens of East African countries tend to see their choice as this: "abundant wildlife and human misery" versus "wildlife elimination and human prosperity." They ask, "Can we use this land to feed ourselves, or must we maintain a gigantic zoo for rich foreigners?" The question virtually dictates the answer.

Some farsighted East Africans see a possibility for compromise. Tourism is a major source of foreign exchange. By charging enough of visitors, it should be possible to use the fees collected to buy more food than is foregone by not converting animal parks to farms. In such cases, one farms the visitors. For several decades this policy has been followed by Kenya and Tanzania. But Uganda abandoned it with the rise of Idi Amin, and the policy is being eroded in the other two countries.

We could preach to the Africans, of course, but there's little profit in preaching. Why should they listen to outsiders, especially outsiders who have not openly faced this moral dilemma on their own turf?

"Physician, heal thyself," is good advice. The conservation problem in Africa is no different fundamentally from the conservation problem in America—which we have yet to face fully. Condors are becoming extinct not because sportsmen are hunting them to death, but rather because the birds' habitat is being taken over for other purposes. Ranchers want the land for grazing cattle and sheep, and the ways in which they manage their grazing lands pretty well rules out the condors. Oil companies want to drill wells in the Sespe, where the most important nesting sites are. The pandemonium of a vigorous energy search is likely to disturb the nesting of these shy birds. Workmen drilling wells may, in their spare moments, take pot shots at the birds just for the hell of it. Drill crews are a tough bunch, hard to control: not for nothing are they called "roughnecks." They are more than willing tools in what has been ambitiously called the "Reindustrialization of America," which translates into "Full speed ahead for energy and industry, and damn nature and the environment!"

With meticulously careful entry into condor breeding areas it might be possible to have both birds and oil. But such care costs money and takes time. Inflation and the energy shortage lead our reindustrialists to say, "You can't have oil and condors, too. People need energy to live. They don't need birds. Which do you want—oil to keep your homes warm, or birds for a few elitists to stare at while the rest of us freeze in the dark?"

The stark question polarizes discussion and tends to dictate the answer. "People, of course." But the polarization is wrong, and the answer is too.

The real question is not "Wildlife or people?" but "People-with-wildlife or people-without-wildlife?" At some point we will use up the last economically available barrel of oil and cover over the last acre of good farm land with solar energy collectors. From then on humanity will have to live on a constant energy budget. If we are going to have to live on such a budget someday, why not do so now? Why not bite the bullet while there are still so many wonderful creatures in our world?

Every wild thing competes with man in some way: Deer graze parkland that could grow cattle and trash trees for biomass, sea otters "steal" abalone from fishermen, and fish ladders for salmon "waste" part of the hydraulic head that could be used to generate more electricity.

A few years ago the Chinese boasted that there were no birds in large areas of China because the people had caught and killed every one of them, thus keeping grains from being eaten while the people enjoyed a few bird pies. Rachel Carson's *Silent Spring* with a vengeance!

The reindustrialists are city boys bent on increasing the figure on "the bottom line" of the financial report of energy business. But the most effective attack on wildlife will not be launched in the name of business. It will be made in the name of the people. Reindustrialists have learned from the far Left: demagoguery is what brings home the political bacon. How, our newest bleeding hearts will ask, can we justify maintaining groves of useless 2,000-year-old trees when there are poor people who cannot afford housing? Let's cut down the trees and eliminate the housing shortage. While we are at it, we can plant potatoes to feed those poor people.

In the process of making profits, the reindustrialists would work the system to maximize the number of human beings. This will necessarily force the lowest possible quality of life on the multitudes rather than allow a much smaller number of human beings to live a life enriched with birds, flowers, game, and redwood groves.

Our desire to conserve wildlife for our children and our children's children forces us to bring out into the open conservation's secret question:

*Does God give a prize for the maximum number of human beings?*

Put another way, which shall we bequeath to our grandchildren: human life with nature, or human life without nature?

If we opt for life with nature we opt for fewer human beings and boldly assert that God gives no prize for the maximization of human protoplasm. We deny that human life—mere human life deprived of nature—is the most precious thing in the world. Such a denial shocks many people. But can anyone familiar with the grandeur of wildlife give any other answer? Can any trustee for posterity consent to a step-by-step sacrifice of the variety of nature, merely to make possible the maximum number of human lives?

Concern for wildlife is no Sunday avocation. To be effective it must be courageously carried on seven days a week, year in and year out. Stewardship of wildlife takes guts.

# 23

# *The Born-Again Optimist*

If the reception of *The Limits to Growth* and *The Global 2000 Report* taught us nothing else it should have taught us that the Greeks were right. In the public relations game only optimism sells. Cassandra spoke the truth, but she was not believed. As Teiresias in Euripides's *The Phoenician Women* says: "A man's a fool to use the prophet's trade. For if he happens to bring bitter news he's hated by the man for whom he works."

In an engagingly frank introduction to his book *The Ultimate Resource*, economist Julian L. Simon tells us that he used to be a Malthusian. At a particular, well-remembered moment in 1969 he had a revelation that turned him into a born-again optimist. He is now making a very good thing out of his salvation, selling optimism by the bucketfuls to newspapers, magazines, and television.

The ultimate resource, Simon says, is people, and no limit can be set to what people may accomplish. What we usually call resources are mere phantasms. Simon's conclusions are highly palatable to budget evaders, car salesmen, realtors, advertisers, land speculators, and optimists in general; scientists find them appalling. According to Simon, natural resources are getting less scarce; pollution is decreasing; worldwide, food per person is increasing; the faster the population grows, the greater the prosperity; every additional person born into the population is a boon; larger is better than smaller; the more immigrants we take in, the better off our economy will be; diminishing returns is a meaningless concept; and there are no diseconomies of scale.

This is more than optimism: this is euphoria. There has been nothing like it since the Marquis de Condorcet wrote his hymn to hope in 1793, *An Historical Picture of the Progress of the Human Mind*, while hiding from the French Revolution (which he had supported from the beginning). Condorcet made a grand survey of the history of humanity. The succession of stages—tribalism, pastoralism, agriculturalism, the Greek experience, the Dark Ages, the birth of science, etc.—he divided into ten epochs, of which nine had been completed. Humanity was now moving into the tenth and last (Utopians apparently cannot free their dream worlds from the illusion of finality). Affiliating his persona to the panorama of time, Condorcet was, despite the bleakness of his prospects, intoxicated with the future of history. Speaking of himself as "the philosopher," i.e., the lover of wisdom, he concluded his book with this paean: "How admirably calculated is this picture of the human race [to console the philosopher] for the errors, the crimes, the injustice, with which the earth is polluted, and whose victim he often is!" We cannot but admire his courage in writing so optimistically of mankind when his personal situation was so hopeless. Shortly after finishing his book (which was published two years later), Condorcet left his refuge and immediately met the fate he foresaw—death at the hands of the Revolution.

That alarums should breed euphoria may seem strange, but on closer examination it makes sense. Nature has her own dialectic: when the future looks really hopeless you might as well be euphoric. Since no future is ever absolutely determined, psychological denial puts you in the best shape to seize whatever opportunities fortune may throw your way.

The parallel between Condorcet and Simon is more than superficial. The revolution that threatens Simon's peace is not political but intellectual. The simpleminded concept of progress (largely technological progress) that governed most policymaking during the past 200 years is now under severe attack, and the bitter news of real limits is more than the naive devotees of progress can bear. Denying reality, they embrace euphoria. Simon gives them an intellectual base for being born again as optimists.

Simon's first problem is to exorcize the terror of the finite, which he does by trend analysis and theory. Since the price of refined copper and wheat, in real dollars, has (ignoring short-term fluctuations) been on a downward trend for the past 200 years, it follows (he implies) that these commodities will forever become cheaper. But, as René Dubos has said, "Trend is not destiny." The last two centuries are only a moment in the life of the human species. What does the future hold?

The most important unknown in the future is the rate of development of new technology. Unfortunately there is no simple way to measure this rate. For a variety of reasons, the number of patents applied for and the number of scientific papers published per year do not give us the answer. For one thing, the "publish or perish" policy of universities encourages a cancerous growth of scientific papers. A measure of true progress has not been devised, but that does not stop Simon from pronouncing, "The pace of development of new technology in general is increasing." The Pope is not the only one who can speak *ex cathedra*.

That there might be theoretical limits to the supply of resources or the development of technology Simon denies on the most general grounds. The method he uses to establish the essential limitlessness of the world was exactly prefigured by Condorcet. In Simon's words:

> The length of a one inch line is finite in the sense that it is bounded at both ends. But the line within the end points contains an infinite number of points; these points cannot be counted, because they have no defined size. Therefore the number of points in that one inch segment is not finite. Similarly, the quantity of copper that will ever be available to us is not finite, because there is no method (even in principle) of making an appropriate count.

The translation of this statement is simple: anything that is infinitely divisible is infinite in quantity. So Simon says.

If this is the proper way to analyze resource problems Simon should, as a licensed economist, also tell people: "Don't worry about the small size of your bank account. You can always divide the dollars into cents, and if you still don't have enough divide the cents into mils. If that still isn't enough we can create a yet smaller unit so that you can have as many units as you want. You're rich!" Had Simon illustrated his argument with the appropriate economic example he would surely have seen his error.

Or would he? Possibly sensing the preposterousness of his position he falls back on two other arguments. As concerns our copper resources we must consider "the possibility of creating copper or its economic equivalent from other materials." Create copper from other materials? This is sheer alchemy, which science abandoned three centuries ago. True, nuclear physics furnishes a marginal—to use a favorite word of economists—defense of this possibility. With high energy radiation it is possible to produce a tiny amount of copper from other metals, but the yield is so slight that no one has ever bothered to calculate the cost. This is hardly the way to create what a responsible economist would call an infinite supply of copper.

As for the "economic equivalent" of copper, this raises the popular thesis of the "infinite substitutability of materials." It is true, of course, that as copper becomes higher in price we find that we can substitute aluminum for the copper. What happens as aluminum becomes scarcer? Presumably we could substitute some other metal—perhaps silver or gold. But each new substitute also exists in finite supply. There can hardly be an infinite number of substitutes, and in any case the mass of the earth (or of the solar system, or of the Milky Way, if you wish) is limited. The substitutability game is a game of musical chairs. Substituting one element after another for copper eventually brings us back to copper itself. We cannot transcend a finite supply.

Simon's other attack on the concept of finitude can only be called jesuitical. Discussing the petroleum situation he says: "The number of wells that will eventually produce oil, and in what quantities, is not known or measurable at present and probably never will be, and hence it is not meaningfully finite." One can only conclude from this that whatever is "not meaningfully finite"—whatever that may mean—is infinite. I am sure mathematicians will be delighted with this new insight into the meaning of the infinite.

Important though Simon considers his theoretical approach, he mostly relies on empirical facts to beat the reluctant reader into submission. "Information overload" is endemic in our time so every expositor can present only a fraction of the published material available. As one might expect, Simon chooses optimistic reports. For instance, he bases his rosy view of the future of petroleum resources on the pronouncements of Vincent McKelvey, a longtime director of the U.S. Geological Survey. McKelvey spoke from a prestigious platform, but it is astonishing that Simon does not realize how thoroughly McKelvey's pronouncements have been discredited. For nearly a quarter of a century there was a running battle between McKelvey and his fellow geologist M. King Hubbert. In effect Hubbert said, "The end is nigh," while McKelvey said, "Don't worry—there's plenty for everyone." Like Cassandra, Hubbert was not believed. Then, as the 1973 oil crisis approached, other geologists reexamined the arguments of McKelvey and Hubbert and concluded that Hubbert was right, noting that his projections had been uncannily accurate for two decades. Director McKelvey had been talking through his hat—his political hat. For the past ten years everyone who follows energy closely has known that M. King Hubbert is right, but his name is not to be found in Simon's book. Neither is there any recounting of his analysis. This is a pity because Simon, who leans heavily on the most simpleminded trend analysis, could learn much by a careful study of the sophisticated, ingenious, and open-minded methods of analysis used by Hubbert. Leaving Hubbert and his work out of a book-long discussion of resources is like omitting the names and works of Adam Smith and John Maynard Keynes from a treatise on economics.

Simon is, he admits, a "cornucopist," a person who thinks there's always plenty more in nature's cup. In his idiosyncratic view agricultural productivity will increase forever. Is water scarce? Drill more holes in the ground. The fact that water secured in this way is mined water and hence subject to depletion (as are all mined substances) goes unmentioned by Simon. Anyway, if water becomes more expensive we can resort to trickle irrigation. The fact that the benefits of this will soon be eaten up by the exponential growth of demand is never considered.

Discussing the stock of agricultural land under the pressure of population growth, Simon, like the fast change artist at a county fair, befuddles the reader with rapid rhetorical interchanges of "arable land" and "cultivated land," whereby he "proves" that the amount of agricultural land is increasing in the world. To Simon, as to a legion of economists, an acre is an acre, and a table of figures is the ultimate reality. Such economists are unable to see the difference between the rich glacial soil of Iowa corn land and worn-out tobacco land in Georgia. True, it is astonishing what a farmer can do with generous amounts of fertilizer and irrigation, but every corrective costs money (and energy). Agriculturalists are appalled when rich glacial till or fertile alluvial soil in an old flood plain is covered over by shopping malls, factory buildings, and highways. As M. Rupert Cutler, formerly Assistant Secretary for Agriculture, said: "Asphalt is the land's last crop." So it is in the rich countries; in poor countries the last crop is desert.

The Department of Agriculture estimates that the United States is losing a million acres of prime farmland each year to urban sprawl. Does this bother Simon? Not a bit! The paragraph in which he demolishes this bugaboo of the environmentalists is worth quoting in its entirety for it gives the flavor of the entire book.

> The idea that cities devour "prime land" is a particularly clear example of the failure to grasp economic principles. Let's take the concrete (asphalt?) case of a new shopping mall on the outskirts of Champaign-Urbana, Illinois. The key economic idea is that the mall land has greater value to the economy as a shopping center than it does as a farm, wonderful though this Illinois land is for growing corn and soybeans. That's why the mall investors could pay the farmer enough to make it worthwhile for him or her to sell. A series of corn-y examples should bring out the point.

Note the sleight of hand by which the economist substitutes "prime land" for "prime farmland," thus preparing the reader to evaluate the land solely in terms of price on the open market. At a particular moment an acre may indeed be more "valuable" (more revenue-producing) as a part of a shopping mall than as a grower of crops. A purely economic decision focuses on the moment. In practice, economics makes no allowance for future shifts in relative values. In the future the price of corn *relative to* the price of such competing economic goods as the stuff stores sell may rise precipitously. It certainly will if population growth gets out of hand.

A change in relative prices calls for a change in the economist's definition of "prime" and "highest use." If economic calculations could allow for such quite likely future changes, then society could safely put the future in the hands of free-market economists. But the standard technique of "discounting" the future with a negative exponential function lays waste to the real future. With the high rate of interest prevailing now, the future—as the economist anticipates it—virtually disappears. When money is earning 20 percent interest, land anticipated to be worth a million dollars as farmland a generation from now (thirty years) would command only $1,238 of today's money. What counts most is what income the land can bring in right now. High interest has the effect of virtually destroying the future—in the economist's calculations.

The professional inability of the economist to deal adequately with the future has an equally unfortunate corollary: economics is blind to the irrevocable. Thirty years from now a change in the relative prices of grains and commercial gewgaws may make land more valuable as farmland than as shopping malls; but the cost of clearing millions of tons of concrete, asphalt, glass, and chromium from what was once prime farmland can make the correction of the earlier error in judgment economically impossible. A society that listens only to economists ratchets its way to destruction.

Economic libertarians and doctrinaire free-market economists who concede no limits to the simpleminded method of discounting the future are today's providentialists. Pure economics will, in their view, create the best of all possible worlds. We need another Voltaire to write a new *Candide*.

Only political restraints (which are unacceptable to libertarians) can keep a laissez-faire system from destroying itself in a limited world. It is probably their inchoate realization of this truth that leads so many libertarians to deny the reality of limits. If limits can be set aside as some sort of unreality, then growth can continue forever without an increase in the price of money. Everyone can then forever prosper in a free market. The specter that haunts the minds of libertarians and cornucopists is the specter of material limits.

The exorcism of this specter has been greatly aided by a recurrent confusion between material and immaterial resources. Condorcet's book was an account of the progress of the human *mind*; he said that "nature has assigned no limit to the perfecting of the human faculties." This is perhaps true; for the sake of argument let us grant that it is. But where does "mind" fit into the scheme of things? Science deals with three kinds of reality: information, matter, and energy. The second and third are material and are bound by conservation laws. The first, information, is immaterial and is not constricted by conservation. Mind operates in the realm of information.

From Condorcet to Simon, compulsive optimists have shown the utmost ingenuity in confusing information with the material aspects of the world. A thesis proved in one realm is surreptitiously transferred to the other. Where nonconservation holds sway, limits may not be terribly important; but in the conservative world of matter and energy, limits are central to all disciplined thinking and planning. Economics professors love to tell their students that "there's no such thing as a free lunch," thus expressing an orientation that aligns economics with the natural sciences as a conservative discipline. But the usefulness of economics to commerce, which thrives on providential thinking, corrupts some economists into denying limits and abandoning conservative thinking. Pollyanna becomes the patron saint. Intoxicated with the progress of technology during the past two centuries, some economists now say there must be a free lunch somewhere.

The literary world has long realized that the putative subject of a work of fiction may not be the real subject. Pretending to tell the story of Raskolnikov or the Ludlow lad, the author seeks to resolve his own psychological problems. It is not so widely recognized, however, that economists and scientists, when they set forth what they conceive to be the policy implications of their disciplines, may also be trying to free themselves through psychoanalysis. Simon puts his confession at the beginning of his book, and he frankly uses the first person. The source of his anxiety is not external, as was Condorcet's, but internal. Simon's mind used to be caught in the Malthusian mode, and he was "in the midst of a depression of unusual duration." He escaped this depression by freeing himself of the Malthusian belief that material limits are real. Now he wants to free others—and to find companions. "Some others hold a point of view similar to mine. But there are far too few of us to provide mutual support and comfort. So this is a plea for love, printer's ink, and research grants for our side."

Malthus, a devout and practicing Christian, would not begrudge Simon the love he seeks. But would Malthus—or should we—grant him his other requests? Observation shows that printer's ink and research grants (publicity and power) are bestowed in abundance on the Pollyannas of this world. Simon is being greedy when he asks for more than the plethora he has been receiving since he became a born-again optimist. Cassandra is the one who needs support. If the limits of the material world are real—if Cassandra is right—continued denial of those limits will be disastrous for our descendants.

# 24

## *Ending the Squanderarchy*

What would the mythical Man from Mars write home if he were asked to characterize the kind of government we live under? Probably something like this: "These people say they live in a democracy, but that's just window dressing. Nor can their system be called an oligarchy, because there are too many fingers in the pie for the *oligo*: 535 Senators and Congressmen served and advised by 18,500 aides—68 per Senator, 27 per Congressman. From the way everyone wastes fuel and materials I would say that King Squander is in charge. Challenged to conserve, most citizens say they are individually helpless to stop squandering. If one person were in charge we could speak of a monarchy; but *things* are in the saddle (as their philosopher Ralph Waldo Emerson said). These poor wretches sweat under a *squanderarchy*."

How did we get into this predicament? Paraphrasing Rousseau, we can say that every bad idea is born good. The squander imperative grew out of the idea of progress, which was given birth by the Marquis de Condorcet (1743–1794), just before he lost his life to the French Revolution. The long title of Condorcet's book speaks of the "Progrès de l'Esprit humain," but the idea of spiritual (or intellectual) progress was soon displaced by material progress. Science and technology were the agents of progress, and (in the United States at least) the existence of a free enterprise system was said to be a necessary precondition. Progress became identified with all that was open, free, limitless. The optimism of the Victorian age was well expressed by Henry George (1839–1897) in his refutation of Malthusian views of population:

> I assert that in any given state of civilization a greater number of people can collectively be better provided for than a smaller. I assert that the injustice of society, not the niggardliness of nature, is the cause of the want and misery which the current theory attributes to overpopulation. I assert that the new mouths which an increasing population calls into existence require no more food than the old ones, while the hands they bring with them can in the natural order of things produce more. I assert that, other things being equal, the greater the population, the greater the comfort which an equitable distribution of wealth would give to each individual. I assert that in a state of equality the natural increase of population would constantly tend to make every individual richer instead of poorer.

In brief, more is better. Why? For two reasons: because of the progress of knowledge in the scientific-technological-industrial revolution and because of economies of scale. Would more be better *forever*? The way George treated this question is significant:

> Twenty men working together will, where nature is niggardly, produce more than twenty times the wealth that one man can produce where nature is most bountiful. The denser the population the more minute becomes the subdivision of labor, the greater the economies of production and distribution, and, hence, the very reverse of the Malthusian doctrine is true; and, *within the limits in which we have reason to suppose increase would still go on*, in any given state of civilization a greater number of people can produce a

larger proportionate amount of wealth, and more fully supply their wants, than can a smaller number.

Every economy of scale ultimately peters out in a diseconomy, and every cultural revolution is finally afflicted by diminishing returns. Did George acknowledge these facts? On the basis of the passage that I have italicized above he could maintain in a court of law that he had. But it is rhetorically significant that he did *not* italicize this passage, leaving the average, not very critical reader with the impression that economies of scale will rule always. This melioristic view pervades all 565 pages of *Progress and Poverty*, rhetorically overwhelming the feeble qualification hinted at in the fifteen words italicized above. In pursuit of social justice, George, like most sociologists in the following century, found overpopulation unthinkable.

The idea of limitless, accelerating growth was welcome to the power elite of the commercial world. Growth, change, "development," spending, and rapid turnover were viewed as goods without limits. Conservation, thrift, and stability were bads. Paradoxically, while this nonconservative line of thought was flourishing in technology and the commercial world that benefitted from it, the contrasting view of universal conservation was becoming established in pure science (on which technology and commerce ultimately depend). Curiously, the effective beginnings of conservative thought also began in France, in the work of another man of privilege who also lost his life to the Revolution. Lavoisier (1743–1794) imposed the discipline of the analytical balance on chemistry. Following his lead the world of chemistry and physics was soon ruled by the dogma that input must precisely equal output: no creation, no destruction, nothing unaccounted for. By the middle of the nineteenth century explicit statements had been made of the Law of Conservation of Matter and the Laws of Thermodynamics. All such laws—and they are not many—are generically called "conservation laws." Despite the marvellous possibilities revealed by science in its applied aspects—technology—fundamental science came to be seen as a search for "impotence principles," as the physicist E. T. Whittaker called them. The most profound minds of science look for the limits of the possible; they seek *closure* of the intellectual systems.

The inherent conflict between minds that worship openness and those that seek closure was largely overlooked because of social barriers between the two groups. The wheeler-dealers of the world had open minds; theoretical scientists, more cloistered and seeking no personal potency in the world of commerce and politics, had closure-seeking minds. Popular semantics favored the first group, implicitly setting up these equivalences: open = liberal = creative, while closed = conservative = timid.

We need not wonder then that the publication of Rachel Carson's *Silent Spring* in 1962 led to an avalanche of denunciations. The essential message of the book was this: we live in a world of real limits, to which we must adjust our demands. This theme was taken up again ten years later in the first Report to the Club of Rome, *The Limits to Growth*. Once more, those not yet weaned from the idea of progress produced a mountain of refutations, some of them quite witty. Yet the Establishment of Progress was beginning to quiver. By 1979 the Establishment was definitely moving: in this year a committee in the Harvard Business School brought out its report, *Energy Future*, which acknowledges that limits are real. The worlds of Condorcet and Lavoisier were coming together.

The union was taking place in the realm variously called "ecology" or "environment." The conservation laws of ecology are not as neat as those of physics but they are at least as important. Two in particular should be noted. First: The extinction of a species is irrevocable. (Exceptions to this are few and of no practical importance.) Second: The destruction of an ecosystem—a stable association of many species—is either totally irrevocable, or, on the ordinary time scale of human history, essentially irrevocable. A tropical rain forest, once destroyed, cannot be reestablished in a few hundred years even when all the species composing such a system are still in existence. These two ecological principles counsel caution and hesitancy, in sharp contrast to the usual inference from the idea of progress which is *Innovate now, pay later*.

Some of the ecological changes now taking place affect the entire world. The addition of $CO_2$ and other vapors to the atmosphere is creating a greenhouse effect and raising the temperature of the globe. How far will this process go? We don't know. But there is at least a small probability that the process may enter into the runaway feedback mode, ultimately converting the Earth into another Venus, with a surface temperature of several hundred degrees Fahrenheit. Such possibilities bring us face to face with what Edward Teller calls the zero-infinity paradox (ZIP)—a near zero probability of a disaster of near infinity seriousness. What should be the rational man's response to a ZIP? Teller, an advocate of nuclear power plants, says *Let's take a chance*. Ecologists, almost unanimously, say *Let's not*. Unfortunately, the definitive answer to a ZIP cannot be worked out in a test tube or with a computer.

In 1966 the ecological point of view received a powerful boost in the world outside the natural sciences with the publication of an influential essay by Kenneth Boulding, "The Economics of the Coming Spaceship Earth." Boulding contrasted the wasteful "cowboy economy" promoted by the idea of progress with the conservationist ethic of the "spaceship economy" dictated by the recognition of limits. Boulding's images are vivid but not without dangers.

As interpreted by many (though not by Boulding), the spaceship image is used to justify treating the entire world as a commons. A necessary (though not sufficient) condition for the preservation or wise use of finite resources is that there be a sovereign power, which Thomas Hobbes (1588–1679) called a *Leviathan*. To share resources without the discipline of such power is to head toward universal ruin. Failure to make the limit of sharing coincide with the limit of sovereignty ensures that the system will move into a destructive runaway feedback mode of operation. Given sufficient intelligence a community may be able to survive in a *managed* commons. Socialism is a managed commons, which, with good planning and eternal vigilance, *may* work. But so long as a commons remains unmanaged in a world of ever-increasing demands, intelligence is almost irrelevant: overconsumption and overpollution are inevitable.

A few problems are truly spaceship problems, e.g., atmospheric pollution. For such as these we may have to create a limited spaceship sovereignty, that is, a *Leviathan* constitutionally limited to the oversight of only certain resources. We should not allow mere fashion to lead us to define as "global" those problems that are merely ubiquitous, for the sufficient reason that we have not yet been able to invent a global *Leviathan*, not even a limited one. The pollution of rivers and lakes is ubiquitous, but we are making progress in cleaning up Lake Erie not by defining it as part of a global commons that includes Lake Baikal and the Rhine River but by treating it as a purely local problem (where "local" includes an entire drainage system). Most people recognize that eutrophication is a local problem, and so we have been spared the nonsense of "global eutrophication."

Starvation also is a local problem, one created by allowing the resident population to grow beyond the carrying capacity of the sovereign nation in which it lives. Unfortunately, the essentially local nature of this problem is denied by people who speak of "global hunger." In the absence of a global sovereign, the phrase "global hunger" cannot give rise to practical policy recommendations.

In recent years the public has often been misled by the thoughtless repetition of the fashionable word "interdependent." A population that has grown beyond the carrying capacity of its home territory often makes demands on other populations because (it is said) "we are interdependent." At the present time populations in desperate need of food are typically increasing at 2 to 3 percent per year, so the "solution" of sharing tends to perpetuate unidirectional *dependence*. (Some people apparently do not know what *inter-* means.) The concepts of "global" and "interdependence" are counterproductive when they foster parasitism. Parasitism is not a wise use of resources; if nothing else, it involves wasteful transportation of materials.

Returning to the local scene we note a multitude of ways in which the squandering of resources, particularly energy, is encouraged by institutional arrangements created and defended by individuals or groups pursuing their own interests. Railroads charge more to transport steel scrap destined for recycling than they do to move new iron ore. Soft drink bottlers oppose laws that would compel the recycling of bottles. The taxicab that takes you to a distant airport is, in many cities, legally forbidden to pick up a return passenger. Intercity trucks are often compelled to travel long distances empty. Industries that produce excess heat are forbidden to use it to generate some of their own electricity ("cogeneration" of product and electricity). Railroad unions indulge in "featherbedding" and bureaucrats pad their rosters to create demands for larger budgets that will enhance their political power. Wasteful throwaway packaging enriches the makers of packages. For every four trees cut down for newsprint only one ends up in the news columns, the other three being devoted to advertisements, most of which most people most of the time do not look at. And so on. It is the seeming compulsiveness of all this waste that leads the Man from Mars to conclude that progress has spawned a squanderarchy.

The pathological processes that led to the present state of affairs are not hard to understand. The "invisible hand" that Adam Smith uncovered in 1776 was, for a while, thought to be universal. Then closer observation showed that quite often politico-economic evolution is governed by a contrary sort of process: in serving his own interests *directly* the individual may go against the interests of society as a whole (and of himself indirectly, though only marginally). In such cases society is, as Herman Daly has said, kicked by an "invisible foot." We might rewrite the relevant passage in *The Wealth of Nations* thus: "Every individual, laboring to increase his revenue as much as possible, and never trying to promote the public interest when doing so would diminish his direct gain, is moved, as it were, by an invisible foot that makes matters worse for society, though this is no part of his intention." The invisible foot is, of course, involved in the tragedy of the commons.

Changes in public attitudes since Earth Day, 22 April 1970, justify a certain amount of optimism about the prospects of our changing from a squanderarchy to a conserver society. How far we will go in this direction, and how rapidly, are questions on which there are justifiable differences of opinion. Before discussing the problems of making the transition, let us look at some of the more obvious differences between the two kinds of economy. The accompanying table does not pretend to be exhaustive; it should, however, be useful in provoking discussion.

A squanderarchy (line 1 of the following table) presumes a limitless world in which the insatiable demands of consumers promote a rapid turnover of materials and a swift degradation of useful energy ("negative entropy"). By contrast, a conserver society presumes a limited world in which people try to conserve materials and energy. Squanderers, as Thorstein Veblen pointed out long ago, make a fashion of "conspicuous consumption." Conservers, by contrast, quote with approval lines from the Talmud: "Who is rich? He who rejoices in his lot." Conservers recommend that we learn to be content with what we have. At its extreme the conserver ethic tries to create a fashion of "con-

## Contrasts Between a Squanderarchy and a Conserver Society

| Characteristic | Squanderarchy | Conserver Society |
|---|---|---|
| 1. Universe assumed | Limitless | Limited |
| 2. Basic good | Consumption | Conservation |
| 3. Esthetic ideal | Rapid turnover a joy | Lingering enjoyment |
| 4. Fashionable ideal | Conspicuous consumption | Conspicuous penury |
| 5. Consumer credit | Wildly promoted | Discouraged, restricted |
| 6. Vacation travel | Good | Bad |
| 7. Worker mobility | A public good | A public danger |
| 8. Labor-saving devices | Virtuous | Sinful, given unemployment |
| 9. Energy saving | A sin | A virtue |
| 10. Damage: burden of proof | "Innocent until proven guilty" | "Guilty until proven innocent" |
| 11. Commercial innovation | Fast | Slow |
| 12. Objective freedom | Greater | Less |
| 13. Psychological freedom | Less (?) | Potentially greater |
| 14. The Seven Deadly Sins | Only sloth a sin; pride, lust, covetousness, envy, gluttony, and anger are virtues | All are sins (except pride and lust, in moderation?) |
| 15. Advertising | | |
| a. Informational | A public good | A public good |
| b. Seductive ("Spend!") | A public good | A public bad |
| c. Competitive | A public good | A public bad |
| 16. Semantics used when Demand exceeds Supply | "Shortage"—of Supply | "Longage"—of Demand |

spicuous penury." For example, some rich young women pay high prices for prefaded, prepatched blue jeans (line 4 of the table).

Consumption is encouraged in the squanderarchy by the vigorous promotion of credit cards and "buying on time." Conservers should discourage most forms of consumer credit, perhaps outlawing some. Vacation travel, extravagant of energy, must be strongly discouraged in a conserving society. For example, we should discontinue the recent practice of shifting a national holiday to Monday because this arrangement creates a long weekend which allows—as was intended—workers to leave home. A return to midweek holidays, by making extensive automobile journeys impossible, would reduce the consumption of petroleum energy (line 6).

Worker mobility in general will be more discouraged in a conserver society. Business managers have long favored worker mobility, finding the task of planning easier if workers can be moved around the country like chessmen on a chessboard (line 7). The economies claimed for this practice are partly, perhaps largely, spurious: most of the social costs impinge first on the worker and his family when they are moved from the old environment in which their social positions are secure into a new one in which parents and children are to some extent aliens. Part of the cost, in the form of increased juvenile delinquency and crime, are ultimately passed on to society at large. It is the commonization of such social costs that enables decision makers in business firms to be unaware of the true costs of the social mobility they praise and encourage.

In getting the world's work done, energy and labor are trade-offs (lines 8 and 9). In the past we have been told that every labor-saving invention is *ipso facto* good, being assured that in the long run it will increase employment. The persistence of unemployment (the full perception of which is obscured by many forms of "hidden unemployment") now makes us doubt this simple faith. The rapidly-increasing cost of fossil energy is making more and more people seriously consider the desirability of reversing history, in part, by substituting muscle power for fossil fuel power. Recently, a Secretary of Agriculture announced that the government will not continue to finance research aimed at developing new machines to displace human labor in agriculture. In line with this change in policy, an organization of attorneys called California Rural Legal Assistance has sued the University of California to cease channeling agricultural funds into research designed to replace men with machines. Almost two centuries ago English workmen, under the banner of a mythical King Ludd, tried to stop the march of the machine, only to be massacred, jailed, and transported. History, which is written by the victors, said the Luddites were wrong then; will it repeat this verdict as we change into a conserver society?

Among the most striking differences between the squanderarchy of the past and the conserver society we are becoming is in the attitude toward innovations in products or processes. In the past each new product put on the market has been assumed to be innocent of danger (line 10). "Innocent until proven guilty" is an old principle of Anglo-Saxon law. When a new product proved faulty or dangerous, the expense of litigation discouraged law suits. Innovation flourished. Then came the disaster of the thalidomide babies, resulting in the passage of the Kefauver-Harris amendments to the Food, Drug, and Cosmetic Act. Thus, in the year of *Silent Spring*, was the assumption of Anglo-Saxon law fundamentally revised (as far as medicine was concerned), resulting in a new presumption: "Guilty until proven innocent." The National Environmental Policy Act (NEPA) carried this revolution over into the environmental area beginning 1 January 1970. With ever greater frequency, proposed alterations in the environment (building of dams, filling in of sloughs, and construction of thermonuclear plants) are held up until the results of an "environmental impact study" (EIS) are examined and approved by some authority. This change in the presumption of the law unquestionably slows up commercial and technological innovation (line 11). The change is both good and bad.

Objectively, the people living under a squanderarchy are certainly freer (line 12). Subjective truth is another matter. "Freedom is the recognition of necessity," said Hegel. Perceiving the necessity of the restrictions imposed by conservation may actually make conservers psychologically more free than squanderers (line 13). But the adjustment will take time. In the interim the public outcry against the loss of freedom may slow, or even stop, the shift to a conserving society.

One of the most profound differences between conserving and squandering societies is essentially religious. In the sixth century St. Gregory the Great named the Seven Deadly Sins: pride, covetousness, lust, envy, gluttony, anger, and sloth. For over a thousand years Christians viewed these sins seriously. Then came the idea of progress and its subsequent melding with commitments to innovation and consumption. As Lewis Mumford has pointed out, the "insatiability of demands" took on the status of a sacred principle, and—except for sloth—all the deadly sins were, in effect, converted into virtues because they promoted consumption. Ministers of religion ceased to dwell on the Seven Deadly Sins, no doubt because they subconsciously sensed the latent antipathy in their commercially oriented congregations. As we move toward a conserver society it will be interesting to see if the Seven Deadly Sins once more become fashionable topics for sermons.

As things stand now I think the Man from Mars would identify *Playboy* magazine as one of the sacred documents of our squanderarchy, not because of its photographs but by virtue of the advertisements with their incessant glorification of all forms of consumption. *Playboy* can stand as the exemplar of all advertising.

As a medium of information—a way of telling people what is for sale, where, and for how much—advertising serves a useful purpose in every sort of economy (line 15). But modern advertising has grown far beyond this simple function. The major purpose of advertising now is to seduce people into buying more than they need, and to do this it subtly glorifies every sin except sloth. When needs are satisfied, customers are badgered into changing brands. This is usually a socially trivial act. (What difference does it make whether you use *Tweedledum* toothpaste or *Tweedledee* toothpaste?) The purely competitive aspect of advertising is largely a social bad, since it increases waste.

In 1978 the cost of advertising in the United States was $44 billion. Because this sum was only 2 percent of the gross national product (GNP) we might be tempted to dismiss it as trivial. But before doing so we should ask, How much wasteful consumption was fostered by this 2 percent of the GNP? There is no objective answer to this question because "wasteful" implies standards on which opinion is divided. Nevertheless it is probable that most people who are committed to the conserver ethic would estimate that the waste caused by advertising far exceeds 2 percent of the GNP.

Of much greater importance is the bearing of advertising on human freedom. Television is the most important medium of information in the lives of Americans, "information" being used in the widest sense. There are 168 hours in the week. Let us assume that 40 of these hours are used for work, 56 for sleep, 8 for necessary local transportation (to offices, schools, and shops), and 10 for eating. Subtracting these 114 hours from the weekly total leaves a supply of "disposable time" of 54 hours per week. According to A. C. Nielsen, the average American in 1978 spent 30.4 hours per week viewing television. That figures out at 56 percent of the disposable time. Most of the programs watched are commercial programs. Considering the great skill with which TV advertisements are constructed and the pervasiveness of their messages, how free are people, really, to do their own thing? We still thrill to John Milton's praise of free speech and condemnation of censorship: "Let Truth and Falsehood grapple; who ever knew Truth put to the worse in a free and open encounter?" But is it a "free and open" encounter when an unknown but certainly quite small sum spent on denouncing the Seven Deadly Sins is opposed by $44 billion spent in praising six of them?

We have gone far beyond Milton. Many psychologists, notably B. F. Skinner, have convinced us that—to a large extent—we are what we are conditioned to be. The key issue in freedom is this: Who controls the conditioning process—and who controls the controller? This is a deep and subtle problem. It is central to the problem of changing from one type of society to another—or not changing.

The preceding analysis has implicitly assumed that a historical change of the following sort is possible:

$$\text{Squanderarchy} \rightarrow \text{Conserver Society} \qquad (1)$$

But is it? We can find many reasons for doubting this. For one thing a large and influential literature has treated perpetual growth as the only conceivable—or only moral—state of affairs. A civilization that has scoffed at the fatalism of traditional societies has created a fatalism of its own, a "Grow or Die" fatalism. In the depths of the Great Depression, Stuart Chase wrote:

> Abundance demands no compromise. It will not operate at half speed. It will not allow retreat to an earlier level and stabilization there. Pharaoh did not tell the Nile what to do; the Nile told Pharaoh what to do. The industrial discipline must be accepted—all of it—or it must be renounced. The only retreat is back one hundred years to the Economy of Scarcity.

The unacceptability of restraint was underlined by Nicholas Rescher a generation later when he said: "An *economy of scarcity* is, by definition, one in which justice . . . cannot be done, because there is not 'enough to go around'. . . ."

Despite the conservation literature of the past two decades fatalism is still evident in the writings of influential commentators of today. Consider, for instance, Irving Kristol:

There is far too much easy and glib talk these days about the need for Americans to tighten their belts, accept a reduction in their living standards, even resign themselves to an economic philosophy of no-growth. It is dangerous and irresponsible talk. Yes, of course, the American democracy can cope with a *temporary* cessation of economic growth, as it has done in wartime. But only if it is perceived to be temporary. What few seem to realize is that a prospect of economic growth is a crucial precondition for the survival of any modern democracy, the American included. . . . It is only so long as economic growth remains a credible reality that democracy will remain an actuality.

The interest vested in promoting perpetual growth is enormous. The most important fraction of this interest is probably that of the $44 billion advertising industry. It is, therefore, of considerable interest to note that many influential members of this segment are seriously examining the role they might play in a world devoted to conservation rather than to squandering. At a conference on "The Conserver Society" held at the University of Texas in November of 1979 and sponsored by the American Marketing Association, many leaders of the industry expressed confidence in the adaptability of their art to the needs of conservation. The skills of "marketing" (which includes advertising) can, they said, promote conservation as well as consumption. But one thing bothered them: who would pay marketers to persuade people to *not* consume?

It is not only marketers who must be paid to facilitate conservation; so also must many other people, and it is not obvious how this is to be done. The long-term trend toward bureaucracy may seem to imply that a no-growth (or low-growth) conserver society will be a coercive society run by bureaucrats, but Charles L. Schultz suggests another possibility: a society that makes better use of market mechanisms to serve the public interest. Market-like arrangements can "minimize the need of coercion as a means of organizing society. . . . A market approach . . . stresses incentives, not rights and duties. People or firms act in certain ways because their self-interest dictates doing so, given the existing set of incentives."

As the comic-strip character *Pogo* says, we are faced with overwhelming opportunities. If the inventive genius so evident in science and technology during the two centuries of "Progress" can be transferred to the realm of politics and economics, we may be able to make a moderately smooth transition along the line indicated by Equation 1 above. But if our abilities prove unequal to this task, the transition may take a different course:

$$\text{Squanderarchy} \rightarrow \text{Poverty \& Chaos} \rightarrow \text{Conserver Society} \quad (2)$$

We may have to pass through a new Dark Ages before emerging into the light of a sensible, comfortable, conserving society. Between the beginning and the end there may have to be a painful political discontinuity.

If I were betting on the future where would I place my bet—on passage (*1*) or passage (*2*)? If I were the Man from Mars I daresay I would bet on the second passage. But, as a participant observer of the human comedy, I confess that I will be satisfied with myself only if I do what I can to promote the first passage.

It is part of the conventional wisdom of our time to suppose that a no-growth economy is inherently unstable—this despite the fact that most human societies, most of the time, have lived under no-growth conditions. As Kristol worded the unexamined assumption of our day: "It is the expectation of tomorrow's bigger pie, from which everyone will receive a larger slice, that prevents people from fighting to the bitter end over the division of today's pie."

No doubt there is much truth in this, yet we cannot forget the Talmud: *Who is rich? He who rejoices in his lot.* We need to be quite explicit about the possible roads to wealth.

The definition of wealth can be given as an equation:

$$\text{Wealth} = \frac{\text{Supply}}{\text{Demand}} \quad (3)$$

The technique of dimensional analysis, as developed by physicists, can be applied to this. "Supply" has the dimension of material things, the sort of things listed in handbooks of resources (multiplied, of course, by a fractional factor standing for the technological "state of the art"). Demand, by contrast, in both its origins and its enduring meaning is psychological in its dimension. Wealth is therefore also psychological in dimension—as the Talmudist (and many others) realized centuries ago. *No technological advance can take wealth out of the psychological dimension.*

There are two ways for an individual to become rich: by increasing the supply (if he can), or by decreasing his demand. If the supply cannot be increased the wise person seeks to decrease his demands (expectations, aspirations, desires, wants—call them what you will). Such is reality for the individual.

When we consider a population of individuals the wealth equation needs to be expanded:

$$\text{Wealth} = \frac{\text{Supply}}{(\text{Per capita demand}) \times (\text{Size of population})} \quad (4)$$

With a limited supply, wealth can be increased by either of two routes: lowering the expectations of the average individual, or decreasing the number of individuals. The two forms of demand control can be combined.

In a world of limits we can become wealthy only if we subject ourselves to the discipline of demand control. This will not be easy for many reasons, not the least of which is a semantic one. Confronted with a painful discrepancy between supply and demand the prisoners of a squanderarchy invariably speak of a *shortage* of supply. Why do they never speak of a *longage* of demand? Logically, one expression is as apt as the other: why do we always choose the first?

It must be admitted that only the word "shortage" can be found in the dictionary. The earliest usage recorded in the *Oxford English Dictionary* dates from 1868. The word "longage" seems not to have been coined until 1975. It is easy to see how natural selection favors egotistical organisms that make demands on their environment, organisms which (if they can speak) readily complain of "shortages." It is hard for selection to favor organisms that are willing to curb their demands when in competition with organisms that will not. Demand control, though recommended by gurus for millennia, has not been the practice of the masses. Competition has not favored demand control. Yet this is precisely what a conserver society must achieve if it is to be happy in a limited world.

Confronted with an unconventional way of looking at common realities the human mind has a wonderful ability to quietly and instantly repress language that threatens egotistical impulses. Boulding's attempts (in 1945 and 1949) to get economists to reexamine their world view of "throughput" and "stock" in terms of consumption and conservation produced (he reports) no response whatever for more than twenty years. Not until his classic paper of 1966 did his ideas get the attention they deserved. The shift was no doubt attributable in part to a change in the intellectual climate; but it may also be that a novel idea takes several decades to mature to the stage in which it is visible to the masses.

To speak of "shortage" is to predispose the mind to look only for ways to increase supply. By speaking of "longage" we force our minds to consider the possibility of decreasing demand. "Shortage" is the semantics of a squanderarchy, "longage" the language of a conserver society.

If the world is indeed limited, conservation is required; but the level of living at which conservation is practiced is theoretically a matter of choice. A community can opt for the largest possible population; in this case individuals will be happy only if they succeed in minimizing their per capita demands. Alternatively, a community can opt for population control; if population is kept at a low level, the per capita demands (desires, aspirations, standards) can be correspondingly high. Population control offers the *possibility* of achieving psychological wealth without a policy of penury. Of course we do not yet know how to control population by "acceptable" means because the word "acceptable" has psychological dimensions that are as yet unexplored. Therein lie the problems of population and prosperity.

# LANGUAGE, THE SUBTLE ENEMY

# 25

## *The Threat of Clarity*

He who speaks in favor of unclarity raises a justifiable suspicion that he merely seeks to attract attention; or worse, that he is promoting a subtle form of anti-intellectualism. To be accused of either is a serious matter, but every now and then, I think, someone must run the risk in hope of sensitizing us once more to the ever-present dangers of language. Language should periodically be put on trial, and when it is, even its accepted virtues, *e.g.*, clarity, must be doubted. Those who judge must listen to a devil's advocate. This is the role I play here in pointing out the dangers of clarity—or, if you wish, of "clarity."

Language subserves two functions: communication and thinking. As regards the first, it is perhaps not possible usefully to doubt the desirability of clarity. Of course, there is the superficial unclarity of tact, of poetry and parable, and of the replies of a skilled psychiatrist—but all these art forms can, from a more profound standpoint, be defended as real (though subtle) kinds of clarity in communication.

It is only when we come to consider language in its role *in thinking* that we begin to see a sense in which it is doubtful if clarity is always desirable. Ours is a language-limited world. We not only speak our language: we think in it, as a fish lives in water. For the most part we see the world as our language tells us to. Each of the many languages has its peculiar limitations which shut out certain aspects or views of reality to those who speak but one language. He who "masters" but one language may thereby be mastered by it. To be completely "at home" in a language is to be structured to fit one particular and limited world of thought.

A few simple examples of the coupling of words to perception may be useful. Eskimos have separate words for falling-snow, snow-on-the-ground, wind-driven-snow, snow-packed-into-ice, etc.; we make do with one word—*snow*. Half a world away, Argentine gauchos have names to distinguish some 200 different color patterns in horses. The reason for diversity is obvious in both cases: interest dictated by culture. But distinctions, once made, "feed back" into the mind and cause it to perceive as much or as little variety in the world as language has words for. The gaucho who distinguishes 200 colors of horses lumps the vegetable world into 4 "species": *pasto* or fodder; *paja* or bedding straw; *cardo* or woody material; and *yuyos* for all other plants, including lilies, roses, and cabbages. (The class of *yuyos* reminds us of the grab-bag group *Chaos*, which Linnaeus, the father of taxonomy, resorted to when he despaired of completing his analysis of the living world.) It would be going too far to say that the gauchos can see only four kinds of plants, but undoubtedly their perceptual world is impoverished by their linguistic one. Experimental evidence for this principle has been obtained by Lenneberg who has found that an English-speaking person can, in a nonverbal test, more easily identify those colors that have recognized names in English than he can the distinguishable hues that have no names.

Cautiously interpreted, the language of another people is a clue to their psychology. Rabbi Blau has remarked how curious it is "that the Hebrew language, though impoverished in many respects has preserved [in Leviticus xxi and in both *Tochechoth*] so many words that describe unsightly malformations and loathsome diseases. We lack classic Hebrew terms for many of the beautiful sights and sounds of this world— for colors, flowers, trees, birds—but we do not seem to be wanting in terms that bring before us the seamy side of life, that echo the groans of the sufferers, that reflect the gloom of darkened lives. One is reminded of those old-fashioned books on theology that contained nine chapters on hell and only one chapter on heaven." There are many chances for error, of course, in deducing a people's psychology from their language, as is suggested by the following puzzle. The two Greek words *chloros* and *achros* both have dictionary translations of "yellow." But usage indicates that the former sometimes means yellowish green, sometimes grayish brown; and the latter sometimes means greenish yellow, and at other times red (of all things). What's going on here? It is hard to believe that the words refer only to color, but attempts to include intensity or luster in their meanings have only made the snarl worse. In desperation, one linguist has suggested that all the old Greeks must have been color-blind!

Does perception produce language, or language produce perception? This question is clearly in a class with "Which came first, the chicken or the egg?" and there is no need to take sides. Whatever the origin of linguistic distinctions, once made they are part of a cybernetic system of mutual support of language and perception. Call it a vicious circle, if you will. But it is not unbreakable: new cultural demands may force a finer analysis. Thus, in our own part of the world, we observe ski enthusiasts enlarging the language about snow to make it as finely discriminating as the Eskimos'. Regarding objective things like snow and horses and trees, we need not concern ourselves over much with the limitations of a particular vocabulary, for it will enlarge when there is a cultural need for it to do so.

It is words of another sort that give us trouble—the words that stand for large classes of things, or for abstractions or difficult concepts. Here the coupling of word and reality is often excruciatingly *loose*. "What is intelligence?" "What is the cause of insanity?" "How can we control the unconscious?" Who has not winced at such questions? How can one possibly answer them? Yet, grammatically speaking, they look so simple, so clear! What is wrong?

The simplest objection to them is that each key word covers a confused multitude of concepts or things. Intelligence, for example, is a grab-bag term including at least four—and possibly nine or more—different abilities. "The unconscious" is capable of at least sixteen different interpretations. And "insanity"—who is so mad as to attempt to catalog its complexity? But the real problem posed by such words is far deeper than appears at first.

It must not be supposed that an attempt to find out what is behind such "big" words as "intelligence" and the "unconscious" will be warmly welcomed. These words, besides having the support of a long tradition, play an important role in the sociology of knowledge: they stop inquiry where it is most painful and difficult (and, it must be admitted, most likely to fail). When we say that "Intelligence solves our problems," or "The mind resists change," we think we have explained something. But an honest examination convinces us that we have "explained" only by resort to words whose meaning is so vague that they can "explain" almost anything. A word which acts as an explain-all has been called a *panchreston*, a word coined on the analogy of panacea, a cure-all. The history of human thought is littered with discarded panchresta: the many personal and omnipotent gods, the soul, and the "humours" of medieval medicine, for example. Bergson created an *élan vital* to explain the properties of living things; Driesch conceived an *entelechy* to explain the mysteries of embryology. "Mind," "instinct," and "love," though they may have defensible denotations, are certainly often used panchrestically. The literature of psychoanalysis is riddled with explain-alls: a single (and by no means exceptional) quotation should suffice: "The ego becomes suspicious: it proceeds to invade the territory of the id."

If the physiology of language is to promote communication and thinking, the inhibition of these functions may be regarded as part of language's pathology. Always, of course, in a deep sense, pathology is as "normal" as the normal physiology in which it has its roots. "Every language," said the linguist Benjamin Lee Whorf, "incorporates certain points of view and certain patterned resistances to widely divergent points of view," and it is these points of view that determine both the strengths and the weaknesses of each language. As in so much of biology, discovery is greatly aided by comparative study. Experience has shown that the comparison of Indo-European languages among themselves has yielded only modest increments of knowledge: the greatest gain has been made when our languages have been compared with strikingly different tongues, for example with the many Indian dialects of

North America, a program of study in which Sapir and Whorf have been leaders.

The comparative study of two languages should throw as much light on the strengths and weaknesses of one as on the other—if carried out by a really neutral observer. In fact, however, the very few observers who have been equipped for this difficult work have been Indo-Europeans, and the most they have been able to do is lay bare the structure of *our* kind of language, using the exotic language as a probe. The reciprocal knowledge, desirable as it would be to have, is scarcely available. It is for this reason that only the characteristic weaknesses of Indo-European languages will be pointed out in the paragraphs to follow. The one-sided presentation does not stem from a Rousseau-like belief in the "noble savage." The savage has his troubles, too, but we should consider ourselves lucky enough if we come to understand our own.

We can begin with a very simple example, the analysis of which shows that our language is more mysterious than we ordinarily realize. Consider the declarative sentence, *"It rains."* What is the *it* that rains? Well, *rain* rains . . . but that is an odd sentence, isn't it? "Rain" must be the implied antecedent of "it," but we never, in ordinary conversation, say "Rain rains"; always we assert the predicate of some vague and unspecified subject "it." We also say "It thunders," and we may say "it lightnings." Why? As Whorf has pointed out, we are compelled to make such sentences because of an overriding metaphysical assumption of the Indo-European languages that everything in the world has two poles—an actor pole and an action pole, and that one cannot exist without the other, any more than a magnet can have a north pole only. The actor we represent by the subject of the sentence; the action by the verb. Always there must be both; so when we have trouble finding the actor for such processes as raining, thundering, and flashing (of lightning), we invent a subject called "it" to stand as actor. We would feel uneasy just saying "Rains!" or "Thunders!" or "Flashes!"

Other peoples feel otherwise. Hopi Indians, confronted with the same objective realities, use only the verbs without subjects, and feel quite secure. The metaphysic of their language is different and permits—even insists—that they use verbs-without-subjects to represent the events we denote by the nouns *lightning, wave, flame, meteor, puff of smoke,* and *pulsation.* The decision to invoke the noun category or the verb category in giving name to fact is as unconscious in the one language as in the other. As Émile Meyerson has said, "L'homme fait de la métaphysique comme il respire, sans le vouloir et surtout sans s'en douter la plupart du temps." Comparative linguistic study makes it immensely easier for us to discover the unconscious metaphysic of our language and to make allowance for it.

Failure to appreciate the role of the structure of Indo-European languages in affecting perception has repeatedly led western science into error. The "luminiferous ether" of classical physics was created for the express purpose of standing as a subject of the verb "to wave." When the Michelson-Morley experiment and Einstein's analysis finally showed that the substantive ether had to be abandoned, the decision was a traumatic one. Similarly, in biology, the substantive "protoplasm" was created to stand as the subject of such verbs as "to metabolize." Led by F. G. Hopkins, biologists are now abandoning the substantive as a scientific concept.

The structure of our language has probably played an important role in determining the order in which we have uncovered natural phenomena. Compare, for example, the ease with which we discovered and accepted the germ theory of disease with the difficulty encountered by the vitamin theory of nutrition. The former advance was made in a few decades in the latter half of the nineteenth century. Vitamins, by contrast, had to be discovered and rediscovered repeatedly—by Hawkins (1593), Lancaster (1601), Woodall (1639), Lind (1753), and Captain Cook (1772), among others—and yet at no time was the knowledge stabilized until Hopkins clearly defined the phenomenon (1906) and Funk named it (1912). Why was a vitamin so hard to accept and a disease germ so easy? Was the reason not, at least in part, because the latter fitted in with the metaphysic of Indo-European languages so much more easily than the former? We already had sentences of this sort, "A spirit makes him sick," in which we had only to substitute a new actor, *e.g.*, *Eberthella typhosa*, to create a new doctrine. In contrast, the sentence "What he doesn't eat makes him sick," failed to make sense to men who spoke, and thought, Indo-European. Biochemists had to find a substance to name, and had to create the substantive "vitamin" to stand as actor in a new sort of sentence, before the new idea could carry conviction. Even today, we still backslide frequently and say "He has an avitaminosis," though how one can *have* a lack of something is most mysterious. Such sentences are just part of the pathology of our language.

The comparative historical study of the germ theory and the vitamin theory leads us to realize that there are at least two different kinds of analysis involved in scientific advance. The first kind we may speak of as the analysis by simple subdivision. The type question may be given in symbolic form: "Is all fruit, fruit—or are there apples and oranges?" Once the question is asked, success in finding an answer is almost assured. When one suspects diversity, he usually finds it. Thus the skier discovers many kinds of snow and the physician many kinds of fever. The "typhus" fever of 200 years ago was found to be differentiable into two diseases—typhus and typhoid. Malaria gave way to malarias, and unitary hemophilia to many different hemophilias. Similarly, such classical psychiatric entities as schizophrenia must yield to *subdivisive analysis*. The work is not easy, but we always know what it is that we are trying to do.

The second type of analysis is far more difficult for it involves changes in the categories of thought. We may call it *categorical analysis*. The type question takes this symbolic form: "Is it an apple or an orange that I'm dealing with—or is it perhaps the singing of a bird?" So stated, it sounds ridiculous; but inability to ask such an odd-sounding question has repeatedly delayed the progress of science.

Consider "heat," for example. From the time of the ancient Greeks down to, and including, the work of Robert Boyle, the facts connected with heat were terribly confused because "heat" was assigned to the wrong category—that of the substantives. Being a substance, it should have weight, of course; convinced of this, a British physician, George Fordyce, found that heat did indeed have weight. The first experiments of Count Rumford seemed to confirm this belief. But Rumford was convinced that the wrong category of thought was being employed in calorimetric studies; so he went to a great deal of trouble to look for experimental errors, which he found and corrected, thus arriving at the correct conclusion that heat, like the singing of a bird, is an activity, a process—and not a substance or object, like apples or oranges. Its category has rather more to do with verbs than with nouns.

Subdivisive analysis is (comparatively) easy. Categorical analysis is always difficult. There are no rules for it. It requires insight and courage (or insanity) to slash away the unconscious strictures of language. Such action may generate an almost unbearable load of insecurity in the analyzer. Traditional language always *seems* clear. There seems to be great clarity in such sentences as these: *Heat flows. Life left him. He is possessed of a devil. He has a disease. He has a neurosis.* But, for all their apparent clarity, they are surely all wrong. Their categories are wrong. All of them assert false substantives, when the discussion should be couched in terms of processes.

It is not easy to abandon false language, nor need it always be completely abandoned when it is traditional. There may be no words, or only awkward language, for correct ideas that are new, and we cannot, as human beings cut ourselves off from the support of our fellow men while we grope for new speech. As Thomas Mann said, "The word, even the most contradictory word, preserves contact—it is silence that isolates." We cannot let linguistic perfectionism isolate us while we indulge in analysis. In the meantime, we must speak, even though we recognize that our idiom is, in some sense, false. So we say, "The sun sets" and "Heat flows," though we know these are false statements. So also may we continue to say, "He has an avitaminosis," or "She has a neurosis," though we know these statements are also false. For the sake of the present we must continue to speak; but for the sake of the future we must continue to analyze our language. And analysis, as Wittgenstein has said, is "the battle against the bewitchment of our intelligence by means of language." This battle is not part of a push-button war waged from afar. We are in the midst of this battle as we are in the midst of life itself, using as a weapon against language, language itself. There is no other.

# 26

## *The Ghost of Authority*

The controversy over the propriety of contraception, which has raged for almost a century, seems on the verge of being settled. Propaganda in favor of contraception was begun by Francis Place in 1822, but discussion of this tabooed idea was muted until the subject was brought into the open in 1877 by the trial of Charles Bradlaugh and Annie Besant. Thereafter, decade by decade, the volume of disputatious literature increased, the rate of production reaching a climax in the late 1950s as it became clear that birth control is not only a private matter but is also an issue in which population growth has created an inescapable public interest.

Two recent collections of materials written by Roman Catholics suggest an imminent settling of the dispute in a way that will be reasonably satisfactory to both Catholics and non-Catholics. Once resolved, a controversy ceases to be of keen interest per se; but since it is certain that comparable differences of opinion on other issues will appear in the future, it is of more than antiquarian interest to identify the factors involved in the resolution of past difficulties. In the sexual sphere alone we see several issues that threaten public peace: abortion, sterilization, and artificial insemination, to mention only the more obvious. What can we learn from the course of the birth-control controversy that may help in resolving the disputes ahead of us?

Dipping into the rather large literature on this subject I have been forcibly struck by the remarkable and (to me) unexpected change that has taken place in the attitude of practicing Roman Catholics toward the concept of authority. For the most part the change is no more than implicit in the discussions; but once the reader has become sensitive to it he finds it all pervasive. Because quotable, explicit statements are so few, there is a danger that the remarkable developments in this area will be entirely lost from sight in a short time and hence will fail to serve the valuable pedagogic function of history. We like to believe that "history teaches," but, as Thomas Kuhn has demonstrated, in the evolution of science at least, there are self-healing processes in the recording of history which tend to cover the wounds of each resolved controversy, leaving visible only the final conclusions, thus depriving posterity of useful insights into the processes by which controversies are brought to an end. The recording of history by even the best intentioned of people is uncomfortably reminiscent of that depicted in George Orwell's *1984*.

What we may call the classical attitude toward authority is displayed in the following quotation from Patrick J. Ward: "The Catholic Church teaches that the artificial prevention of conception by mechanical, chemical or other means is intrinsically evil. Since this is the universal moral law, it applies with equal force to Catholic and non-Catholic." Notice that this statement not only asserts a particular doctrine about contraception but also asserts the authority of the Catholic church to settle questions of right and wrong. Implicit, but just as real, is the assertion that authority exists—that there are documents, men, or institutions whose pronouncements determine or define the truth. Is this true? Does authority exist?

It should be clear that the word "authority" in this context has quite a different meaning from its use in scientific literature. When we say "Smith, 1961, found that . . ." we are not establishing the subsequent statement as true but merely assigning Smith the responsibility for correctly reporting the evidence. In principle, science is built on indefinitely repeatable observations; but in practice, as a matter of economy, we do not establish from the ground up every observation on which a particular conclusion is based. He who doubts a particular fact can repeat the work himself. "If it isn't true, don't blame me, blame Smith"—this is the meaning of authority in science.

The authority theologians confront us with is quite a different thing. This authority validates, proves, establishes, or defines truth. It is somehow prior to, or superior to, observation and reason; and it is certainly not to be questioned. Every western religion—if one excepts borderline institutions like the Unitarian church—assumes the validity of authority. The greatest and most powerful church of all asserts its authority most explicitly, particularly since the Vatican decree of 1870 which established as apparently inescapable orthodoxy a belief in the infallibility of the Pope. Because of this belief, consequences of great moment were set in train by the encyclical *Casti connubii*, which Pope Pius XI published on the last day of 1930. In it he said: "Any use whatsoever of matrimony exercised in such a way that the act is deliberately frustrated in its natural power to generate life is an offence against the law of God and of nature, and those who indulge in such are branded with the guilt of a grave sin."

One might expect that such a solid statement would put an end to dissension and aberrant practice within the church; but it did not. Public opinion surveys during the next thirty years showed that an increasing number of Roman Catholics were using methods of birth control that had been condemned by papal authority.

How did the communicants justify their sin (as defined by the Pope)? No doubt in many different ways, but their rationalizations were almost all made in private, and hence it would be hazardous to discuss them. The ordeal of conscientious members of the church finally came out into the open with the publication of *The Time Has Come* by John Rock, a Catholic physician who had played an important part in the development of the contraceptive progesterone pill. Dr. Rock argued that "the pill" should be licit for Catholics. An important part of his argument revolved around the meaning of "Natural Law," a concept which (in spite of its name) does not lie in the realm of the natural sciences but is, rather, a theological invention. This aspect of Rock's book will be by-passed here in order to plunge directly to the heart of the problem of authority. Rock does not devote much space to this matter, but (signifi-cantly) he places his remarks at the very beginning of his story. In the preface he recalls a day from his childhood. He was a shy boy of four-teen, and Father Finnick, a curate of his parish, had invited him to come on a visit to the Poor Farm.

> I shall never forget the short slow ride in the small buggy down East Main Street to the Sudbury road. . . .
> I don't remember how the conversation started, if you could even call it that. We did not interrupt Father in class, as he gently but firmly expounded Catholic doctrine to us: now also, I listened intently. I noticed, as we jogged along, the big Walcott house set back behind a wide lawn on the right side of East Main Street about halfway to our turnoff at the Sudbury road.
> It was just then that he said, "John, always stick to your con-science. Never let anyone else keep it for you." And, after but a moment's pause, he added, "And I mean *anyone* else."

When Father Finnick said, "Never let anyone else keep it for you," did he have any mental reservations? From the following sentence it is surely clear that he made no exceptions. From John Rock's remem-brance and repetition of the story, one presumes that Rock also makes no exceptions. That neither of them has been more explicit is under-standable; perhaps those of us who are bystanders should decently join them in this reticence.

A few years after Rock's book, an even more astonishing document came from England, from a Roman Catholic convert, the mother of seven children, a physician who had opened up a birth-control clinic. The author, Dr. Anne Biezanek, was led to her unusual position by painful personal experience. She tells us:

> Suspicion dawned that a domestic crisis was approaching. Our house went with my job. I could see for myself and quite clearly

that I could not continue to hold this, or any other job, if I continued to give birth to children with such regularity. . . . I explained the danger I felt I was in to the Roman Catholic chaplain at the hospital where I worked, and he seemed to understand for he had doubtless come across problems like this before. He advised that I should procure the services of an able spiritual director, and he then recommended one to me by name. He also explained to me that for spiritual direction to work in accordance with the whole Roman Catholic spiritual theory one must place oneself in a position of total submission to the advice of the director, and orientate oneself to this opinion as though it were the Lord in person giving it. . . . In the course of the next eighteen months, as total physical and emotional collapse assailed me (I had my fifth child and a miscarriage in this period), I repeatedly queried it. On each occasion I received the same answer: I was not free to abandon my profession. I was accused at the time, by colleagues and relations, of acting irresponsibly in thus allowing myself to reach a dangerous point of exhaustion. My defense to them was: "I was acting under obedience." I see now of course that this is no defense. The responsibility for putting myself under a director was mine. If my director considered any of the responsibility his, he has certainly kept marvellously quiet about it, and has done so to this day.

It is interesting to note the closely parallel experience of another convert to Roman Catholicism in the last century, St. George Mivart (1827–1900). The material issues were different, but the conclusion was the same. As his biographer tells the story: "By the end of his life, he had thrown off the last and strongest external authority to which he had been subject. In the midst of his last great controversy, he announced to his archbishop and through him to his Church: 'All of us, however submissive to authority, must in the last resort, rest upon the judgment of our individual reason. How otherwise could we know that authority had spoken at all or what it had said?'"

In the light of these factual accounts, it is interesting to note that the dramatist George Bernard Shaw deduced that Joan of Arc must have traveled the same intellectual path in the fifteenth century. In Scene VI of *St. Joan* we see the young heretic—it would be antihistorical to call her a saint at this point—chained by the ankles, submitting to questioning about her "voices."

> *Ladvenu*: Good. That means, does it not, that you are subject to our Lord the Pope, to the cardinals, the archbishops, and the bishops for whom his lordship stands here today?
> *Joan*: God must be served first.
> *D'Estivet*: Then your voices command you not to submit yourself to the Church Militant?
> *Joan*: My voices do not tell me to disobey The Church; but God must be served first.
> *Cauchon*: And you, and not the Church, are to be the judge?
> *Joan*: What other judgment can I judge by but my own?
> *The Assessors (scandalized)*: Oh! (*They cannot find words.*)

The conclusion to be derived from all these witnesses is surely obvious. Put bluntly it is this: *Authority does not exist*—not in the sense that is meant by those who would have us govern our lives by Authority with a capital *A*. If I accept authority, says Biezanek, the responsibility for acceptance is mine. "What other judgment can I judge by but my own?" asks Joan. "All of us," says Mivart, "however submissive to authority, must in the last resort, rest upon the judgment of our individual reason." The external agent referred to is an illusion. Whether one calls the internal agent "conscience" or "reason" is perhaps only a matter of taste. But it is clear that, from an operational point of view, "authority" is empty of content since it is a redundant word for "conscience." The operational meaning of *this* word is not easy to establish, but we make no progress by introducing "authority" as a mere synonym for it. It would be naive to argue that one word is as good as another, for the very reasons for preferring the word "authority" are the reasons why it should not be used. If I justify my actions by reference to authority, I thereby announce my intention of rejecting reason and its demands for rigorous honesty. Acceptance of personal responsibility necessarily requires the rejection of authority.

Authority is a ghost. Why is this truth not more widely advertised?

The error of believing in this holy ghost is shared by millions. An error so widespread and so persistent must serve important psychological and sociological functions. These are not difficult to discover.

In the first place, if I cite authority as the reason for my actions, it may well be because I have a sneaking suspicion that I cannot justify them by reason. Authority, by definition, is unexaminable; reason is always subject to scrutiny. Acceptance of authority arises naturally from the facts of individual psychological development. Normal development necessarily begins with a childhood phase in which authority resides in *other* persons: the child is not competent to assume control. The complete life cycle, however, includes also an adult phase in which the individual is now his own authority; he does not try to foist responsibility for his actions and beliefs onto others. Needless to say, a considerable, and sometimes dangerously large proportion, of the legally adult population is not psychologically adult.

Whether or not I personally accept authority, I may urge others to do so for reasons of personal aggrandizement. Each of us, to a greater or lesser extent, wants to control others. *I* want to control *you*. How can I do so? One of the first things each of us learns is the feebleness of naked power. If I tell you to do something, you instinctively ask "Why?" If I then say, "Because I say so," I make no progress in furthering my will to power. But if I can first insinuate into your mind the idea that there exists a being or spirit who is always right—say the Zoroastrian god Mazda, to take a nonprovocative example—and if I then say you should do thus and so because Mazda says so, I may then succeed in controlling you. If I am successful, it is because I have succeeded in putting Mazda in the psychological locus formerly occupied by your parents (hence the term "father figure") without your catching on to the fact that Mazda is really *me*. In general, the more distant in time and space, the less questionable authority is, hence the more authoritative. As an ambitious, aggressive individual, it is to my interest to maintain in you the illusion that authority exists.

The on-going associations of individuals that we call institutions have an equally strong interest in maintaining the fiction of authority. It is not unreasonable to ask if the most successful institution ever devised by man, the Church of Rome, has to any extent suppressed (or at any rate failed to publicize) thoughtful discussions of authority. One might

suspect that some of the church's most profound thinkers in the past
may have reached a conclusion similar to that of Shaw's fictional
St. Joan.

I have not found it easy to document this suspicion. I thought that I
might be led to relevant passages by the syntopicon volumes of the great
books of the Western world, but I found them more wonderful than
useful. The *Syntopicon* subsumes all knowledge under the headings of
"102 Great Ideas." It is hardly to be expected that any two persons
would agree on the 102 most seminal ideas of the Western world, but it
seems rather odd that the list established by Mortimer J. Adler and
William Gorman should omit both *conscience* and *authority* while including such relative trivia as *monarchy, eternity,* and *angel.*

At one time I had thought to canvass the writings of the most revered
of Catholic writers, St. Thomas Aquinas (1225–1274). I found this task
too great for one not disciplined in the Thomistic idiom, and so I can do
no better than present a paraphrase of Aquinas made by Eric D'Arcy.

> The proper object of the will is not the good as it exists objectively,
> or as it is known to some moral genius with a skill and an insight
> superior to one's own: it is the good as apprehended and presented
> to a man by the judgment of his own reason. Of course, one of the
> elements of the decision which one's reason ultimately makes will
> be the guidance of authoritative and skilled moralists whose stand-
> ing we accept; but it has to be the individual's judgment of con-
> science that this *is* an authority which we may safely accept.

If we grant the accuracy of D'Arcy's paraphrase, we are justified
in saying that St. Thomas Aquinas anticipated the discoveries of St.
George Mivart, John Rock, Anne Biezanek, and George Bernard Shaw.
There is no evidence that any of these people drew on the wisdom of
"the angelic doctor" in reaching their conclusions. Neither is there any
sign that this aspect of St. Thomas's thought has been, or is being
given, unduly wide publicity by the church of his affiliation.

The conclusion that authority does not exist comes as no surprise to
scientists, whose working life is built on this premise. The Royal Society of London has as its motto *Nullius in verba,* which may be collo-

quially translated as "We don't take anybody's word for it." Can other phases of human effort be infected with this attitude?

There is little question but that this infection is already proceeding, and with some success (from a scientist's point of view!). However, every cluster of human beliefs is a homeostatic system with immense powers of repair in the face of logical attack. Put another way, each truth that is contrary to a well-established system seems to have a very short half-life; such truth has to be discovered over and over again, each new statement of it being speedily transmuted into innocuous intellectual isotopes by the internal forces of Freudian denial.

The decay of truth is aided by kindly and practical men. An incident from Victorian history will serve as an illustrative example. When anesthesia was introduced into England, it was forcibly resisted on the grounds that it was unnatural and hence contrary to God's will. This argument might have been countered by a general discussion of the nature of evidence and authority—though probably without much effect. A wiser approach (at least in the short run) was that of the physician James Y. Simpson, who played the game of authority by arguing that the users of chloroform were but following the example set by the Lord, who, intent upon extracting one of Adam's ribs for the fabrication of Eve, considerately "caused a deep sleep to fall upon Adam" before beginning the operation (according to Gen. 2:21). Most written authorities are sufficiently prolix, inconsistent, and ambiguous to make this method of counterattack effective in the hands of kindly and witty men. Playing the game of authority, Simpson won his particular point by implicitly reassuring his audience that he would not tackle the more general issue of authority itself. Tact paid off. The welcome given to tact is part of the homeostatic mechanism of tradition.

Because tactful victories are limited in scope, each new problem must be attacked *de novo*, as if nothing of its sort had ever been seen before. Thus, in our own time, we witness literally hundreds of fine Catholic minds wrestling with the meaning of "natural" as concerns contraception, because few will face the logically simpler issue of authority. It now seems likely that the theologians will soon find a suitable key to contraception. But the insight that authority is a ghost would be more in the nature of a skeleton key that would open many doors. In this day of an accelerating rate of appearance of new ethical problems, we stand sorely in need of more general, more powerful methods of analyzing them. Progress would occur much faster if we could persuade the common man that authority is a ghost.

Is this persuasion possible? I think this question is not answerable by armchair research. To determine how one can replace one homeostatic epistemology by another requires, I think, nothing less than experimental work with human beings. If a label is needed, such an activity might be called experimental anthropology. It can be argued with some degree of plausibility that the development of this science is essential for the survival of mankind.

# 27

# An Ecological View of International Relations

In times of perceived scarcity the desire to help others (which comes naturally to the human animal) conflicts with self-helping impulses. Reconciliation of the two drives was not overly difficult in ancient times when the individual was aware only of poverty near at hand, but now that technology enables us to see, in a single instant, poverty all over the world, the problem of setting practical limits to altruism becomes pressing. Like all recalcitrant problems this one generates rhetoric that tends to confuse the issues.

As an ecologist I am disturbed by what seem to me to be careless habits of thought developing in the brotherhood of economists. Let me illustrate by commenting on a brief paragraph from a 1979 report by the Joint Economics Committee:

The world has become an increasingly integrated, interdepen-

dent economic community. Goods, money, people, ideas and problems travel across national boundaries as never before.

Interdependence may or may not be increasing, but it is certainly not
new. Trade is a manifestation of interdependence, and trade between
peoples began long before there were any nations as we understand
them—even long before writing. The principal forms of international
transfer are three: plunder, gifts, and trade. If there has been a relative
increase in trade (the interdependent form of transfer) in modern times,
it is principally because we have "improved" warfare to such an extent
that it no longer yields any plunder.

More significant than the doubtful increase in trade (interdependence) has been the genuine increase in gifts from rich nations to poor
nations. The gifts are seldom called by their proper name, being variously labeled transfers, aid, "loans," and concessions. Gift-giving establishes a relation of dependence, not interdependence. In the interest
of truth almost every assertion of the "interdependence" in recent literature needs to be labeled for what it is: a plea not for more interdependence but for accepting and creating more dependent relations between
nations. Perhaps the goal is praiseworthy, but let us not gild the lily
with the word "interdependence." We should also examine the argument for fostering dependent relations.

What sorts of things can be transferred from one nation to another?
The categories in the passage quoted ("goods, money, people, ideas,
and problems") are ill-chosen. Better are the fundamental entities of
physics: matter, energy, and information. For each of these, what is the
physical cost of transferring it from one nation to another, and what are
the human consequences of a policy that encourages such transfers?

The physical cost of transferring matter, energy, and information has
diminished greatly in the past thousand years. The cost always includes
a loss of energy (strictly speaking, an increase in entropy). The cost argument against transfers is much less important now than it was in the
past. With information, the cost argument has almost disappeared with
the advent of incredibly cheap information transfer by communication
satellites. Nearly instantaneous and nearly cost-free communication of
disasters at the other side of the world creates a cost of another sort, the
psychological cost of anxiety about distant disasters. It is far easier to

know of disasters than to do anything about them, e.g., to transfer food, blankets, and building materials. The Good Samaritan of the Bible (Luke 10:30–37) had an easy task because the man he helped was one he could both see and touch. But now that we can see more than we can cure we must learn to accept the rediscovered limitations of action. Our hallowed ethical precepts are unfortunately devoid of reference to quantities; but quantities matter. Time, distance, ergs, and ohms (in a metaphorical sense) must enter into the calculus of action. Ethics, to serve the modern world, must be made quantitative.

The most important difference between information and the other two fundamental entities is this: matter and energy are subject to conservation laws, information is not. Transfers of matter and energy cannot escape the zero-sum principle: A's gain is B's loss. Not so with information: the gift occasions no loss. In fact, the receiver may act on the gift of information and pass it back in enriched form to the original giver. Even from a strictly selfish point of view one can urge rich nations to be generous with information, because a supposedly more "backward" receiver may make improvements on the information it receives. When it comes to information, sharing is a plus-sum game.

Not so with matter and energy. In the first accounting, the giver obviously loses in a zero-sum transfer. Is there a second accounting that turns the loss into a gain? There are many now who say so. One argument for gifts between nations raises the fear of force: it is said that the rich must give or the poor will simply take. This is hardly a high-minded argument, and it may not be true. It takes great wealth to wage modern war, so how can a country that is too poor to buy what it needs pay for an invasive war? Terrorism is cheaper, of course, but is preemptive surrender the only response to terrorists?

A more elevated argument for international gifts rests on the dream of One World. Nations are regarded as transient divisions of the world. The rhetoric of "global hunger" and "global problems" implies that the accounting unit should not be the individual nation but the entire world. Distribution of goods is to be made according to the principle enunciated by Karl Marx, "to each according to his need." In effect, the global view seeks to turn national goods into common property. Is this wise?

It is not. More than 2,000 years ago Aristotle spotted the fatal flaw of commonization. "What is common to the greatest number gets the least amount of care. Men pay most attention to what is their own: they care less for what is common." The enormity of the danger is being made clear in our time by the growing literature on "the tragedy of the commons."

Human nature ensures that the distributional system of the commons fails to create justice. If I can take from the commons according to my perception of my need, I am not encouraged to be either energetic or innovative. Those who exploit the commons are rewarded at the expense of those whose consciences lead them to refrain from doing so. The system of the commons is worse than irresponsible: it is negatively responsible. It is counterproductive: it fosters the opposite of the kind of behavior that created the finest products of civilization.

The perils of commonization are exacerbated by population growth. The "each" in Marx's "to each according to his need" stops ethical thinking at the singular level. In the international arena the need is very plural, and the plurality escalates. The 800 million malnourished poor of today will be 824 million a year from now; and another 3 percent—compounded—a year later. Worse: if we succeed in improving the nutrition of the desperately poor we will surely increase their fecundity. The cross-cultural negative correlation between national fertility and national wealth has led to the comforting belief that improving the nutrition of the very poor will decrease their fertility. Possibly it might in the long term—say two generations—but the weight of the evidence falls on the opposite side. At the lower levels of income at least, people act rationally: when their circumstances improve they have more children. Fewer people would be seduced into adopting the Marxist ideal if it were more exactly but less elegantly phrased, "to the multiplying each's according to their escalating needs."

The unacknowledged assumption of the "New International Economic Order" is that need creates right. This is a Marxist assumption; accepting it creates an international commons. If Congress wants to support NIEO it should do so in honest language. The supporting bill should begin: "In order to establish an international commons from which all nations may draw at will, in accordance with the Marxist principle 'to each according to his need,' we do hereby. . . ." A bill so worded would not have a ghost of a chance of passing of course, which is why those who seek to establish an international commons use other language. They speak not of gifts but of "transfers," or "loans at concessionary rates of interest." When a debt shows no prospect of being repaid they may manage to get it "forgiven," as the United States forgave India's debt of 3 billion dollars in the early 1970s. When the costs of debt-service rise too high, the debt is refinanced at a lower rate of interest, sometimes with an additional loan. The expropriation of American property is seldom protested; many Americans even look on expropriation as a desirable step toward the globalization of property. No mention is made of commonization and the tragedy of the commons. Instead there is much diversionary talk of exploitation, colonialism, inequity, injustice, and imperialism. Rhetoric is wonderful at concealing the truth!

One other consideration dictates caution in trying to diminish the suffering in other parts of the world. No poor nation is a unity: it is made up of the governors (a small fraction) and the governed (the vast majority). Desperate need is confined to the latter group, which is the group our compassion leads us to want to help. But unless we are to revert to imperialism (in the form of a new charitable imperialism) we must honor the sovereignty of other nations and treat them as units, dealing with their de facto rulers, who then control the distribution of our largesse.

Two evils follow from this necessity. First, the well-fed governors may well be corrupt; they are all too likely to distribute the goodies preferentially to themselves, their relatives, and their friends. Second, the largesse strengthens the position of the governors and diminishes their motivation for tackling their difficult national problems. Internal reform is made less probable by gifts from the outside. Incompetence becomes entrenched. The aim of NIEO and other forms of international commonization is to benefit the poor of the world. Unfortunately such well-intentioned efforts will generally benefit only the governors of the poor. So NIEO is only the latest in a series of well-intentioned proposals that in fact are counterproductive. The road to hell now has one more paving stone.

# 28

## *Perishable Euphemisms of Foreign Aid*

If you are well off and want to speak of those who are not, you have no linguistic problem: you just call them *poor*. But if you want to help them, and propose talking about their situation in their presence, you have to consider the effect of your language on the objects of your charitable attention. Words intended to be merely descriptive then become more than descriptive; they become social operators.

In the nineteenth century smug and ethnocentric Europeans felt no compunction in speaking of "primitive people" and "savages." The rise of anthropology in the twentieth century made these terms unacceptable, and the adjectives "backward" and "poor" were favored for a while.

When these words in turn were criticized as cruel, "undeveloped" came in as a substitute. It was a hopeful term: it implied that improvement was possible, perhaps inevitable. It was accepted as the justification for charitable interventions designed to hasten the inevitable. Yet, with usage, this term too began to grate on some people's nerves, and "underdeveloped" made its appearance, spawning a derivative, "less developed," as in "less developed countries" ("LDC's"). "Developing" and "emerging" appeared after World War II.

In the early 1950s a French sociologist introduced a new thought: "The Third World." At the purely descriptive level this was defined as what was left of the world after subtracting the First World (the democratic rich countries) and the Second World (the centrally controlled economies). But because "The Third World" was coined by a Frenchman it implies a threat. The new term is an echo of the Third Estate, the aggregation of common citizens who brought about the French Revolution to end injustices committed by the First and Second Estates of the nobility and clergy. Implied—and often more than implied—was the threat that the Third World would some day enforce international justice through world revolution.

Perhaps in reaction to this too-activist a term, an American demographer introduced a geographic note in proposing "The Non-West" as a collective for the poor countries. In this scheme, Russia and Japan— but not China—were parts of the West. The etiquette of foreign aid discussions presumes a rather rubbery geography.

The geographic motif was momentarily abandoned in the 1960s when a congress of poor and demanding nations identified themselves as "The 77." Others soon joined the party, and the number swelled to "The 119" before the term was abandoned.

Geography came back into the picture in the 1970s when "The South" was created as an antagonist and supplicant to the rich North. Again, rubber-sheet geography determined the categories: Australia and New Zealand, the southernmost of nations, were assigned to the new North. The Brandt Report, on which the United Nations based its 1981 conference at Cancún, Mexico, popularized the "South versus North" debate.

If history is any guide, "The South" won't last long. The unending succession of perishable euphemisms suggests some unacknowledged psychological resistance to calling things by their right name, a reluctance to acknowledge publicly the Emperor's nakedness. What is the common feature of these countries that we keep calling by inappropriate names? Individually, and as a group, these countries complain that their needs exceed their resources. They complain of shortages of supply (though never of longages of demand, all the while their populations grow at fantastically high rates). Could it be that the unifying word we are looking for, but hesitate to say, is "overpopulated"?

# 29

## *The Toughlove Solution*

Why should the United States be concerned with the suffering of poor countries? Two sorts of reasons are given, one moral and the other prudential.

The prudential reasons are plausible, but basically unsound. We are told that if we don't take care of a poor nation it might attack us. Nonsense. Modern warfare is so expensive that even rich nations cannot afford it. If a poor country can't afford bread, it certainly can't afford guns. International terrorism comes cheaper, of course. So long as there is envy in the world—which is forever—terrorism will be a tempting option. The answer to terrorism is police action: this is not a perfect answer, but it is the best there is.

What about this: "If we don't take care of poor people in their own countries, won't they migrate into ours?" Unfortunately, there are 2.5 billion poor people in the world, and they are increasing by 40 million per year. We cannot possibly keep up with this need. Our responsibility is to keep our country from being overwhelmed by immigrants. The responsibility of each poor country is to keep the excess population from being produced.

What remains are the moral reasons for helping other countries, and these are weighty. But we must remember what we have learned from domestic experiences: we can't solve social problems by blindly throwing money at them. We've had a salutary lesson in the development of India and China during the past three decades. Since 1950 India has received massive foreign aid from many countries, but China from only one country (the Soviet Union) and that only until 1957. At the outset the two countries were equally miserable and had equally poor prospects. Today? Without question the people of China are far better off. Foreign aid did not rescue India from poverty; lack of aid did not handicap China. In fact, it may be that China did so well precisely because she was not "helped" by "aid."

Back in 1945 Mao Tse-tung committed China to a policy of "regeneration through our own efforts." Fertilizers and factories are splendid things, but far more important than technology is what is inside the heads of men and women. Foreign aid can supply technology: the people must be willing to make the social changes that will make technology work.

It is essential that we distinguish between crisis and crunch. When an earthquake killed 23,000 people in Guatemala in 1976, *that* was a crisis. The world responded generously, and it should have. But when thousands—or millions—of people die of starvation in an overpopulated country like Bangladesh, what we are confronted with is not a crisis but a crunch. Ninety-four million Bangladeshi live in an area the size of Iowa—which has only 3 million people. Bangladesh, with its fertile soil and a climate that permits three crops a year, is a rich country, but not rich enough to add three-quarters of an Iowa every year to a population already thirty times as large. Direct food aid to such a country merely subsidizes further destructive population growth.

Sensing that gifts are bad, we generate euphemisms to hide our tracks. "Concessionary rates of interest" is a euphemism; anyone who can borrow money at 3 percent when the going rate is 8 percent is getting a gift. A loan forgiven is certainly a gift. Poor countries ask for, and get, loan after loan. As their debt mounts, the burden of "servicing the debt"—paying the interest—becomes unbearable. Finally, since fore-closure is out of the question, the lender has no choice but to forgive the debt.

Way back in 1953 John Foster Dulles saw the direction foreign aid was taking. "You know," he said to a friend, "aid is like opium. There are withdrawal pains when you remove it." I think we have now reached the stage when foreign aid addicts should be subjected to the "cold turkey" treatment. Most of the world's wretchedness is caused by the crunch of overpopulation, which will only be made worse by the drug called "aid." That this drug is addictive is shown in a statement made by the President of Kenya in 1980: "No country can maintain its economic independence without assistance from the outside." What a long way from Mao, and what a curious definition it implies of "independence"!

Now that rich countries are catching on to the corruption of the word "loan," poor countries are taking a different tack: they are demanding concessions in foreign trade. They want to be paid more than market prices for their exports and to buy at less than the market—gifts under another name.

Times are changing. Notice what is happening to parenting. We are relearning what has been known for thousands of years: love must be combined with discipline. Recently, a group of American parents, driven to distraction by their children's drug taking and rampant he-donism, joined forces to lay down the law to their children—with love. These parents meet to exchange ideas, and they meet with their chil-dren to say, "Shape up or ship out." Significantly, the parents called their organization Toughlove.

Toughlove parenting is perilous, but it has at least the possibility of solving problems permissiveness has created. Toughlove takes courage. Some of the children clear out. This is hard on parents, but they accept the risk because the alternative of continuing to support irresponsible behavior is worse.

Relations among nations must be guided by Toughlove, too. Spokes-men for poor nations now threaten us with the loss of their love if we do not give them everything they demand. We must be prepared to lose their love out of genuine concern for the long-term interests of their people. Most of the poor countries are, in fact, rich—rich in natural resources. It is their governments, usually, that are poor.

To realize a country's inherent richness, a government must see to it that population matches the carrying capacity of the land. China has shown how to use incentives and disincentives to work toward this goal. China's methods may not be acceptable everywhere, but the goal should be universal. Each country must choose the means that meshes with its culture. Outsiders can furnish the technology of birth control, but population control must grow out of the will of the people, expressed through their political decisions.

There is no survival without self-reliance, which cannot be donated from the outside. Self-reliance must be generated inside each nation, by the people themselves. There is no other way.

# 30

## *Limited World, Limited Rights*

When a deaf woman who tried to enroll in a school of nursing was turned down, she sued, claiming that her rights were being violated. After reviewing the case in 1979 the Supreme Court unanimously found against her: neither the Rehabilitation Act of 1973 nor any reasonable conception of natural rights justified imposing the handicap of a deaf nurse on hospital patients. Some time later, a hundred and fifty handicapped protesters of the decision marched through the Westwood region of Los Angeles chanting, "Rights have no price," and "How would you feel if it was you?"

These chants nicely revealed two important characteristics of rights, as popularly understood. The first is a feeling that a right is something outside of—beyond—all systems of pricing and evaluation. This view implies that rights are immune to rational discussion. The second chant tries to shore up what is essentially an egotistical demand with the altruistic authority of the Golden Rule. The implied argument is this: "Wouldn't you want this privilege if you were in my shoes? Therefore must you not support me when I claim this privilege as a right?" Logic aside, this is a powerful emotional argument.

Claiming rights is a major oratorical sport of our time: it is a marvelous substitute for reasoned argument. Julius K. Nyerere, the president of Tanzania, once said: "In one world, as in one state, when I am rich because you are poor, and I am poor because you are rich, the transfer of wealth from the rich to the poor is a matter of right." Note the implied reference to the Golden Rule by a speaker who intends to be on the receiving end of the transfer. The same pattern is seen, perhaps at a more elevated level, in a statement made shortly before his death by Robert Kennedy, who based his claim to more political power on right: "At stake is not simply the leadership of our party, and even of our own country, it is our right to the moral leadership of this planet." Some of Kennedy's advisers recommended against his saying this in public, but hubris prevailed. "Whom the gods would destroy . . ."

Perhaps nothing that most people want has not been claimed as a right by someone: the right to work, the right to an adequate standard of living, the right to liberty of movement, the right to conscience, and the right to dignity. (How defined?) Even the right to treason has been claimed. (Why not the right to rob, the right to murder?) My favorite is the "right to hold religious pizza parties in the prison chapel" claimed by a group of penitentiary inmates in Michigan. The petitioners wanted to hold a pizza party, and since fifty-two of them had foresightedly paid two dollars each to be made ministers in the California-based Universal Life church (which ordains by mail, no questions asked), it seemed only politic to claim that eating pizzas was a religious exercise (as is eating consecrated wafers in the Catholic church). When their petition was denied by prison authorities, the dissatisfied petitioners sued the state for $110,000 for violating their rights. (They lost.)

Given examples like this, we sympathize with the utilitarian Jeremy Bentham, who, almost two centuries ago, said that the idea of natural rights "is simple nonsense . . . rhetorical nonsense, nonsense upon stilts." The no-nonsense approach of the utilitarians to such transcendental entities as natural rights was kept alive by August Comte and the positivists of the nineteenth century, as well as by the logical positivists stemming from the Vienna Circle in the twentieth. The operational approach of science, explicitly described by physicist Percy W. Bridgman, falls into the same category. Names change, but the spirit remains the same. The opposing spirit survives also: belief in the existence of translegal rights is probably more widespread today than it was in Bentham's time.

I believe it was religious historian Ernest Renan who invented the "Man from Mars," that thoroughly rational, inquisitive being who asks earthlings to explain what they do in terms that can be understood by an intelligence completely free of all traditional terrestrial beliefs, assumptions, and prejudices. Renan's Man from Mars is, of course, completely in the Bentham-Comte-Bridgman tradition (which just shows that tradition cannot be *completely* escaped). What would the Man from Mars make of the multitude of rights now being vociferously claimed? If the idea of religious freedom supports the right to eat consecrated wafers, why does it not also support the right to eat pizzas? How can a real translegal or natural right be distinguished from a fraudulent one? Looking for a common denominator to the many rights claimed on earth, the Man from Mars would find only one: the implied demand, "I want it."

This is an egotistical demand, of course. It is the weakness of egotistical demands *openly expressed* that they provoke defensive denials by other egotists, lest they be sucked into satisfying the demands. To forestall such denials the egotist casts his demands in the apparently personality-free language of universal natural rights, thereby improving the chance that he will get what he wants. *Right* is the rhetoric which, if unchallenged, transforms personal desire into universal virtue. So say the operationalists.

The principal intellectual opposition in our time comes from those who see the concept of translegal rights as a necessity for the evolution and rationalization of law. H. L. A. Hart and Ronald Dworkin are distinguished proponents of this view. Dworkin says we cannot understand statute law without presupposing deep principles which, though not stated explicitly in the statutes, pervade all laws and all proposals to change law. This is certainly a plausible view; yet a scientist cannot but note the family resemblance between this concept of natural law and the concept of the "ether" held to be indispensable in physics for more than two centuries. The wavelike properties of light were regarded as evidence of the existence of a medium—"ether"—in which waves could move, even though there was no positive evidence for the existence of such an ubiquitous, substanceless entity. Around the turn of the present century, the Michelson-Morley experiment and Einstein's relativity theory removed the intellectual underpinnings of "ether," and physicists found they could get on quite well without the concept. Perhaps the concept of translegal rights will some day be recognized as being equally dispensable.

Without settling the eventual fate of natural rights, we can usefully point out a number of the properties of rights, whether natural or legal. Rights imply more than they say. When a right is demanded by a human being from a nonhuman universe, no controversy ensues. If Robinson Crusoe feels that he has a right to food, let him set about getting it. Either he will succeed and live, or fail and die; in neither case is controversy created. But when a human being in a world crowded with some 4 billion other human beings asserts a right, he asserts a claim upon his fellow beings, a claim that cannot be accepted without proof of its value to the community.

The point is well illustrated by an exchange of views between columnists in *Newsweek*. When Shana Alexander asserted that people have a basic human right to food, clothing, shelter, and medical care, Milton Friedman replied: "The heart approves Ms. Alexander's humanitarian concern, but the head warns" us of the dangers in her statement. "If I have the 'right' to food . . . someone else must have the obligation to provide it. Just who is that? If it is Ms. Alexander, does that not convert her into my slave?" Friedman's language is perhaps too blunt, but the fact asserted, namely that a right is a claim *upon other people*, is undeniably true. This is apparent from one of the earliest definitions of right by Samuel von Pufendorf, a statement that was influential in the writing of the Declaration of Independence: "A right is an active moral power of a person to receive something from another as a matter of moral necessity."

One person's right is, then, a demand upon others. Pufendorf follows his definition with a two-word précis: *Vocabuli ambiguitas*. Rights are ambiguous words, literally "words that drive both ways." This fact is conveniently neglected by those who fight most vigorously to establish new legal rights on the basis of supposed translegal rights. The desirability of the right to the person benefitted may be admitted by all; but before acquiescing in the establishment of a new legal right, we need to examine its drive in the other direction, in the demands it makes on those who must pay the cost of the right.

The highly individualistic view implicit in rights as currently conceived is not adequate for a world of more than four billion human beings. Our world is not the world of Robinson Crusoe or even of Daniel Boone. It is preeminently a social world, and social relationships are fantastically complicated and subtle. Whenever we contemplate intervening in an existing social system, we must be acutely aware that we can never do merely one thing. Quantities matter. A right that may be bearable and even beneficial at one level of population, may be unbearable or disastrous at another. Situation ethics is the only ethics that works.

In the past, freedom to move about as one might wish has been regarded by many as a right. Clearly, this right must be reexamined in the light of population increase. In the days when people were few, movement presented little social problem. In general, there was no reason to deny a person the right to move out of a community (though for the serfs of old this right did not exist). An American colonist moving into the wilderness seemed to present no social problem: either he made it or he didn't. A person living in a wilderness is not obviously infringing upon the rights of others. But 4.5 billion people have pretty well covered the face of the earth. Except for Antarctica, there are no parts of the earth unclaimed by one or another of the 150 nations. Under these circumstances, to claim the right of immigration would be to assert the right of invasion. It would be suicidal for the invaded country to accede to a right to immigrate. It is noteworthy that the United Nations, though prone to assert far-reaching rights, has not yet asserted the right of immigration.

However, the United Nations has asserted the right of emigration. One has sympathy with this claim, but we should admit there is also something to be said for the contrary position. The USSR, for example, has denied the right of emigration to Jewish citizens who want to go to Israel. I am one of the many who have signed petitions appealing to the Soviets to relax their restriction on emigration, and yet I can see a sort of defense for their policy. It could be maintained that my petition is just the knee-jerk reflex of a person so immersed in Lockean individualism that he cannot see the social picture. An adult individual, after all, represents a considerable investment in the maturation process. In a simple society living largely by private enterprise, the investment may be made almost entirely by the family, so only the family need be concerned if an individual proposes to emigrate. But in a complex, modern, socialistic state, it is the state that invests most in the maturation of the individual. From a purely economic point of view, it is appropriate for the state to claim a right to control emigration since the would-be emigrant proposes to take human resources, for which he personally has not paid, out of the state which did pay. Such is the strict economic, nonindividualistic view. I do not think this is all that matters, and I think it would be only prudent for a nation sensitive to the views of other nations to soften the purely economic conclusion. For our part, a recognition of the basically individualistic nature of western rights might make our international demands less shrill, and hence more effective.

What about the movements of citizens within a nation? Should they be free to travel from one part to another and change their place of residence? The largest nation in the world, China, with its approximately 1,000 million people, denies this right to its citizens. To most westerners, China's policy seems a retrogression to the days of serfdom; but before we condemn it we should look for the positive benefits of a policy of restricted internal migration.

One of the problems resulting from free internal migration is excessive urbanization. The concept of *urbanization* is not precise, but in round numbers it can be said that 75 percent of Americans live in urban centers, as compared with only 20 percent of the Chinese. *Excessive* is also not a precise concept, but attests to the evils associated with heavy urbanization—crowding, crime, pollution of many sorts, and anomie. If a policy of restricted freedom of movement can diminish "natural" excessive migration to urban centers, it is conceivable that a just accounting of the benefits and costs of the right to move freely might work out to the disadvantage of the claimed right. At any rate, the governing powers of China seem to think so; other countries should seriously examine the issue.

What happens to the beauty of an exceptionally favored locale when people are free to move into it if they want? Hawaii is an example in point. Many of the people long resident in Hawaii feel their state long ago grew beyond the optimum population level; they would like to restrict further entry into it from the other forty-nine. Any such restriction would appear to be unconstitutional, but Hawaiians are desperately seeking an argument to compel a reexamination of this point. To the biologist, the theoretical issue underlying such a situation is clear: the argument for restriction should be based on the "carrying capacity" of the environment. "Carrying capacity" is not a figure that is uniquely determined: it depends on the quality of life presupposed. In the case of Hawaii, the very peculiar merit of the environment is its beauty. Beauty is a complex concept, difficult to pin down in law, but clearly crowding has an adverse effect on beauty. The present state of Waikiki Beach compared with its condition in 1930 indicates a marked depreciation in esthetic values. Further population growth can only make the beach worse. Ultimately, Waikiki may be Coney Island West. In the allocation of natural beauty we face a problem in the diseconomies of scale. Hawaiians have no argument with New Yorkers about the desirability of Coney Island for the East Coast—they merely do not want to see their state turned into a western version. Is the Constitution of the United States incapable of supporting the desire of a state to control the number of its entrants in the name of quality of life? It is not easy to see how such control could be exercised without a fundamental change in the Constitution, but this question will be raised increasingly in time to come.

There is another reason for suggesting that we may some day restrict movement in a country like the United States. All travel requires energy. As the energy budget of the average citizen becomes increasingly restricted, this reason alone may force us to accept restrictions on travel and on change of residence. This possibility is only one among many raised by the contraction of the energy budget. The diminution of per capita energy supplies is moving us into a world that will be categorically different from the one we have known for the past century. Only dimly can we see the psychological adjustments we must make if we are to live with a reasonable degree of happiness in this new world.

Probably no right now claimed is so revolutionary in its consequences—and, I shall argue, so indefensible—as the right to food. On 23 March 1976 an organization called Bread for the World presented the following statement to the American Congress: "We believe that every man, woman and child on earth has the right to a nutritionally

adequate diet. This right is not ours to give or take away. It is fundamental and derives from the right to life itself. The Declaration of Independence identifies the right to life as an unalienable human right coming from God who has created all persons equal. Without the food to
sustain life, that right is meaningless."

This is lovely rhetoric, but it is ecological nonsense. In a limited
world, indefinitely continued exponential growth, if food is equally
shared, will lead ultimately to starvation and misery for all—and "ultimately" is not far off. Every year another 90 million mouths clamor for
food—another Egypt and Vietnam, as it were. The World Health Organization says that 800 million persons are now malnourished. The
advances in agricultural productivity, most conspicuous in the already
advanced countries, give little promise of decreasing the number of
malnourished, in either absolute numbers or relative to the total global
population.

The people in poor nations are increasing faster than those in the
rich: about twelve times as fast, in absolute numbers. (The poor are
about four times as numerous as the rich, and they are increasing at a
relative rate that is three times greater.) Before we support a right to
food, we should ask what this will do to us if we support also the right
claimed in the 1948 United Nations Universal Declaration of Human
Rights in Article 16: "Men and women of full age, without any limitation due to race, nationality or religion, have the right to marry and to
found a family." In practice, this statement has been repeatedly interpreted to mean that the right "to found a family" means the right to
determine the size of one's family. If people in poor countries persist in
producing larger families than people in rich countries, and if poor nations are unable to feed all their citizens, and if we hold that the right to
food means that the rich must ship food to the poor, then we are setting
up a one-way siphon that moves food from slowly-growing rich countries to rapidly-growing poor countries. Charity then finances suicidal
growth. If the world's resources are indeed finite—and few doubt this
any more—then at some time in the future the right to food will produce disaster. Considering the magnitude of malnutrition in the world,
we can say that the future is already here.

Why are we not more acutely aware of this fact? There are several
reasons. First, chronic misery is not news. A dog set on fire by an un-

known sadist in Massachusetts gets more newspaper space than 800 million people *continuing* to suffer from malnutrition throughout the world. Second, where chronic misery is greatest, newspaper reporters are scarcest. How many reporters are there in Bangladesh and central Africa as compared with the District of Columbia? Third, we do not know what to do about chronic misery anyway. We have great dreams, we make periodic plans; but in our more realistic moments we see that nothing much has come of these plans. We doubt our political potency.

We do not keep our attention focused long enough on the problem of chronic misery to see that simultaneously asserting the right to food and the right to breed ensures the perpetuation *and increase* of need. Every right must be evaluated in the network of all rights claimed and the environment in which these rights are exercised. When the human population was periodically decimated by such crowd diseases as cholera, typhoid, plague, and smallpox, claiming both the right to breed and to be fed may have done no long-term harm (though such double claims were seldom made in those days). But the new limit to growth—sheer want—created by substantially eliminating the old limits (disease, principally) turns the right to food and the right to breed into a suicidal combination.

If these two rights have a translegal existence—if, to use the language of earlier days, they are God-given rights—then we must bitterly conclude that God is bent on the utter destruction of civilization, that He must intend to reduce human existence to the level of the Iks, so movingly described by Colin Turnbull. Saying that both such translegal rights exist in unqualified, unquantified form is fatalism of the most extreme sort. On the other hand, if we hold that every right, "natural" or not, must be evaluated in the total system of rights operating in a world that is limited, we must inevitably conclude that no right can be presumed to be absolute, that the effect of each right on the suppliers as well as on the demanders must be determined before we can ascertain the quantity of right that is admissible. From here on out, ours is a limited world. Right must also be limited. The greater the population, the more limited the per capita supply of all goods; hence the greater must be the limitation on individual rights. At its heart, this is the political meaning of the population problem.

# SOURCES AND SECOND THOUGHTS

## Sources and Second Thoughts

With few exceptions, the chapters of this book were originally published in popular periodicals or professional journals. The original publishers have generously given permission to reprint, for which I express my thanks. Some of the pieces are printed exactly in their original form but most have been modified in minor ways to make them fit together better. I confess I have tightened up more than a few sentences, but I have not taken advantage of later knowledge to make my prognostications appear better than they were.

Superscripts referring to documentation affect many readers like pox marks. In a general audience, not one in a hundred readers cares to see the documentation. I refer the few who do to the original publication, the citation of which is given for each of the numbers reprinted. A few of the more obvious questions that may occur to the readers have been anticipated; in those instances I have given the relevant citations here.

Editors of popular periodicals have an irritating propensity to change the title submitted by the author to one of their own choosing. In my opinion, the change is usually for the worse. I suspect the practice is a symptom of the NIH Syndrome—Not Invented Here—that accounts for a good deal of the Brownian motion in the realm of ideas. I have not hesitated to restore the original title when, after the passage of years, it still seemed the better one. Sometimes I have even devised a new one.

## 2
## Immigration—America's Peculiar Population Problem

The original title of the longer article was "Population and Immigration: Compassion or Responsibility?" published in the British journal *The Ecologist* 7:268–272 (1977). I thank the editor, Edward Goldsmith, for permission to reprint. I have borrowed some ideas from John H. Tanton's essay "International Stability as an Obstacle to Achieving World Stability." Dr. Tanton was then president of Zero Population Growth, Inc.; he has since moved to the same position in the Federation for American Immigration Reform (FAIR).

While this piece was in manuscript it benefitted greatly from the criticisms of Justin Blackwelder, Judith Blake, Jane Hardin, and William Ophuls.

Those who wish to look further into the theory within which immigration must be evaluated are urged to read the two essays "The Tragedy of the Commons" and "Living on a Lifeboat," both of which may be found in *Managing the Commons*, edited by Garrett Hardin and John Baden (San Francisco: W. H.

Freeman, 1977). Also to be highly recommended is Michael Teitelbaum's sensitive treatment of the subject, "Right versus Right: Immigration and Refugee Policy in the United States," *Foreign Affairs* 59(1):21–59 (1980).

# 3
# Smokescreens and Evasions

This is abstracted from "The Limits of Sharing," published in *World Issues* 3(1):5–10 (1978). This was a publication of the Center for the Study of Democratic Institutions, now known as the Hutchins Center. The introductory six paragraphs have been added to the original text.

# 4
# Thinking Hearts Are Better Than Bleeding

Act I was originally published in the *Los Angeles Times*, 8 July 1979, Part V, pages 1 and 3 under the title "We Need Thinking Rather Than Bleeding Hearts."

Act II is from the same paper, 11 May 1980, Part V, pages 1 and 3. Original title: "Refugees: Should Compassion Have Limits? Yes: Our Hearts Must Be Made to Think Too."

The idea for Act III was derived from Chapter 9 of *Famine—1975!* by William and Paul Paddock (Boston: Little, Brown, 1967). This book has been much derided since 1975 by anti-Malthusians who ask "What happened to that famine?" Well, various experts in such organizations as the United Nations, the World Health Organization, and the World Bank estimate that something like ten to thirty million deaths (most of them of children) occur each year due, in part, to malnutrition—this in spite of a statistical upward trend in world-wide per capita grain production over the past fifteen years. We should at least wonder what will happen when "unusual weather" (that is, unwanted weather) drives food production down for several years in a row.

"Who next?" is not an idle question. It may not be simple hunger that drives multitudes to our doors, it may be political persecution. The practical problem of sharing with multitudes is the same, whatever the reason for their coming to us.

## 5
### Throwing Facts in the Jurymen's Eyes

The gist of this essay was first presented as a letter to the editor in *Not Man Apart* (Friends of the Environment), June 1981, pages 21–22.

For the facts on illegal immigrants see David S. North and Marion F. Houstoun, 1976. *The Characteristics and Role of Illegal Aliens in the U.S. Labor Market*. Washington, D.C.: Linton.

Julian Simon's transgressions are treated at length in Chapter 23. The passage discussed here is from pages 274–275 of *The Ultimate Resource*, where Simon asserts that he has carried out a cost-benefit assessment that proves that "the rate of return from immigrants to the citizen public is of the order of 20 percent per annum, a remarkably good investment for anyone's portfolio. The return from illegals must be even greater, of course, because the public services they receive out of the taxes they pay are almost non-existent."

The citation given for this analysis is "Simon, forthcoming." It is to be hoped that Professor Simon will not keep the world waiting for long. In its importance, this discovery must be judged on a par with the discovery of perpetual motion. Operating on the Simon principle every nation can grow rich "beyond the dreams of avarice," to quote Dr. Johnson, simply by importing immigrants as fast as possible. With infinite wealth in sight, the danger of international war should subside—until national leaders realize they have a new natural resource (immigrant bodies) to fight over. Under the new enlightenment we would cease promoting family planning abroad. In fact, more aggressive nations that did not hesitate to intervene abroad would try to force foreigners to have more babies. Simon is now doing no more than his duty in pointing out the new opportunities. As he says, "The economist worth his or her salt should offer a cost-benefit assessment for policy analysis." Oh Brave New World, that hath such assessors in it!

## 6
### Immigrants and Oil

The information in the table came from the U.S. Department of Energy by way of page 15 of Robert Stobaugh and Daniel Yergin, editors, *Energy Future* (New York: Random House, 1979).

This chapter is an expansion of a letter to the editor in the Santa Barbara *News-Press* for 21 December 1978.

The per capita use of energy has dropped somewhat since 1977, but no significant change need be made in the conclusions.

7
## "Scientific Creationism"—Marketing Deception as Truth

Originally published under the title "What to Say to These People" in the magazine of the Public Broadcasting Corporation, *The Dial 1*(1):46–51, 1980. For a good account of the legal and publicity battles, see Dorothy Nelkin's *Science Textbook Controversies and the Politics of Equal Time* (Cambridge, MA: MIT Press, 1977). To bring this up to date, follow the daily news.

Gosse's bellybutton approach to truth continues to be followed just as if the Reverend Charles Kingsley and the philosopher Karl Popper never existed. In 1972 Henry Morris, director of the Institute for Creation Research, revived the idea of *Omphalos* in his book *The Remarkable Birth of Planet Earth*. Astronomers are agreed that some stars are so far away that their light takes 10,000 years to reach the earth. If the universe was created only 6,000 years ago, as Morris maintains, how does it happen that we can see this light now when we should not be able to see it until, say, 5972 A.D.? No problem, says Morris: when God created the universe in 4004 B.C. he created such stars with their light rays already extending 4,000 light-years out from them. "Real creation," he says on page 62, "necessarily involves creation of 'apparent age.' Whatever is truly created—that is, instantly called into existence out of nothing—must certainly look as though it had been there prior to its creation." So: Adam *did* have a bellybutton.

It is unfortunate that Fundamentalists are cut off from their historical roots—from their fundament, if you please. Fundamentalism arose out of Protestantism, and Protestantism out of Catholicism. In this twofold transition there has been lost—or jettisoned—some useful intellectual baggage. Fundamentalists could justify their position much more easily if they would borrow from Tertullian in the third century or St. Augustine in the fifth. Tertullian is variously credited with saying *Credo quia impossibile* ("*I believe because it is impossible*") and *Certum est, quia impossibile est* ("It is certain because it is impossible"). St. Augustine wrote: "Understanding is the reward of faith. Therefore seek not to understand that thou mayest believe, but believe that thou mayest understand."

But it is no good using the tongs of reason to pull the Fundamentalists' chestnuts out of the fire of contradiction. Their real troubles lie elsewhere, as Nelkin has pointed out. Fundamentalists are panicked by the apparent disintegration of the family, the disappearance of certainty and the decay of morality. Fear leads them to ask, if we cannot trust the Bible, what can we trust? The truth or falsity of evolution is a secondary matter. Rationalists must listen to the complaints of the Fundamentalists with a psychiatrist's "third ear," and respond to the more subtle messages.

## 8
### Sociobiology—Aesop With Teeth

Originally published in *Social Theory and Practice 4*: 303–313 (1977). For a discussion of the "Baldwin Effect" see my article, "Genetic Consequences of Cultural Decisions in the Realm of Population," in *Social Biology 19*: 350–361 (1972). The double-blind experiment (a major advance in scientific methodology), so far as I know, first had its logic explicated in a paper by Harry Gold, N. T. Kwit, and H. Otto, "The Xanthines (Theobromine and Aminophylline) in the Treatment of Cardiac Pain" in the *Journal of the American Medical Association 108*: 2173–2179 (1937).

## 9
### Ethics for Birds (And Vice Versa)

I have no second thoughts about this essay, which was newly written for this book.

## 10
### The Moral Threat of Personal Medicine

Originally printed as a chapter in *Genetic Responsibility*, edited by Mack Lipkin, Jr., and Peter T. Rowley (New York: Plenum Press, 1974).

It is perhaps quixotic to include a chapter on eugenics in this book, because in the year of our Lord 1982 the word "eugenics" is a *No-No*. But, in the strictest sense, eugenics is an inescapable part of economics, broadly understood. We must some day conquer our distaste and examine the economic and ecological consequences of the inescapable process of mutation. The medical profession is beginning to do so. But the word "eugenics" is still burdened with a taboo.

## 11
### In Praise of Waste

This chapter is an edited portion (about one-third) of the last chapter of my *Nature and Man's Fate*. Copyright © 1959 by Garrett Hardin. Reprinted by permission of Holt, Rinehart and Winston, Publishers. That waste, coupled with selection, is a creative force is still not widely recognized. Even some apparently well-trained scientists do not understand this power. At the evolution trial in Arkansas in December 1981 an English professor of astrophysics, one N. C. Wickramasinghe, asserted that the theory of evolution was no more credible than "saying a tornado blowing through a junkyard would assemble a Boeing

707." That would be a fair criticism if mutation alone occurred, but selection makes all the difference.

# 12
## An Evolutionist Looks at Computers
This address to a computer conference in 1968 was published in *Datamation* 15(5): 98–109 (1969).

# 13
## Discriminating Altruisms
First published in *Zygon* (1982). Among biologists, the first major step in the development of the idea of altruism-as-discrimination was made by Robert Trivers in his article, "The Evolution of Reciprocal Altruism," *Quarterly Review of Biology 46*: 35–57 (1971). Early critics protested that behavior that followed the rule of "You scratch my back and I'll scratch yours" is not altruism at all—which indeed it is not, in the pure sense. Trivers freed our minds from the shackles of the idealist's unreciprocated altruism, thus turning our attention to discriminating altruisms, the essential elements of social existence.

I have been told that Ralph Barton Perry (1876–1957) coined the term "egocentric predicament," but I have not verified this. The term is seldom used, which suggests that the underlying phenomenon is under something of a taboo. Social intercourse is facilitated by a belief in the sincerity of the "other," which is an unknowable. Most traditional ethics is concerned with intentions, which are also unknowable. The law wisely is built on actions, though it frequently lapses into inferring intentions, as in the case of "fraud." In our desire to shield our minds from the corrosion of doubt, we usually suppress the sure knowledge that we can never know what goes on in the mind of the "other." Social life is permeated with this suppression.

Many disturbing examples of the treatment of whistle-blowers are to be found in Alan F. Westin, ed., *Whistle-Blowing: Loyalty and Dissent in the Corporation* (New York: McGraw-Hill, 1981). For the particular story of a high-level dissident in the General Motors Corporation, John Z. DeLorean, see J. Patrick Wright, *On A Clear Day You Can See General Motors* (New York: Avon, 1979).

Here are the essential references for the bad press of patriotism. E. M. Forster's statement comes from his essay "What I Believe," reprinted on page 68 of his *Two Cheers for Democracy* (New York: Harcourt, Brace & World, 1951). Samuel Johnson's remark was made in 1775, when he was 66 years old. But Johnson was not condemning true patriotism. As Boswell said, "Patriotism having become one of our topicks, Johnson suddenly uttered in a strong determined tone, an apophthegm at which many will start: 'Patriotism is the last refuge of a scoundrel.' But let it be considered that he did not mean a real and generous love of our country, but that pretended patriotism which so many, in all ages and countries, have made a cloak for self interest." (*Boswell's Life of Johnson*, Everyman's edition, vol. I, pp. 547–548.) In other words, patriotism is the last of a scoundrel's many refuges, most of which bear the names of virtues.

Michael Novak's fine epitome of contemporary liberalism may be found in his article, "The Social World of Individuals," *Hastings Center Studies 2* : 37–44 (1974).

Those who need a background in the theory of the commons should consult *Managing the Commons*, edited by Garrett Hardin and John Baden (San Francisco: W. H. Freeman, 1977). Despite the fact that information tends to become commonized there are some advantages to be gained by treating it as a limitable, transferable property (when that is feasible). Copyright and patent laws, which do so, make it possible for the originators of good new ideas to reap profits, thus encouraging inventiveness in others. The transferability of these property rights makes it commercially possible for enterprisers to make the investment needed to convert ideas into products, a possibility foreclosed to a public patent (which creates a commons). But property rights in information are difficult to police; note, for example, the widespread pirating of computer software and tape recordings.

## 14
## Biological Insights Into Abortion

Originally published in *BioScience* (1982). Copyright © by the American Institute of Biological Sciences. Reprinted with permission. The first two paragraphs have been added to the previously published text.

For the evidence that natural abortion is the rule, carrying the fetus to term the exception, see J. D. Biggers, 1981, "In Vitro Fertilization and Embryo Transfer in Human Beings," *New England Journal of Medicine 304* : 336–342. For a discussion of abortion in general see my book, *Mandatory Motherhood: The True Meaning of "Right to Life."* (Boston: Beacon Press, 1974); also see Christopher Tietze and D. A. Dawson, *Induced Abortion: A Factbook* (New York: Population Council, 1973). Father Wassmer's early recognition of the moral implications of delayed menstruation is given in his little known article, "The Crucial Question About Abortion," *Catholic World 206* (1): 57–61 (1967).

I found the information on the meaning of the Japanese term *mabiki* in T. J. Samuel, "Population Control in Japan: Lessons for India," *Eugenics Review 58* : 15–22 (1966).

## 15
## Ecology and the Death of Providence

Originally published in *Zygon 15*: 57–68 (1980), this essay was first given as an address, 9 May 1978, in a symposium honoring LaMont C. Cole shortly before his death.

For the theology of providence see the article on "Providence" in the *Encyclopaedia of Religion and Ethics*.

## 16
## Why Plant a Redwood Tree?

The first three paragraphs have been added to the essay published in *Living in the Environment*, Third Edition, by G. Tyler Miller, Jr. © 1982 by Wadsworth, Inc. Reprinted by permission of Wadsworth Publishing Company, Belmont, California 94002.

The economic calculations were correct when made in 1974. If they were recalculated for today's rate of interest, the point of the argument would be even stronger.

## 17
## Setting Limits to the Global Approach

This essay is modified from a book review published in the *Sierra Club Bulletin 60* (8): 41–43 (1975).

## 18
## Ecological Conservatism

Reprinted with permission from *Chemical and Engineering News 49* (28): 3 (1971). Copyright © 1971 American Chemical Society.

This editorial was solicited by the editor of the journal not long after "Earth Day," 22 April 1970. Editorials I have contributed to other journals have always provoked responses. This one elicited not even a peep from the readers. Was the message so repugnant that chemists could not even think of it? Or so out of their ken that it meant nothing to them? Or are chemists just not given to reacting to public statements? One would like to know.

## 19
## Property Rights: The Creative Reworking of a Fiction

With only minor modifications, this essay is taken from the Foreword to

Christopher D. Stone's *Should Trees Have Standing? Toward Legal Rights for Natural Objects* (Los Altos, CA: William Kaufmann, Inc., 1974).

The passages from Aldo Leopold may be found on page 217 of *A Sand County Almanac* (New York: Oxford University Press, 1966).

## 20
## Cash Crops and Redistribution

This essay is an augmented book review published in *Agricultural History* 54:371–373 (1980).

It is astonishing how often "development" professionals fail to see that the wisdom of growing export crops depends on the relative prices of export crops and subsistence crops. An economist who formerly worked for U.S. AID (Agency for International Development) is reported to have said: "Allocating more resources to export crops [in Africa] is difficult when population growth alone dictates that these same resources be used for domestic food crops." *World Development Letter*, 11 November 1981, page 87.) "Neo-colonialism," Nestle's baby formula, and export crops are all welcome whipping boys to those who hold wealthy nations responsible for the difficulties of the poor. The mere mention of any of these seems to free the speaker of the necessity of close and critical reasoning.

## 21
## Exploited Seas—An Opportunity for Peace

First published as an editorial in *BioScience* 22:693. Copyright © 1972, American Institute of Biological Sciences. Reprinted with permission. The first four paragraphs are additions to the original. Among the minor modifications in the rest of the text I should call attention to the omission of the Panama Canal as a national property that could be internationalized. Since the editorial was written, another decision (to make the canal explicitly the national property of Panama) has been reached, which precludes the suggestion made in this editorial.

## 22
## Conservation's Secret Question

Originally published in *Defenders* 56(2):22, 24 (1981) under the title, "Destroying Wildlife in the People's Name." John H. Tanton contributed useful criticisms in the writing of this essay.

One of the curious characteristics of editors of popular periodicals (as opposed to the editors of scientific journals) is that they do not hesitate to introduce errors of their own into a manuscript. It was only when this essay was published that I discovered that the editor had placed me in the seat of a Landrover (fifth paragraph). It happens that the car was a Peugeot. But Landrover is the cliche image for East Africa and Landrover it had to be.

I should say, however, that the editor proposed other changes which were for the better; these he cleared with me.

## 23
## The Born-Again Optimist
Published under the title of "Dr. Pangloss Meets Cassandra" in *The New Republic*, 28 October 1981, pages 31–34.

The environmental revolution begun by Rachel Carson's *Silent Spring* in 1962 had, by the time Ronald Reagan was inaugurated as President, evoked a powerful reaction. One aspect of this was a revival of the sort of insistent optimism first hawked throughout the United States by the French pharmacist, Emile Coué, following the First World War. Coué's message was personal: everything will be fine, he said, if each of us will daily repeat the formula, "Every day and in every way, I am becoming better and better." The Couéistes of our day have transferred the formula to the public realm: "Every day and in every way everything will get better spontaneously—if we will only free the magic of the market from governmental meddling." Two Bibles for the new religion have appeared, George Gilder's *Wealth and Poverty* and Julian Simon's *The Ultimate Resource*. In pursuit of the new Eldorado, President Reagan, in his first month in office, issued Executive Order 12291 which, without the concurrence of Congress or the people, virtually emasculated all regulatory agencies. The counterreformation is under way.

The more outrageous of the two new Bibles is Simon's. Considering the favorable reviews given it in such prestigious publications as the *New York Times* and *Fortune* one might question my review. For independent support I refer readers to the thorough review by Herman E. Daly in the *Bulletin of the Atomic Scientists*, January 1982.

One of the puzzling features of Simon's book is its publication by a distinguished university press, Princeton's. One is reminded of the publication of Velikovsky's *Worlds in Collision* by a dignified commercial publisher in 1950. A barrage of criticism by scientists persuaded the publishers to divest themselves of this embarrassing bit of nonsense, selling it to a less discriminating house. Will the Princeton University Press be similarly embarrassed? Probably not. The line between sense and nonsense is not so precisely drawn in economics and sociology as it is in the physical sciences. That Simon dreams alchemical dreams and thinks that the laws of thermodynamics are mere matters of opinion apparently does not strike his professional colleagues, or the literary world, as outrageous.

Despite all this it must be said that Simon has written an invaluable book for university teaching. There is no better way to sharpen the critical faculties of the students than assigning them a book replete with plausible but erroneous statements. Not more than once in a generation do we encounter a book as valuable (in this peculiar sense) as *The Ultimate Resource*.

## 24
## Ending the Squanderarchy

This was first published as a chapter in *Energy, Economics, and the Environment: Conflicting Views of an Essential Interrelationship*, edited by Herman E. Daly and Alvaro F. Umaña (Boulder, Colorado: Westview Press, 1981). Copyright © 1981 by the American Association for the Advancement of Science.

So far as I can recall, I first used the term "longage" in 1975 in my poem "Carrying Capacity." See my *Stalking the Wild Taboo*, second edition, page 260 (Los Altos, Ca.: William Kaufmann, Inc., 1978).

For valuable criticisms of the developing manuscript I thank Karl Henion as well as Mortimer Andron and other members of the Little Men's Marching and Deep Thinking Society.

## 25
## The Threat of Clarity

Reprinted by permission from *The American Journal of Psychiatry, 114*: 392–396 (1957). Copyright © 1957, the American Psychiatric Association.

I owe the deepest debt of gratitude to Benjamin Lee Whorf for insights in the essays brought together in his *Language, Thought and Reality* (New York: John Wiley & Sons, 1956). In addition I thank Zigmond M. Lebensohn for initiating this paper, and for his many kindnesses. I am also greatly indebted to Herbert Fingarette, Douwe Stuurman, and Lewis Walton for their searching criticisms. This paper was read at a meeting of the American Psychiatric Association in Chicago in May 1957.

## 26
## The Ghost of Authority

Reprinted from *Perspectives in Biology and Medicine* 9:289–297 (1966). By permission of the University of Chicago Press. Copyright, 1966 © by the University of Chicago.

Since this essay was written, I have found (in Will Durant's *The Age of Faith*, p. 964) a relevant statement by St. Thomas Aquinas: *Locus ab auctoritate est infirmissimus*—"The argument from authority is weakest."

It is a tradition in science that a belief or concept that is found wanting is abandoned *utterly*. Contemporary science textbooks contain no mention of phlogiston, suction, or entelechy. It is a strength of science that scientists are willing to "expose" its defective children (in the Greek sense). Outside of science, the tenderness shown ancient but defective ideas greatly slows down intellectual progress, even causing reversals from time to time. Sloppy ideas get underfoot. It would have been better if St. Thomas had decisively said, *Locus ab auctoritate invalidus est*.

# 27
# An Ecological View of International Relations

Taken from *The Economy of 1981: A Bipartisan Look*. Proceedings of a Congressional Economic Conference on Wednesday, 10 December 1980. Washington, D.C.: U.S. Government Printing Office, 20 April 1981, 73-057-0.

How this came to be written may be as interesting as the final product because it highlights some problems of managing information in a democracy.

Toward the last of President Carter's regime, the Joint Economic Committee decided it would be a good thing if they held a conference that would point out to the next Administration (whomever it might be) the true way to economic virtue. Speakers for the plenary sessions were carefully chosen to unfurl a variety of banners: *Progress! Grow or Die! Re-Industrialize! Get the Government Off Our Backs! Tap the Magic of the Marketplace!* Slightly more than a hundred people were invited to be the captive audience. More than half of these were presidents, board chairmen, or chief executive officers of the *Fortune* 400 corporations—Exxon, Dupont, General Electric, and the like.

But it wouldn't do to let on that the house was stacked, so three known "environmentalists" were on the guest list: Russell Peterson (Audubon Society), David Brower (Friends of the Earth), and myself (The Environmental Fund). When I received the invitation I wondered if I should bother to go; being a rather simple, optimistic sort of person—and a curious one—I accepted.

I did not exactly feel at ease. Russell Peterson, who had at one time been in industry, hobnobbed comfortably with the presidents and C.E.O.'s. As for myself, I looked around for Dave Brower, but didn't see him; I learned later that he, a wiser and more experienced man than I, had elected to attend another Washington meeting scheduled for the same time. So I just stuck it out, suffering through inane speeches by politicians and others who know so well how to say what pays. I was surrounded by people—good people, I am sure—with whom I had nothing in common. After the plenary session we broke up into small discussion groups where one might have a chance to say something useful, except for one thing: no one was listening. Nothing that was said in these groups would ever get out. They were pro forma obeisances to the democratic principle of participation.

In anticipation of this conference every participant was invited to hand in any statement he wished, which would become part of the written record. It is very difficult for a compulsive writer to resist such an invitation, so of course I accepted. So did many others. The published result was a big fat volume.

What did the conference accomplish? It made scarcely a ripple in the press; media people can spot a non-event like this a mile away and ignore it. All of the major speeches could have been turned out by the lower echelons of the Congressional staff at much less expense. As for the published record, who read it? I confess I have read only my own contribution. I will bet that all the other contributors have been equally discriminating. I would be very surprised if even two people out of the nation's 228 million have read the entire volume—unless they were required to in their role as copy-editors or the like. I would be moderately surprised if even ten Americans have read as many as three articles in the book. A government book like this is really a form of non-publication.

What did the conference cost, from beginning to end? Even though most of the participants were paid from nongovernment funds, the total cost to taxpayers must have been considerable. The sad thing is, there are countless conferences and publications like this that have no more effect than a passing breeze. When government tries to manage information it is difficult to do more than waste money. Much of what the U.S. Superintendent of Documents puts out is outside the recognized channels of information distribution and so is ignored.

I don't regret writing this sort of contribution—*once*. I got some things off my chest.

If you want to know the evidence that good nutrition increases human *fecundity* (the ability to produce children) see Rose E. Frisch, "Demographic Implications of the Biological Determinants of Female Fecundity." *Social Biology*, v. *22*, 1975:17. For the effects of perceived well-being on fertility (achieved family size), see the following. Chowdhury, A. K. M. A., A. R. Khan, and L. C. Chen, "The Effect of Child Mortality Experience on Subsequent Fertility in Pakistan and Bangladesh." *Population Studies*, v. *30*, 1976:249. Coale, A. J., "The Demographic Transition." *Transactions of the International Union for the Scientific Study of Population*, 1973:53. Morgan, R. W., *New Perspectives on the Demographic Transition*. Washington, Smithsonian Institution, 1976.

Teitelbaum, M. S., "Relevance of Demographic Transition Theory for Developing Countries," *Science*, v. *188*, 1975:420.

## 28
## Perishable Euphemisms of Foreign Aid

Perhaps my printed statement to the Joint Economic Committee resulted in my being invited to contribute a piece to *Newsweek*, though I doubt it. Busy newsmen have better things to do than comb the vanity publications of the government. In any event, I did write an essay for the magazine (see the following chapter), but it seemed to me that it needed a "backgrounder" to be properly understood. So I wrote a piece on euphemisms from which the present chapter is derived. The editors ignored my unsolicited contribution.

The inspiration for this essay comes from William and Paul Paddock, who first called attention to the chameleon quality of the euphemisms for the poor in their *Famine 1975!* I was long under the impression that "The Third World" was coined by the French demographer Alfred Sauvy, but Cordelia S. May called my attention to a passage on page 264 of Jean-Francois Revel's *Without Marx or Jesus* which states that the French sociologist George Balandier is the originator. Further library research is called for. The significant thing is that the term was coined in France, where it is far more evocative than it is elsewhere.

## 29
## The Toughlove Solution

Reprinted from *Newsweek*, 26 October 1981, page 45. This was a special issue put out just before an international conference at Cancún, Mexico, where poor countries made great demands on rich countries, which the rich ignored. Hordes of diplomats and media people were flown in for several days of rhetoric and gourmandizing. The cost must have been enormous.

I am a great believer in the creative possibilities of some kinds of waste (see Chapter 11). But not in waste of this kind, which is, if anything, counterproductive.

## 30
## Limited World, Limited Rights

Published by permission of Transaction, Inc., from *Society* *17*(4):5–8 (1980). Copyright © May/June 1980 by Transaction, Inc.

# Index of Names